HISTORIC CEMETERIES

of Portland, Oregon

HISTORIC CEMETERIES
of Portland, Oregon

TERESA BERGEN AND HEIDE DAVIS

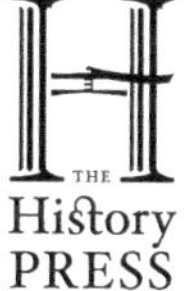

Published by The History Press
Charleston, SC
www.historypress.com

Unless otherwise noted, photos were taken by or are in the collection of the authors.

First published 2021

Manufactured in the United States

ISBN 9781467148610

Library of Congress Control Number: 2021941089

Notice: The information in this book is true and complete to the best of our knowledge. It is offered without guarantee on the part of the authors or The History Press. The authors and The History Press disclaim all liability in connection with the use of this book.

CONTENTS

ACKNOWLEDGEMENTS

First, thanks to our editor at The History Press, Laurie Krill, for taking on this project. Thanks to the many individuals and organizations who helped us by supplying facts, previewing chapters, escorting us on cemetery tours, tracking down historic photos and otherwise aiding our research. These include Debra Allen, Mountain View Oregon City; Bitsie Appleton, Congregation Beth Israel; LeAnn Stephan, Troutdale Historical Society; Jay Ollerenshaw and Edith Aschim, Rose City Cemetery; Alisha Babbstein, Oregon Jewish Museum and Center for Holocaust Education; Ed Bixby and Marie Ferraiolo, Historic Columbian Cemetery; Brian Johnson and Mary Hansen, City of Portland Archives; Karol Miller, Milwaukie Pioneer Cemetery; Jason and Angie Pope, Affordable Family Memorials; Mark Hurlburt, Milwaukie Museum; Karin Morey, Friends of Mountain View Cemetery; Adam Simpson, stonemason researcher; Randal Houle, former cemetery employee; Eric Cordingley and David Anderson, Friends of Multnomah Park Cemetery; Elerina Aldamar and Robert Warren, Oregon Historical Society; Ryan Fernandez, *Oregonian*; Josey Koehn and Michael Salazar, Wilhelm's Portland Mausoleum; Mike Andrews, Gresham Historical Society; Tom LaBonty, Friends of Lone Fir Cemetery; Emma Williams, Oregon Metro; Janice Dilg, historian; Hattie Mead, Greenwood Hills Cemetery Maintenance Association; Lauren Goss, University of Oregon Libraries; David Scheer, Odd Fellows Peninsula Lodge No. 128; James Rodgers and Lucy Capehart, Japanese American Museum of Oregon; Kaylee Guerrero, Humane Society Animal Cemetery; and Joe Collins, Oswego Pioneer Cemetery. And we appreciate our husbands, Denis Davis and Gideon Parque, for cheering on our cemetery sleuthing.

INTRODUCTION

For years, we've enjoyed visiting cemeteries in the Northwest together. We call this cemetery sleuthing—looking for interesting stones with old-fashioned names and trying to imagine what people's lives were like based on their headstone information. During the 2020 pandemic, with most of the world on lockdown, it seemed like the perfect time to methodically visit all our local cemeteries and research some of the residents. This book is the result of those visits and that research.

Obviously, cemeteries are places people go to commune with their dearly departed, and this purpose is foremost. But they are fascinating places to visit even without a personal connection. Studying the evolution of our local cemeteries taught us a lot about the city we live in—from the time it was a village by the river, carved out of the forest, to one of the West Coast's largest cities, with a population of nearly 650,000. Headstones taught us about demographic changes and the influx of different ethnicities that make our area more diverse and cosmopolitan.

Researching early Portlanders helped us appreciate how hard life was and how resourceful people had to be. In 1800s Portland, it was extremely easy to die. People fell off horse-drawn wagons, were crushed by logs, fell victim to steamboat explosions and, of course, died of diseases for which we now have vaccinations and treatments. Childbirth was often deadly, for both the baby and the mother. We never quite get used to seeing areas of cemeteries devoted just to babies—especially when several in a row belong to the same parents.

But early Portlanders are also inspiring. A typical successful pioneer like Oliver Perry Lent, who came to Portland in 1852, had to be versatile. Lent was a stonemason, farmer, homebuilder, road surveyor, sawmill operator, justice of the peace, school director and Grange movement leader, to summarize part of his résumé. All pioneers had to be much more self-sufficient than we are today.

In our book, we introduce readers to twenty-five historic burial places in and around Portland. You'll learn about the origins of each cemetery; read about beautiful, symbolic and unusual markers; and meet some notable residents. In addition to the pioneers, we showcase a diverse cross-section of ethnicity, economic status, religion, morality and occupation. We've included people renowned for their civic contributions or artistic talents, citizens with tragic tales and a few who live on in infamy for their deranged crimes. We report eerie stories and mention a few ghosts—though we can't guarantee the ghosts will appear for you. We also point out recreational opportunities available at cemeteries, including birding, geocaching, biking, dog walking and special programs or historical tours.

Not only are cemeteries interesting places, but they also need us, the living. Most of the cemeteries in this book are run by volunteer groups or by the county. Many are closed to new burials. This makes their future precarious. A full cemetery becomes a financial liability, since it brings in no money to pay for maintenance. If people don't appreciate cemeteries, they quickly become overgrown with weeds. People dump trash in them and tip over markers. Many of the cemeteries in this book have had ups and downs over the years, fluctuating between being valued parts of the landscape and eyesores loathed by neighbors. We want people to value cemeteries—as green spaces, public art exhibitions, historical sites, places for spiritual contemplation, paths to exercise on and part of our cultural heritage.

Putting together the photos for this book was a lot of fun. We took thousands of our own photos—they are ours unless otherwise noted—and tracked down as many historical ones as we could find. Out of respect for people who are still mourning, we've mostly restricted the images to markers of people who died more than fifty years ago.

In addition to being amateur cemetery sleuths, we bring different backgrounds and strengths to this project. Heide is an artist who does both fine art and decorative painting. She loves vintage stuff and worked in the antique business for years. Teresa is a freelance writer who also works in oral history and has a background in historical research. During this project,

Heide honed her research skills and got deeply into people's stories. Teresa's favorite part is the headstones themselves. She's fascinated by how people are commemorated by the art, words and symbols on their markers. We are both suckers for an eerie tale. We hope this book will inspire you to explore and value your local cemeteries.

I

LONE FIR CEMETERY

649 Southeast 26th Avenue, Portland

By far Portland's most famous cemetery, Lone Fir made a National Geographic top ten list of best cemeteries in the world and was listed in the National Register of Historic Places in 2007. The thirty-acre rectangle is treated as a park by people who live in the residential inner Southeast neighborhood. Lone Fir may look familiar even to people who haven't visited Portland, as movies like *Body of Evidence*, *Restless* and, fittingly, *My Summer as a Goth*, feature scenes filmed here.

HISTORY

Lone Fir's story started with a lone resident buried on private land. James Stephens paid $200 for a land claim that reached from the Willamette River to present-day Southeast 23rd Avenue and from Stark Street to Division Street. When his father, Emmor, died in 1846, James buried him on land he'd cleared for the family farm. At that time, the land wasn't even part of Portland, which existed on the west side of the Willamette River.

In 1854, businessman Colburn Barrell bought Stephens's land, promising to maintain Emmor's grave. That same year, the steamship *Gazelle* ended in a tragic explosion that killed twenty-four passengers, including Barrell's business partner Crawford Dobbins and friend D.P. Fuller. Barrell, an investor in the steamship, buried Dobbins and Fuller close to Emmor Stephens. In 1855, the land was platted as Mount Crawford Cemetery in honor of Dobbins.

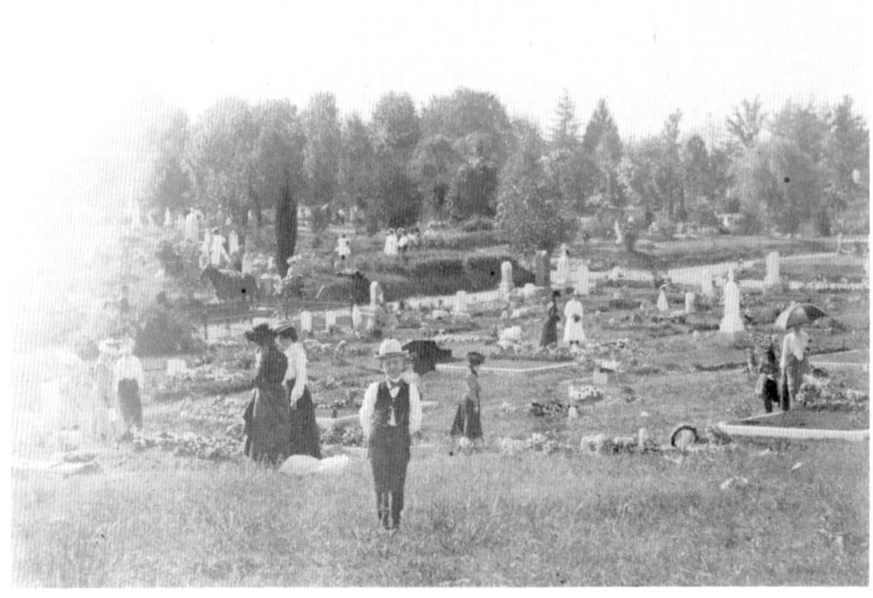

Cemetery visitors, circa 1900. *Architectural Heritage Center Library*.

The cemetery quickly gained business. Portland's previous graveyards suffered from marshy ground. Many bodies were exhumed and reinterred in the better soil of Mount Crawford. Freemasons bought two big plots. Additional purchases of thirteen acres in 1865 and seven acres in 1866 brought the cemetery up to its present size. That same year, Barrell sold the cemetery to a group of Portland families for $4,000. They renamed it Lone Fir Cemetery after the one fir tree then standing.

For the next few decades, Lone Fir was *the* place to be buried in Portland—or reburied, as more bodies from small downtown Portland burial grounds were transported across the river. Unfortunately, the cemetery owners failed to set money aside for perpetual care. By the 1920s, Lone Fir had fallen into disrepair. Many pre-1880s markers were made of wood and had rotted or burned, leaving up to ten thousand unidentified graves covered by blackberry brambles. Multnomah County took over ownership of the cemetery in 1928, but cemetery upkeep wasn't a high priority. Things got even more crowded when Central Catholic High School was built across the street from the cemetery in 1939, and some former residents of Saint Mary's Cemetery moved into Lone Fir.

Fortunately, Metro, a regional agency that deals with land use and open spaces, took charge of fourteen pioneer cemeteries in 1997. It aimed to take better care of the grounds and stop the vandals who were damaging headstones. Friends of Lone Fir, formed in 2000, has also been invaluable in preserving this cemetery. The dedicated group of volunteers has raised awareness of Lone Fir as a cool cultural asset, a treasure-trove of history and a fun place to visit—even for people who never previously pondered the entertainment aspects of cemeteries.

Also, the cemetery—which has a bit of everyone, including Chinese, Vietnamese, African Americans and Japanese along with Portland's many white people—got some new blood. An influx of Eastern European burials changed the look and the feel of the cemetery. Shiny black laser-etched granite stones proliferated, along with relatives who cared about upkeep. "With the Russian community, someone comes by either daily or weekly to maintain the grave," Frank Schaefer, former president of the Friends of Lone Fir, told the Portland *Mercury* in 2009. He said that the Eastern Europeans successfully pressured Metro to pave the cemetery's gravel roads and fix a patchy water main. "They've brought life back into the cemetery," he added.[1] Approximately twenty-five thousand people are buried at Lone Fir.

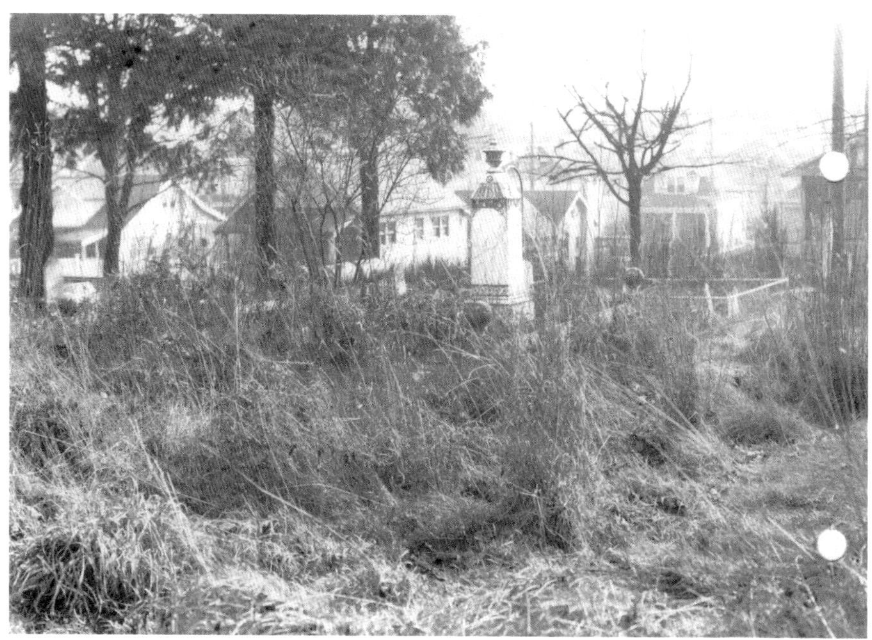

Lone Fir choked with weeds in 1928. *City of Portland (OR) Archives, A2001-008.220.*

MEMORABLE HEADSTONES

Lone Fir is a patchwork of old graves laid out beside new ones, flat headstones and soaring obelisks, pioneers and Masons, with the occasional eclectic or even carved-by-amateurs stone. The influx of shiny black granite stones with laser-etched portraits and Russian writing contrasts with worn old stones with moss filling the carved letters.

Several mausoleums rise above the stones. The biggest and most impressive is the compellingly spooky Macleay mausoleum. Its arched stained-glass windows, corner turrets, flaking gray stone and surrounding pointy black iron fence melt a goth's heart and have attracted many filmmakers. Scottish immigrant and U.S. National Bank of Portland president Donald Macleay paid $13,500 to construct the mausoleum after his first wife died in 1877. Many Portlanders will recognize his name from Macleay Park on Portland's west side. Macleay was the first major land donor to what became Forest Park, that 5,200-acre gem of urban forestry.

Lone Fir's ten or so stone tree stumps look real from a distance, especially considering their layer of moss. On closer inspection, visitors see lettering and all kinds of fancy individualized carving—scrolls, ivy leaves, woodworking tools. While it seems a reasonable assumption that these must have been

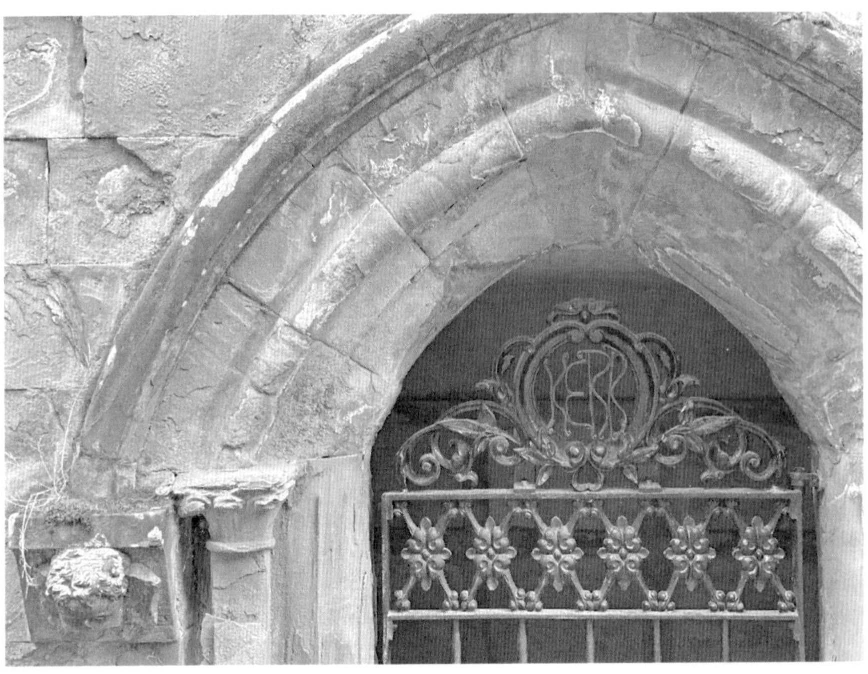

Opposite: Macleay Mausoleum.

Right: Macleay Mausoleum, detail.

Below: This sad marker inspires questions.

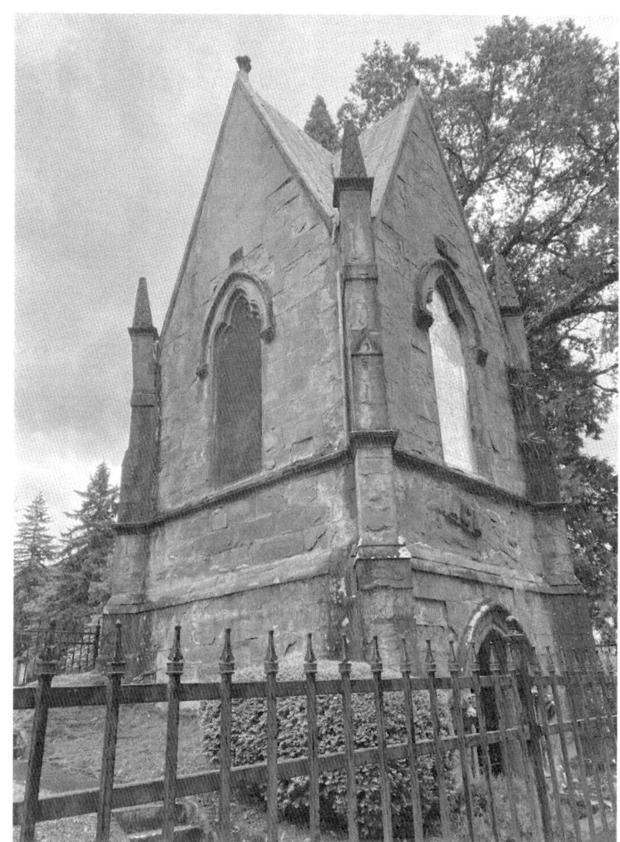

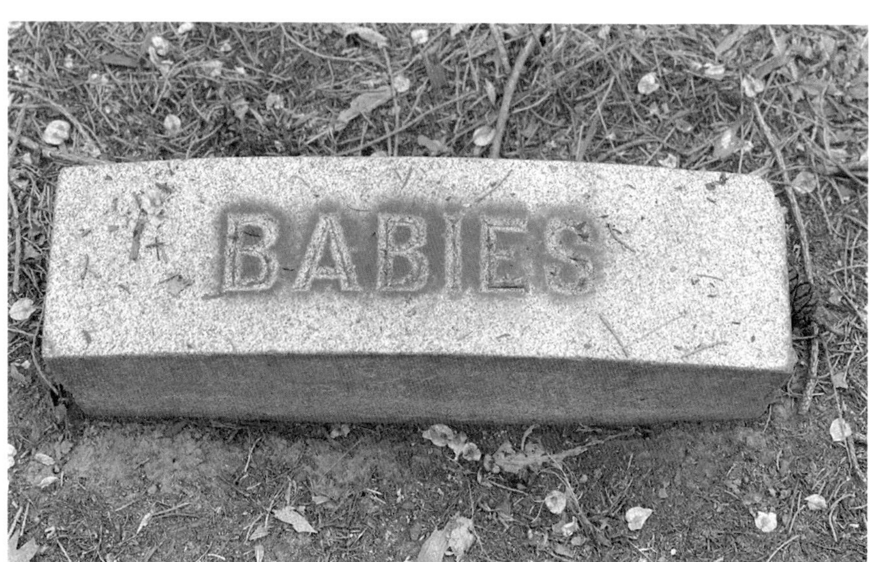

timber industry folks, given that Portland is in the heart of the Pacific Northwest, the stumps mark the graves of people who bought Woodmen of the World insurance. Members received $100 worth of tombstone money as one of their benefits. Legible death dates on Lone Fir's stumps range from 1891 to 1912. Lone Fir has sixty-seven WOW markers, but the others are less elaborate than the stumps. You'll recognize them by the round emblem on the front displaying a log, an axe and a maul and the Latin phrase *dum tacet clamat*—"though silent, he speaks."

While elaborate headstones are eye-catching, sometimes the stones that say the least make visitors wonder the most. One flat rectangle in Lone Fir simply says "Babies."

Local Celebrities

Being Portland's biggest pioneer cemetery, Lone Fir has way too many local celebrities to name them all. But here are just a few.

Asa Lovejoy (1808–1882) co-founded Portland but lost the famous coin toss to name the city. He wanted it to be named after Boston instead of Portland, Maine. He was a businessman who founded the Oregon City Woolen Mills, the city's first Masonic lodge and the first telegraph company. Lovejoy Street carries on his name.

Frank Dekum (1829–1894) also has a street named after him. This German confectioner built much of early Portland.

Anna Hembree Cullen (1840–1932), last survivor of the first Applegate Wagon Train in 1843, co-founded the Oregon Pioneers Association with her husband, John. Their children started the Sons and Daughters of Oregon Pioneers.

Laundry worker Emma Gotcher (1890–1962) became famous for winning a Supreme Court case that limited women's work hours.

A much more recent resident of Lone Fir, Joel Weinstein (1946–2008) was the self-described "famous publisher" of the 1970s *Mississippi Mud* magazine, which published Portland's rising stars in literature. His headstone depicts a full-color Day of the Dead skeleton riding a bicycle, reflecting his interest in Latin American art.

Infamous axe murderer Charity Lamb (c.1818–1879) attacked her husband as he sat down to a family dinner. A judge sent her to the Oregon State Penitentiary, where she was the sole woman prisoner. Later she was transferred to the Hawthorne Asylum. Now she rests in an unmarked grave.

Notable Resident: Harriet "Hattie" Redmond

Harriet "Hattie" Redmond (1862–1952) was one of many local African American women who worked hard to improve the lot of her community. She was born Harriet Crawford in Saint Louis, Missouri, around 1862, and her family moved to Oregon and settled in Portland about 1880. Harriet's mother, Vina Crawford, did domestic work. Her father, Reuben Crawford, was a ship caulker. Her family joined Mount Olivet Baptist Church and quickly became involved in local organizations, including co-founding one of Oregon's first Odd Fellows lodges.

In the early 1900s, Redmond served in African American women's clubs. "These women poured so much of themselves into building community," Avel Louise Gordly told the *Skanner* in a 2012 article. Gordly was the first African American woman to be elected to the Oregon State Senate, serving from 1997 to 2009. "Growing up I was very aware of the activism of these women who always seemed to be doing good in the community. They raised money for scholarships. They read books together. Their motto as club women was, 'Lifting as We Climb.'"

Harriet Crawford married Emerson Redmond in 1893. They had no children. He died at the Multnomah County Poor Farm in 1907. Despite her intellect, education and organizational skills, Harriet Redmond supported herself throughout her life with the limited jobs open to Black women at the time, such as domestic work, hairdressing and as a department store duster. She worked as a janitor for Oregon's U.S. District Court judges for twenty-nine years, retiring in 1939. It's hard to imagine how much energy, perseverance and self-restraint Redmond must have had, moving between her less respected work in the wider whiter world and her leadership roles within the Black community.

In 1952, at the age of ninety, Redmond died of bronchial pneumonia. Her contributions to women's suffrage had been mostly forgotten until historians preparing for the suffrage centennial stumbled across her in the historical record. When they tried to locate her grave in Lone Fir, they found that her simple marker had become buried. So in 2012, as part of the suffrage centennial, they ordered her a new, larger headstone inscribed, "Black American suffragist."

NOTABLE RESIDENT: MCMILLEN FAMILY

Both Tirzah Barton (1832–1903) and her husband, James H. McMillen, were Oregon pioneers. He arrived in 1845, she in 1851. Both were originally from Ohio. James McMillen made a fortune in the California gold rush. By the time he met Tirzah, he was a Cayuse Indian War veteran, a successful millwright and a widower with a five-year-old son. They married in 1851. Their first home together was a big farm in the Tualatin Plains, nineteen miles west of Portland. Tirzah took on the duties of a pioneer farm wife—running the house, helping neighbors as needed and bearing as many children as possible. A regional history book published in 1889 veils the horrific loss of several of her children in gauzy spiritual terms: "It was there that Justus and Union passed to spirit life in 1863, they, with their elder half-brother Frank, departing within a few days of each other. Constant remained until 1882, when he joined his brothers in the beyond. One daughter, Myrtle, was born at Oswego. At the age of twelve she passed to the better life."[2] Constant died in an elevator accident. Elevators were invented in 1857, and early iterations were dangerous. These children are all buried near Tirzah at Lone Fir.

The McMillens left Tualatin to live in Oswego in 1861 and then eventually moved across the Willamette to East Portland. There they lived in an area dubbed McMillen's Addition, which has since been demolished to make room for the Memorial Coliseum Complex near the Steel Bridge. The couple celebrated their fiftieth anniversary before Tirzah died in 1903.

Local newspapers made much of James McMillen's third marriage at the age of eighty-one. Long a member of Spiritualist circles, McMillen's third wife was Adaline Rogers Smith, a much younger clairvoyant. According to contemporary accounts, neither competing clairvoyants nor McMillen's two daughters rejoiced at the union.[3]

The couple swore their marriage was for love, so McMillen was shocked the following year when he returned home from visiting his daughter Ivy to learn his wife had liquidated his assets. The *Oregonian* reported, "Just what can be recovered is doubtful, for it is said that Mrs. McMillen and her daughter, Mrs. E.B. McClure have wasted no time in turning everything available into cash and diamonds."[4] Despite this disappointment in love, McMillen lived into his ninetieth year, dying in Ohio in 1913, where he is buried.

Their daughter June McMillen Ordway wrote plays, songs, stories and poems. Her dedicatory odes were read at the unveiling of military monuments. She wrote "After the Battles" for the soldiers' monument at

Lone Fir. June earned the tragic title "Oregon's first war mother" during the Spanish-American War, when her sons Earl and Eliot were the first Portland men to be killed in action.

Eerie Tales

Anne Jeanne Tingry-LeCoz, commonly known as Emma Merlotin, was born in France in 1850. By the 1880s, she was a high-class prostitute in Portland. In 1885, somebody murdered her with a hatchet in her home at Third and Yamhill. The murder remains unsolved, despite police using a strange technique of the time called optography. The idea was that if you took a picture of somebody's retina, it would reveal the last image they saw—in this case, the murderer. It didn't work. Some say that Merlotin's ghost still walks Lone Fir. If you see a woman dressed in French fashion who throws her hands in the air, screams and disappears when you approach, that's probably her. Other people have reported seeing a happier apparition, a young woman in a red dress calmly strolling the grounds.[5]

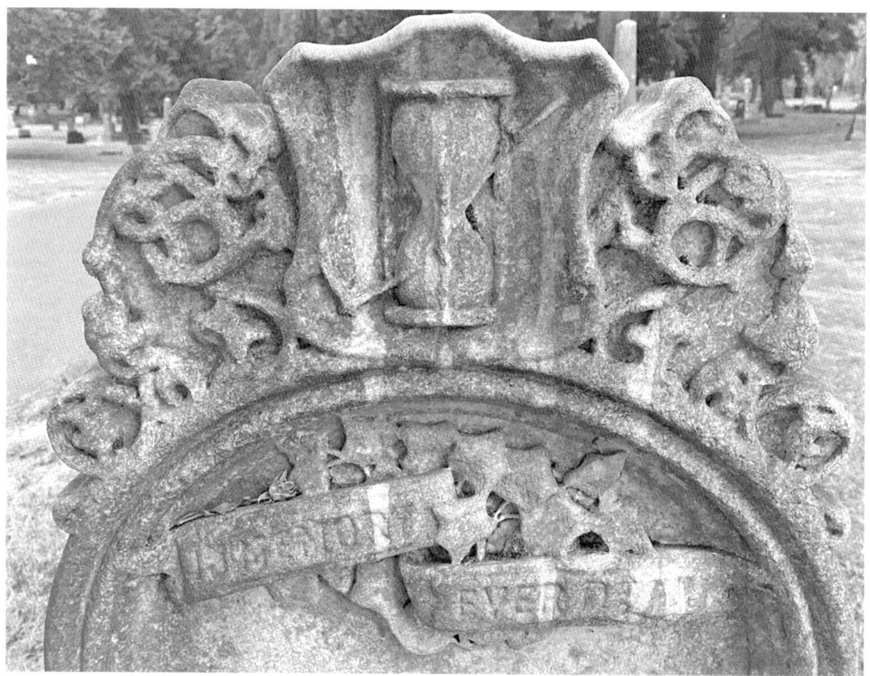

A classic tombstone decoration of the sterner variety, the hourglass reminds visitors that their lives are running out.

Recreational Activities

Walkers, bikers and runners use Lone Fir's paved pathways. A loop of the cemetery is a little less than a mile. Friends of Lone Fir offers organized activities, including history tours, seasonal work parties and grave cleaning workshops. On some years, the group offers the extremely popular Tour of Untimely Departures, a Halloween event featuring monologues by costumed characters and exhibitions of souped-up hearses.

Special Features

Portland's second arboretum. The cemetery has come a long way since being named for the single fir tree that stood on the original one-acre property. Now its collection of trees—more than 550 of 71 different species—is second in the city only to the Hoyt Arboretum. Some of the trees are specific to the graves, such as a eucalyptus tree planted on the grave of Gary Grayson, who worked for Portland Urban Forestry and was fond of eucalyptus trees, or a flowering cherry tree planted in an area with many Japanese graves.

Block 14. Currently, this area resembles a grassy vacant lot. But in 2004, an investigation with ground-penetrating radar found human remains under a county administration building that was built here. The bones belong to Chinese workers who came to Portland starting in about the 1840s. They were meant to be temporarily buried here, with their bones shipped back to China later. While many were, some bones got left behind. This general area of the graveyard also contains the unmarked graves of approximately 200 inmates of the Hawthorne Asylum. The first mental health treatment center in the Pacific Northwest opened in 1861 and reached a height of 327 patients in 1881. Founder James Hawthorne is buried in Lone Fir with an impressive monument. The building that stood over the bones for fifty years was demolished, and Metro plans to eventually plant a memorial garden.

Heritage Rose Garden. The flowers in the small rose garden inside Lone Fir are all descended from clippings brought on the Oregon Trail by pioneer women. In 1936, Mary Drain Albro founded the Pioneer Rose Association and searched the Oregon Territory for old roses. The organization found twenty-three varieties and started five heritage rose gardens in the Northwest with their cuttings. Lone Fir's is the only garden that still survives.

FIREMEN'S PLOT. Early cemetery owner Colburn Barrell set aside a special area for firefighters in 1862 and deeded it to the Portland Fire Department. It now contains about 130 firefighters, 13 of whom died in the line of duty.

STREETCARS TO CEMETERIES

In the 1890s, Portlanders could take an electric trolley right to the cemeteries on Palatine Hill. When the private right of way was extended to River View Cemetery in 1891, the six-mile Fulton line became Oregon's longest electric railway. The line started at Northwest Glisan and Second and traveled on a trestle over a gulch before reaching the summit of Taylors Ferry Road. Local company Vulcan Manufacturing Works made convertible trolley cars with sliding panels that let operators convert them from closed to open in less than two minutes. The Mount Tabor streetcar line later served Lone Fir.

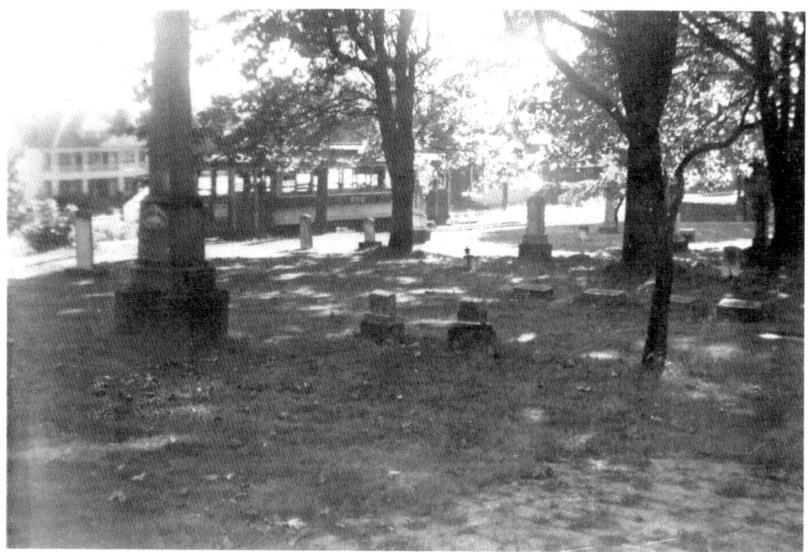

The Mount Tabor streetcar passes Lone Fir in 1946. *City of Portland (OR) Archives, A2011-007.219.*

2

MULTNOMAH PARK CEMETERY

4649 Southeast 82nd Avenue, Portland

Don't let the less-than-scenic setting of Southeast 82nd Avenue put you off. A cemetery sleuth can easily spend hours perusing this interesting collection of headstones stretching from 1850s pioneers to recent Eastern European black granite portrait stones complete with grave gardens.

History

Multnomah Park stands on part of what was once William Kern's donation land claim. Oliver Perry Lent filed the plat for ten-acre Multnomah Cemetery in 1888.[6] Back then, it was all farmlands and orchards, much different than today's view of used car lots and a super Walmart. Together, early Portland movers and shakers Oliver Perry Lent, Gustaf Petersen, George P. Lent, Robert Gilbert and William Kern founded the cemetery, and all are buried there. The earliest graves here predate the cemetery's official founding and may have been moved from family properties.

In the early 1900s, John "Blackjack" Dorsey was cemetery superintendent. After he died from heart trouble in 1919, his widow, Emma Dorsey, took over operations. She was in charge until 1943, when Multnomah County assumed responsibility for the cemetery.

According to Eric Cordingley, who co-founded Friends of Multnomah Park Cemetery with David Anderson in 2010, getting buried here was kind of a budget option. "Mrs. Dorsey did her best, but from everything I've read,

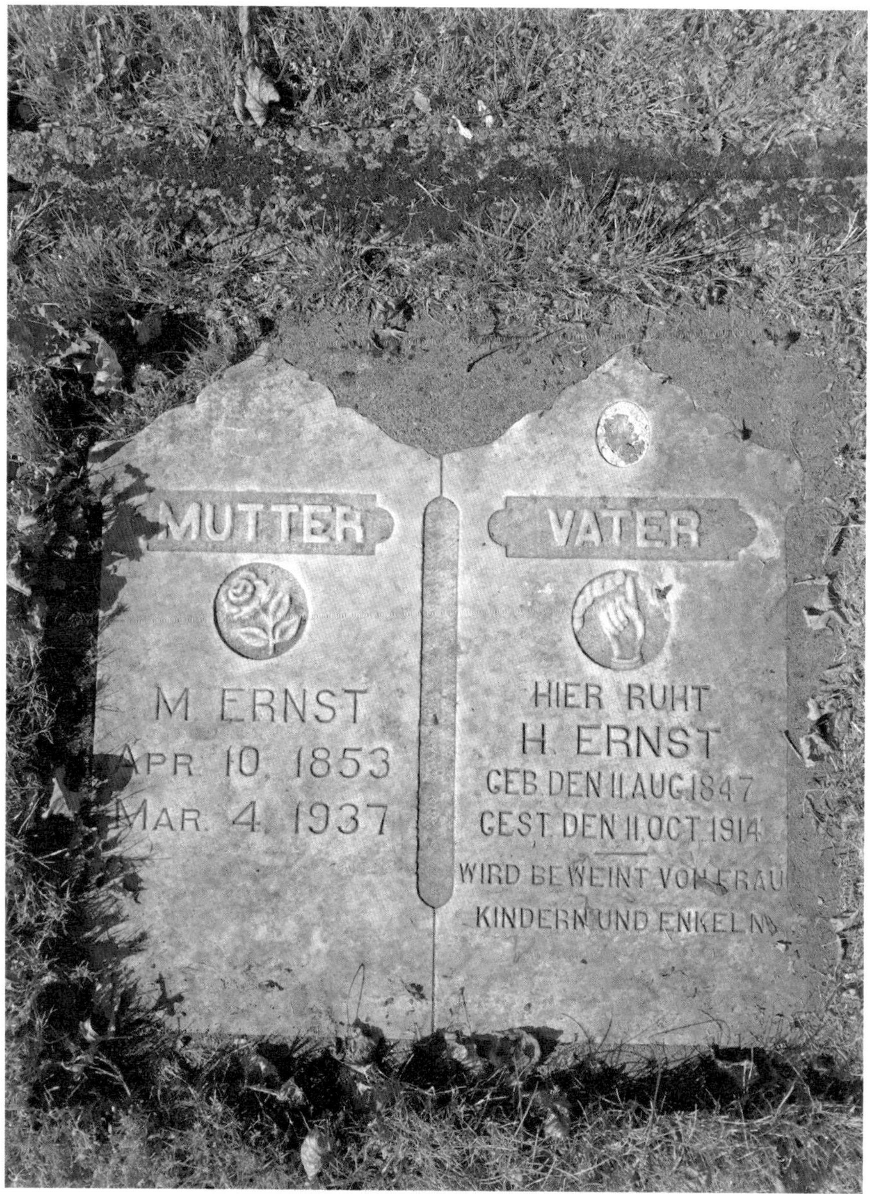

Mother gets a rose, father a finger pointing up to heaven and "weeping from wife, children and grandchildren" on this German marker.

it was consistently overgrown and not kept up well," said Cordingley. "It was basically a cut-rate burial place."[7] This is why Multnomah Park became the final resting place for many residents of the Multnomah County Poor Farm and Morningside Hospital, a private psychiatric hospital formerly located on land now occupied by Mall 205.

After the more upscale Mount Scott Cemetery (now Lincoln Memorial Park) opened in 1906, some people chose to move their loved ones from other Portland cemeteries to the posher digs. Cordingley and Anderson's research revealed at least ten transplants from Multnomah Park to Mount Scott, but there could be more.

The county ran Multnomah Cemetery from 1943 until transferring all cemeteries under its control to Metro Regional Government in 1996. Anderson and Cordingley, both genealogists who lived in the neighborhood, raised sunken cement markers, researched death certificates at the Oregon State Archives and uploaded thousands of photographs to Find a Grave, a database popular with genealogists. They estimate about twenty thousand total interments in Multnomah Park, many unmarked with some graves containing multiple residents.

Memorable Headstones

In addition to plenty of historic headstones, Multnomah Park has a few modern innovations, such as Frederick A. Clarke's (1911–2012) birdbath marker. There are some impressive black granite photo etchings for Eastern Europeans, including one double plot for a pair of Ukrainian sisters complete with a rock garden full of white stones. The Leabo marker is an especially nice example of the zinc, aka white bronze, style popular from the 1870s to the 1910s. Some old stones are a little eerie, such as one cracked flat marker whose moss-filled indented letters spell out "My dear mother" in a spidery font.

The cemetery's standout monument is the Vance Mausoleum, which was controversial when built and has descendants holding a grudge to the present day. Israel Vance was a Gresham-area farmer who died in 1905 with an estate worth about $12,000. He left bequests of $500 each to his three nieces and willed the rest to contractor W.B. Steele to build a grand mausoleum for him and his sister, Isabella Vance Long, who died in 1899.[8] His heirs contested the will, saying Vance was "incompetent, [an] imbecile and unsound of mind, and was under the influence of Mr. Steele." Vance's

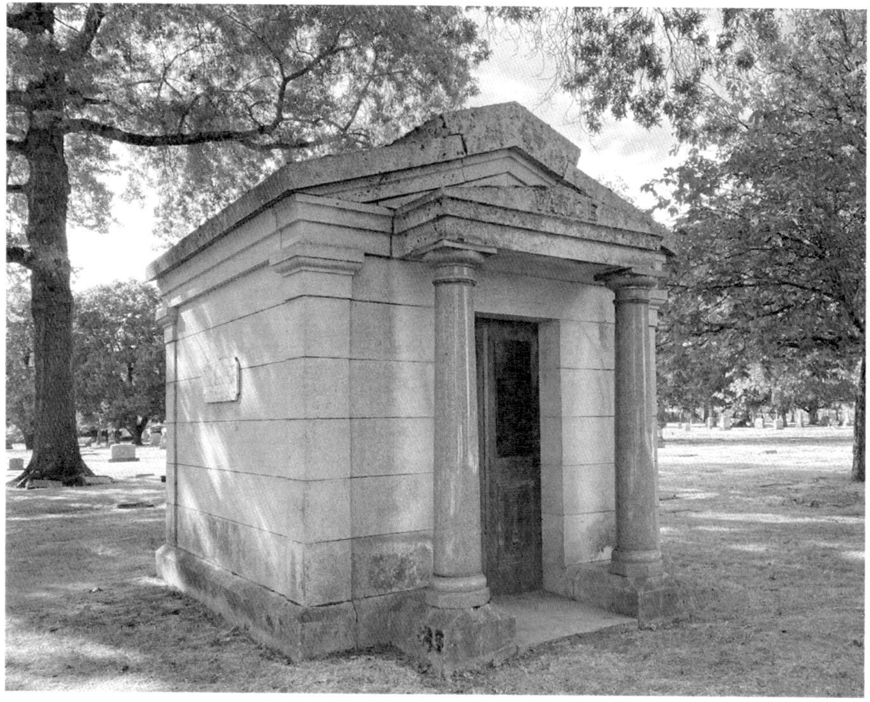

Vance mausoleum. One of the granite blocks used on the roof weighed ten tons.

intentions prevailed. In 1908, the twelve-by-fourteen-foot mausoleum was completed at a cost of $8,000, making it one of the costliest family burial vaults on the West Coast at that time.[9] It features California granite, black and white marble and glass doors with beautifully carved inverted torches.[10]

Local Celebrities

The family that lent its name to the nearby Lents neighborhood has at least ten members buried here. Oliver Perry Lent was born in Ohio in 1830 and came to Oregon in 1852 with his wife, Martha Almira Buckley Lent. A stonemason by trade, he first worked on the penitentiary in South Portland. His other pursuits included homebuilding, farming, operating a sawmill, surveying roads and serving as justice of the peace. Lent was an important figure in the Grange movement and served as school director at Lents.[11]

Members of the Zenger family are also buried here. The Zenger name is now known for Zenger Farm, the center for environmental, farming and healthy eating education that operates out of the historic Zenger farmhouse. William Johnson, who once owned the sawmill on what's now called Johnson Creek, is also buried here.

A well-known but long-forgotten Portland resident, James A. Bennett had a mobile knife and scissors sharpening business. This Indian War veteran pulled a wooden cart around Portland. Upon his death in 1899, the *Oregonian* commemorated him with a line drawing and wrote, "For four decades, he was a unique figure about town, quiet, attentive to business, polite and prompt with his work. He was known at least by sight to most of the pioneer population of Portland."[12]

Multnomah Park has more than its share of infamous stories. Howard Sigsby, a thirty-year-old watchmaker, was one of the victims of a sensational 1922 double murder. When Charles Wesley Purdin found his newly ex-wife Agnes in bed with Sigsby, he shot her three times in the head and hatcheted Sigsby's face to a pulp before attempting suicide by inhaling gas.[13] However, he survived and stood trial twice. His trials were notable for being the first murder trials in the county to include women on the jury. The first jury, which was dismissed for failing to agree, included two women. The second included five.[14] Purdin's dubious claims of both self-defense and insanity paid off. He was given a six-year sentence and a $500 fine but was pardoned in January 1925, less than three years after his conviction.[15] Purdin lived until 1941 and is buried in River View under a military headstone commemorating his service in the Spanish-American War.

Among the Morningside Hospital patients was Lewis Napoleon Lepley. Born in Ohio in 1852, he was part of the Klondike gold rush of 1902 and stayed in Alaska until 1911. His last winter, he and two other men found themselves snowbound in a cabin and unprepared. Lepley survived—by eating his friends. The ordeal ruined his mental health and got him committed to Morningside.[16] Lepley's sister, Nancy Stewart of Wisconsin, suspected that an Alaskan business partner had Lepley committed to deprive him of his valuable mining claim.[17]

Notable Resident: James Roland Leabo

James Roland Leabo (1823–1898) was born in Tennessee. This pioneer was one of the party that rescued the women and children taken prisoner by Indians at the November 29, 1847 Whitman massacre. About sixty Cayuse and Umatilla Indians stormed Marcus and Narcisa Whitman's Protestant

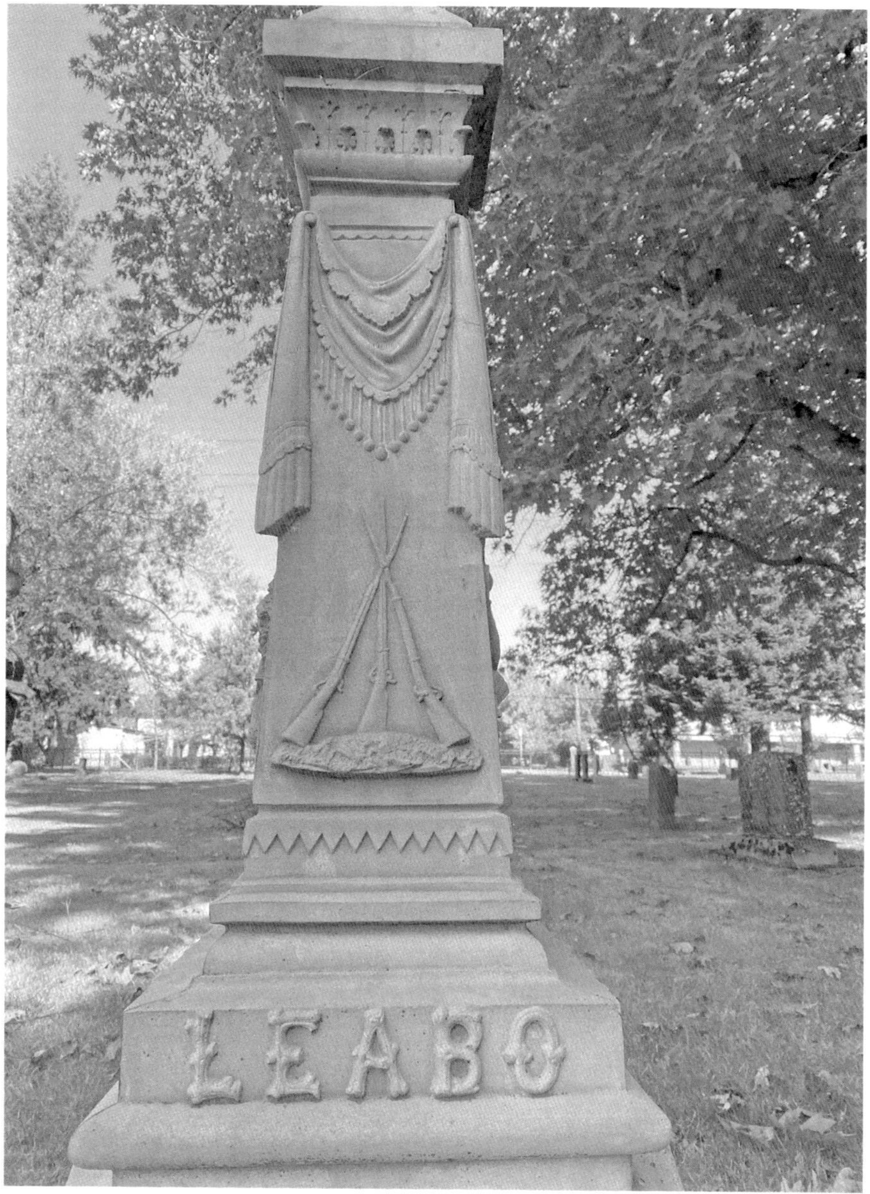

The Leabo monument, an example of the white bronze, aka zinc markers, sold through catalogues from 1874 to 1914. At the time, some people considered them a cheap substitute for solid granite, but they've held up extremely well.

Lost Alaskans

In the early 1900s, when medicine and psychiatry were less evolved, giant institutions housed people with an enormous array of issues and attributes, including advanced syphilis, Down syndrome, deafness and homosexuality. Pre-statehood Alaska lacked such an institution, so the U.S. Department of the Interior was in charge of shipping the mentally ill out of state for treatment. From 1904 into the 1960s, more than 3,500 people were sent to Morningside Hospital in Portland, where Mall 205 sprawls today. Many never returned. These are the Lost Alaskans.*

They didn't voluntarily commit themselves. Instead, a jury of six men decided whether they were of fit mind. Many Morningside patients were people from around the world who'd come to Alaska to make their fortunes. Others were indigenous Alaskans. Those convicted as unfit were often jailed until the spring thaw. Then they'd be sent to Portland by train, dogsled, ship or plane. When Morningside got the government contract in 1904, it received thirty dollars a month per patient. In territorial days, there was a saying that Alaskans could be one of three places: inside (in Alaska), outside (anywhere else) or Morningside.†

Patients who died while in Morningside's care were mostly buried in Lone Fir, Rose City, Multnomah Park and Greenwood Hills, with an occasional interment in the Jewish cemetery Beth Israel or Catholic Mount Calvary. Eric Cordingley and David Anderson of Friends of Multnomah Park Cemetery were among the Portland volunteers who tirelessly searched for death records and unmarked graves to aid researchers in Alaska trying to locate the Lost Alaskans. Cordingley knows of at least three people who have been disinterred and returned to Alaska from Greenwood Hills and Multnomah Park.‡

* Oregonian, August 4, 2012

† Morningside Hospital, https://www.morningsidehospital.com.

‡ Cordingley interview.

mission near Walla Walla, Washington, killing the missionaries and at least eleven others and taking fifty-three people hostage. The Indians blamed Marcus, who was also a physician, for failing to cure a devastating measles outbreak. This infamous incident set off the Cayuse War and increasingly hostile race relations.[18] From 1851 to 1883, Leabo farmed in Clackamas County; he then lived out the rest of his life in Portland. He fathered five children. His pallbearers were members of the Indian War Veterans and the Oregon Pioneer Association.

Eerie Tales

David Anderson told a strange tale about a resident of Multnomah Park. One day he was alone at the cemetery when he uncovered a child's marker with the name Richardine Bates. "When I uncover these markers I just kind of let my mind go and wonder what the person was like," he said. "And all of a sudden I see this shadow off to my right. And it's coming directly toward me. And this thing hits me in the head." Luckily, he still had his bike helmet on when the bunch of fir boughs hit him. He looked up and saw a squirrel in the tree above. "But it was staring at me, just like, 'I got you.' So I'm going okay, this is weird enough."

Later, while researching death certificates in the state archives in Salem he came across Bates's death certificate. "I looked over at Eric and said, 'Look who I just found!' And as I'm showing him Richardine Bates's death certificate, someone was over on the wall of the archives putting or taking a binder off the shelf and the shelf collapses and all the books fall off." After that, Cordingley suggested Anderson leave a toy at her grave and talk to her. "And I have. And everything's been fine."[19]

3
BRAINARD CEMETERY

8950 Northeast Glisan Street, Portland

A huge apple tree is the centerpiece of this small cemetery on a busy street in Northeast Portland. Visitors find a collection of old and new stones, from pioneers to more recent Oregon arrivals, especially Eastern Europeans and Iu Mien people from Laos.

History

Oregon pioneer William Ebenezer Brainard (1832–1911) left Ohio at the age of nineteen and came west to Oregon, where he worked as a steamboat captain on the Umpqua River, operated a tannery and then ran a placer mine. After coming to Portland, he bought 160 acres of land east of Mount Tabor in partnership with C.W. Gay, part of which he officially donated as a cemetery in 1884. Six-year-old Julia Collins was buried there in 1867, as were a few other people who predated the cemetery proper. In 1888, Brainard and his wife, Eliza Maria Brooks Brainard, moved to Southeast 54th Avenue and Morrison Street, where they built a huge Italianate house that today is in the National Register.

By the time Brainard died in 1911, about two hundred people were buried in the cemetery. Two years later, the cemetery made the paper with the headline "Brainard Graves in Danger of Caving into Street." A wooden wall the city had built on Northeast Glisan Street was giving way and likely to spill the contents of at least six graves into the roadway. Mount Scott Cemetery offered space for Brainard's two hundred or so occupants.[20] However, in January 1914, the *Oregonian* revealed that the cemetery's records were a mess. W.E. Brainard had donated some lots to indigent people. Agents had sold other lots, often without deeds being exchanged. At one point, several graves were broken during a widening of Northeast Glisan Street and remains moved to another part of the cemetery.[21] And eventually, all the cemetery's records disappeared with an agent named Mr. Lawrence. Only information on the markers themselves and any paperwork in possession of individual lot owners remained. Since the records were lost, it was impossible to get consent from relatives to move the graves. So instead of a transfer to Mount Scott, a concrete wall was built on the Northeast Glisan Street side of the cemetery to make sure residents stayed put.[22]

Multnomah County acquired Brainard in 1953. Very few people were buried at Brainard from the 1940s until the late 1970s, when the number of burials picked up and it became an active cemetery again. Now it's one of the fourteen pioneer cemeteries operated by Metro.

Memorable Headstones

William O. Heller (1887–1910), an engineer living in Astoria at the time of his death, has an unusual marker carved to look as though it was made from stone bricks.

Two of the most intriguing markers at Brainard are a pair of stumps close to Northeast Glisan Street. These are even more realistic than the Woodmen of the World tree stones and appear to be real stumps from a distance. They're made of a red material, perhaps terra cotta, liberally splotched with yellow and green lichen and moss. The larger of the stumps commemorates three members of the Kennedy family: Dewey and Eva, who died two months apart in 1898, and Oakes (1891–1907). The smaller stump is for Frances Stein, who died in 1892, aged one.

Some of the old markers, like that of Leander James Henry Lenderman (1900–1903), were originally skinny upright stones and now lay flat. Lenderman's especially beautiful white marble stone was put back together after being broken into pieces. It depicts calla lilies, two swans and a lamb and bears a sad inscription: "How much of light, how much of joy, is buried with our darling boy."

The stone of Swiss-born John H. Scherrer (1811–1906) is inscribed, "It matters little at what hour of the day the righteous fall asleep—death

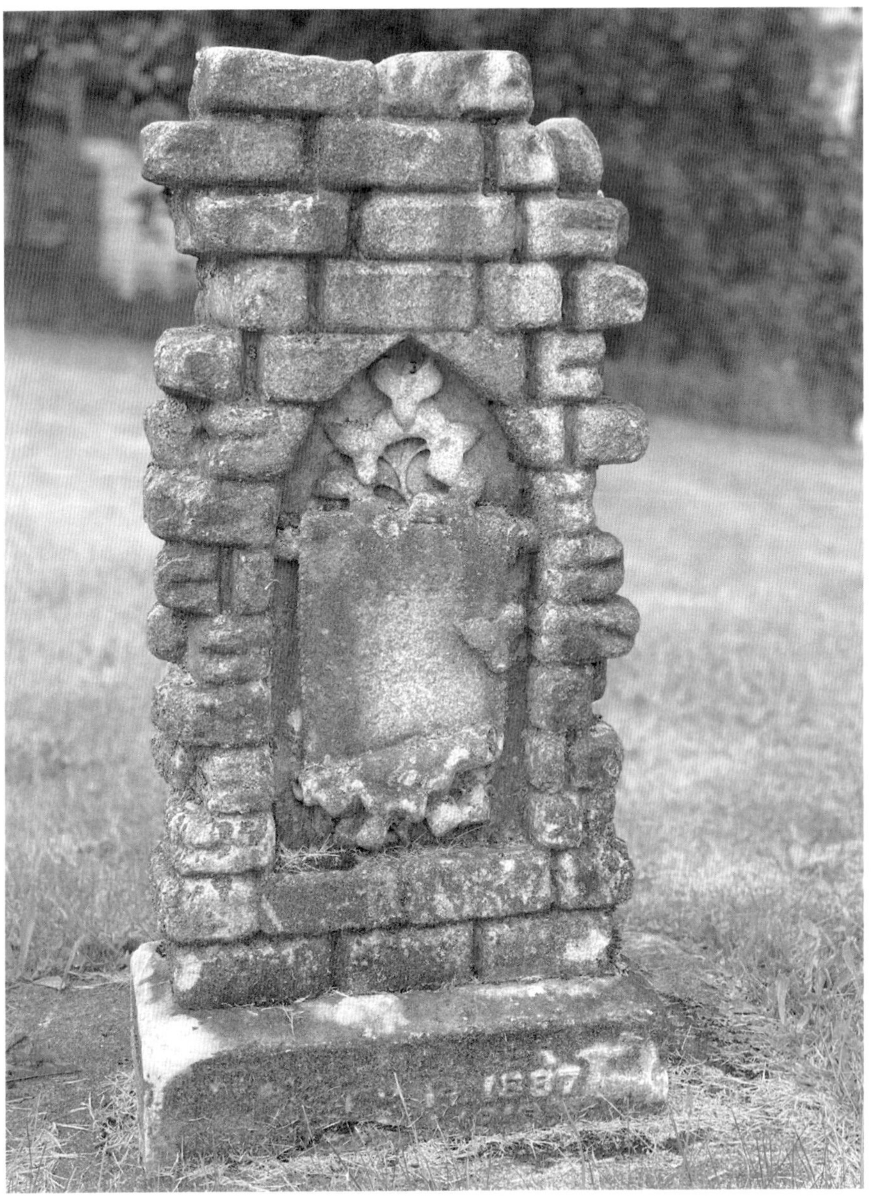

William O. Heller's unusual stone brick marker.

cannot come to him untimely who is fit to die." The second half of this short poem by English historian Henry Hart Milman (1791–1868), not shown on the stone, reads: "The less of this cold world, the more of heaven; The briefer life, the earlier immortality." This poem probably seemed less creepy at a time when circumstances forced people to accept many lives cut short.

Newer stones dominate the heart of the cemetery. Well-tended black granite stones display etched portraits of the residents. The stones are so shiny that they reflect like mirrors fallen apples and the bouquets left by survivors.

Many of the Iu Mien markers feature photo insets of the departed dressed in colorful traditional wear. The dominant name here is Saechao, with about fifty occupants bearing this common Mien surname. Some Iu Mien who lived in Laos helped the CIA during the Vietnam War and then were in trouble when the United States lost. Many attempted to escape to Thai refugee camps. From there, the United Nations helped them relocate to other countries. Of the approximately thirty-five thousand Iu Mien people who live in the United States, most live in California. About five thousand live in Oregon and Washington.[23]

Notable Residents

Nicodemus (1846–1921) and Emilia Ann Fouts Snow (1846–1904) and their three small children left Missouri for Oregon in the late 1800s. Their headstone is the largest in Brainard and striking enough to attract the attention of local musicians. In 2011, an Americana/pop/acoustic blues band named itself after the Oregon pioneer. It released the debut album *Here Lies Nicodemus Snow* the following year with album art based on the tombstone. The band was active until 2017, with its biggest hit being the Christmas song "No Room at the Inn."

In 1892, Mary Jane Lewis (1860–1892), née Hastings, slit her own throat with a knife. She was the first wife of pioneer Leander Lewis. "She had expressed a fear that she would become insane and kill her children, and it is supposed that this led her to commit the fearful deed," the *Oregonian* reported. Her husband found her still alive on the kitchen floor. "She appeared indifferent as to whether she got well or not."[24] She didn't and is buried at Brainard. However, the *Oregonian* reported at the time that she was to be buried in Multnomah Park. This is a typical historical cemetery mystery in times of poor recordkeeping. Was she originally buried at Multnomah Park and then reinterred at Brainard? Or was the *Oregonian* incorrect, and has Mary J. Lewis, as she is remembered on her tombstone, been resting here all along?

Recreational Activities

Geocachers can use info found on Brainard's gravestones to locate a hidden cache.

Earliest Cemeteries

The pioneer cemeteries people visit today aren't Portland's first burial places. The first big cemetery was downtown between Ash and Burnside, west of First near the Skidmore Fountain, with burials dating from 1817 to 1854. By 1887, the *Oregonian* was already reporting on the shortsightedness of new towns when it came to burying the dead, never thinking a city would catch up to the graveyard's "remote" location. Nor did they always take terrain into consideration. "So full was the earth of these veins of water that a grave dug and left open for a few hours would become half-filled from the copious seepage," the *Oregonian* reported of a cemetery south of town.

The bodies in the old cemeteries didn't rest in peace for long. Most were removed to other cemeteries. Others made inconvenient appearances during building projects, when a decaying coffin or naked bones would suddenly emerge. City contractors moved bodies from the original city cemetery near Burnside in 1857—a project that took a while, with graves standing open in the meantime. "While wandering through the gloomy woods after dark, it was no infrequent occurrence for persons to stumble into these sepulchral openings, to their great disgust and discomfiture," the *Oregonian* reported. Supposedly, the bodies were all removed. But considering shoddy early cemetery recordkeeping, we are probably often walking above bones in our modern city.*

* *Oregonian*, April 26, 1887.

4

ROSE CITY CEMETERY

5625 Northeast Fremont Street, Portland

Two beautiful angels on Rose City's entry gates greet visitors. Flat, wide pathways, sculpted trees and bushes and some of the most ethnically diverse tombstones in town make Rose City an extremely inviting place for cemetery fans to stroll.

History

Herman Julius Blaesing Sr. (1870–1959) founded Rose City Cemetery in 1905 on eighty-plus acres of former dairy land. The German immigrant's family first settled in Wausau, Wisconsin, and then came to Portland in 1894. Two years later, he established the Blaesing Granite Company, a business that nicely complemented a cemetery. He built the bases for war memorials and statues of prominent people around the city.

The cemetery name held great meaning for Blaesing, who was at the center of Portland's cultural image as the "Rose City." Blaesing was an original member of the Royal Rosarians when, in 1912, the mayor declared the white-suited gents as official greeters and ambassadors of goodwill for the city of Portland. He was president of the Portland Rose Society and instrumental in the internationally famous Rose Parade.[25]

In 1936, while the Great Depression drove up unemployment, Blaesing hired Jack R.H. Ollerenshaw (1910–1982) to work in the cemetery office.

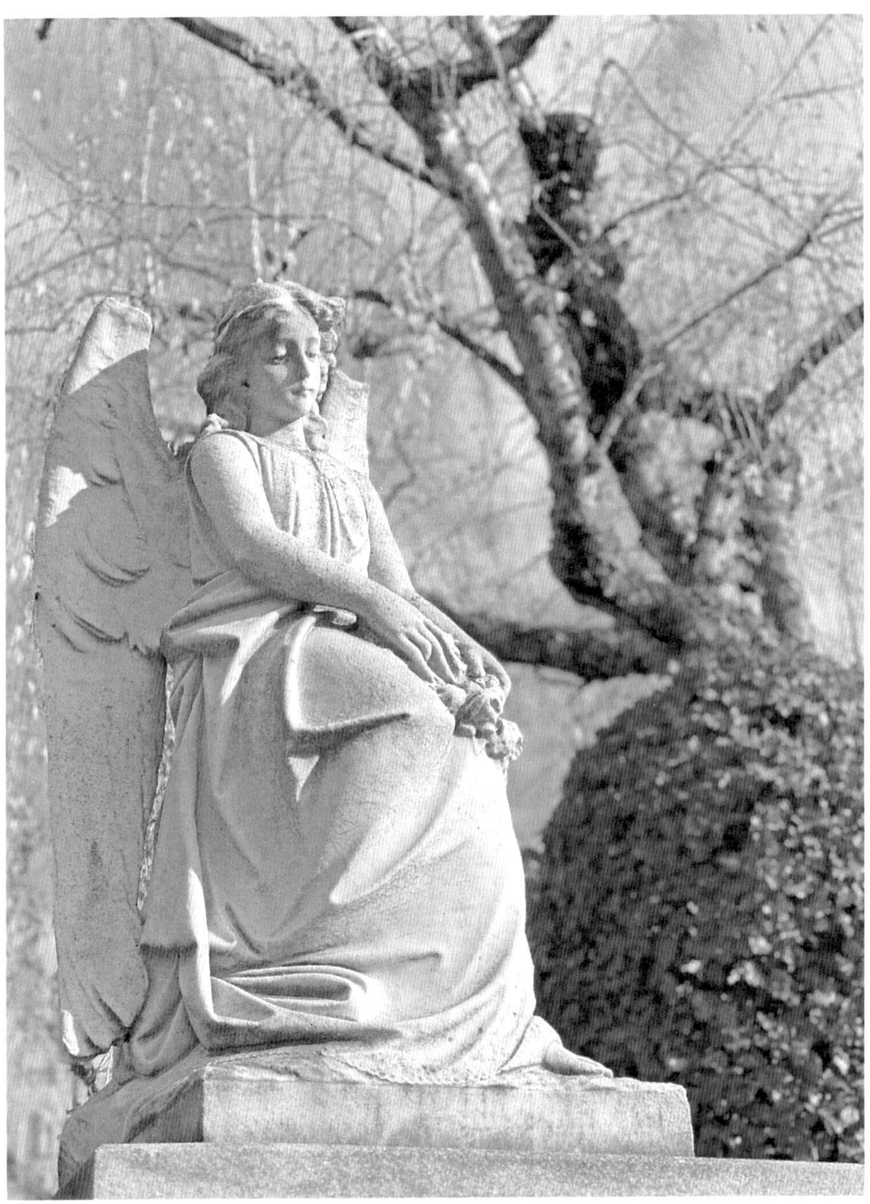

Above: An angel on the front gates of Rose City.

Opposite: Drawing of proposed layout for Rose City Cemetery. *Rose City Cemetery & Funeral Home.*

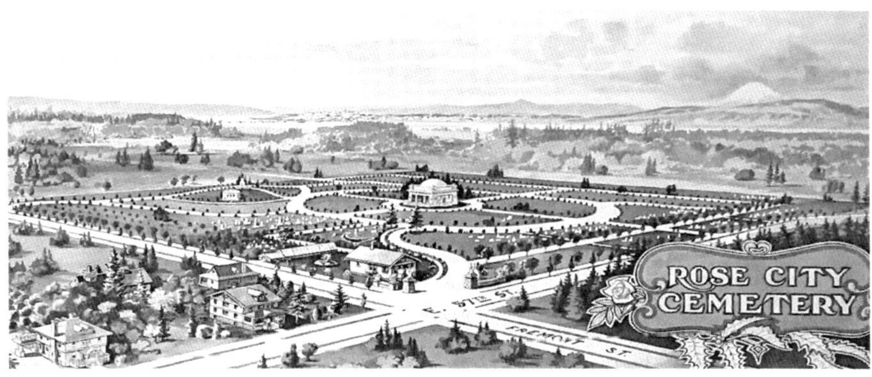

"Quite a number of people applied for the job, and my dad felt that because he was a Mason, he was the one they hired," said Jay Ollerenshaw.

Ollerenshaw's sons Jay and Jon grew up in the cemetery. Jay was only three years old when his father took the job, and Jon was born a few years later. Jay remembers riding around the grounds with maintenance workers and learning to thread pipe in grade school when the cemetery put in a water system. "At twelve years old, I was running a power mower that was seventy-two inches wide. You couldn't get away with that today." Jay remembers digging up horseshoes leftover from the old dairy farm.

Like Blaesing, Jack Ollerenshaw was very involved in civic activities, including the Royal Rosarians. When he died at age seventy-two, he was executive vice president and general manager of Rose City Cemetery. He and Blaesing are both buried at Rose City.

Meanwhile, his sons' interest had made the cemetery a family business, and they grew up to run it. "I loved helping the folks in the situation that they were having to deal with," said Jay Ollerenshaw. "I don't know why, but I just kind of fit in. And I feel that I was pretty good at it."[26]

As extended families and friends buried loved ones together, ethnic "neighborhoods" sprang up within the cemetery, including German, Italian, Russian and Greek. The Japanese have a separate cemetery within Rose City, run by the Japanese Ancestral Society. Rose City Cemetery is famous for having one of the largest numbers of Romani graves in the United States. Many Romas, also known as Gypsies, arrived on the East Coast of the United States between 1880 and 1920. By the 1930s, they had begun migrating west. Traditional Romani occupations include metalcraft, car and horse sales, carnival ride repair and fortune-telling. There are now several thousand Romas in Oregon, with population concentrated in Northeast Portland, just east of Rose City Cemetery.

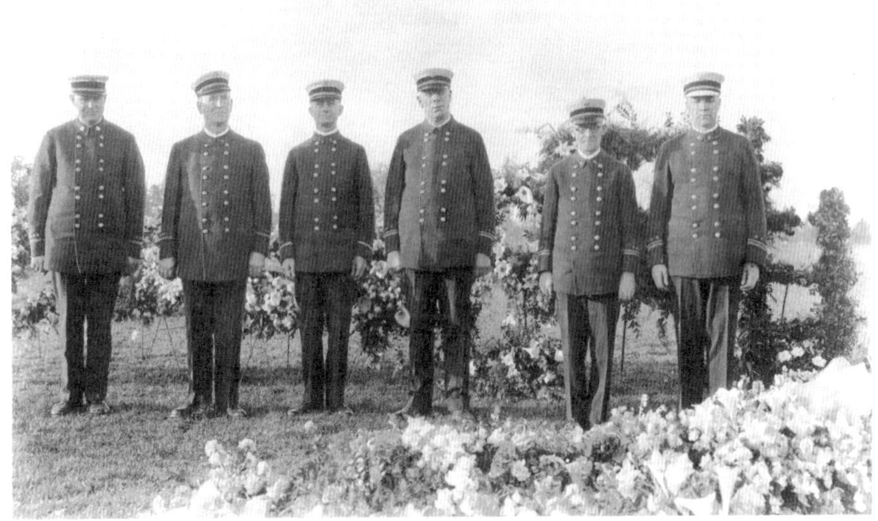

Chief Benjamin Dowell's funeral, 1928. Dowell served as Portland fire chief from 1911 to 1920. *City of Portland (OR) Archives, A2002-007, 1928.*

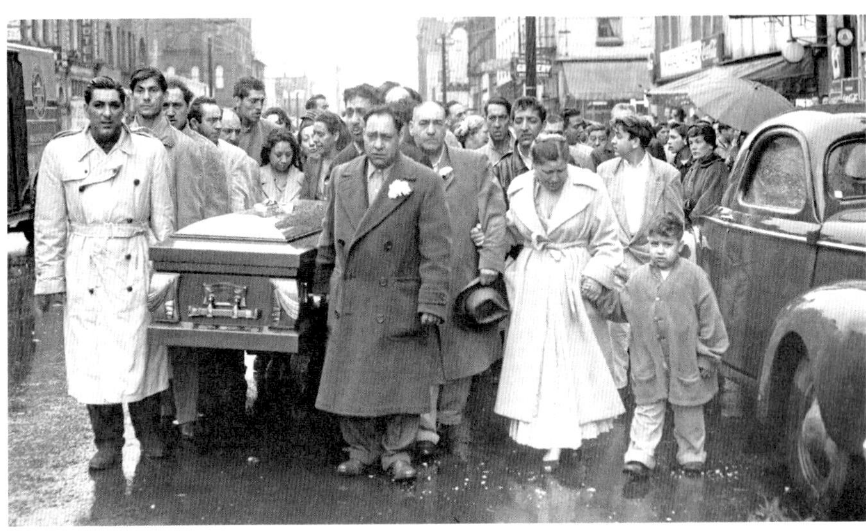

Copper casket of Gypsy king Miller Ristic carried through street to Saint Nicholas Russian Orthodox Church, March 1955. *From the* Oregonian.

Death rituals, funerals and respecting ancestors are important in Roma life. The first Gypsy burial at Rose City was in 1942.[27] The Romanis now have a huge area in Rose City full of colorful and impressive stones, many featuring glass-encased portraits of the departed and several marking the resting places of Gypsy kings and queens. Traditionally, large funeral parties walked through the streets accompanying the casket, stopping at every corner to honor the departed and wash away evil by pouring water on the ground. In addition to wakes, relatives come to visit on birthdays, Easter and other important days, bringing along food and drink to share with the spirits of the departed.[28] Since burying their loved ones with some cash for the afterlife is a Gypsy tradition, Rose City Cemetery pours cement over their graves to make it impossible to get into without heavy equipment.

Rose City is also special because it's privately owned, unlike most burial spots in Portland. "It's been family-owned forever," said Ollerenshaw. "We're not owned by any conglomerate."

MEMORABLE HEADSTONES

It's a joy to walk the impeccably kept grounds, complete with mushroom-shaped holly trees pruned so perfectly round they look cartoonish. And everywhere you turn, there's another interesting stone.

Rose City has many headstones with intact cameo portraits protected by glass from the 1920s–50s. These were especially popular with Italian and Greek families, as well as the Gypsies, and really keep the memory of the deceased alive. The chosen photos are often of the person in his or her youthful prime, regardless of how long they lived, although some also depict people later in life.

Many Eastern European graves feature large Russian Orthodox crosses, some with carvings of Mary. Quite a few headstones are bilingual at Rose City, inscribed with Russian or Greek as well as English.

The newest, grandest private mausoleums belong to Roma families and are located in the middle of the cemetery. On the north side is a fortress of shared mausoleums, the first built in 1955.

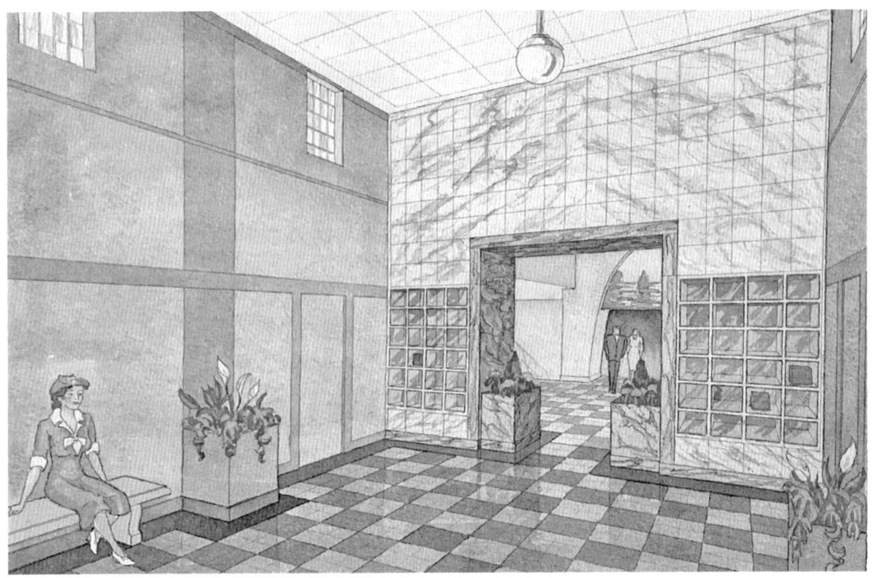

Mausoleum interior. *Rose City Cemetery & Funeral Home.*

Local Celebrities

Two former Oregon governors rest at Rose City Cemetery. Theodore Thurston Geer (1851–1924) was the first governor to be born in the state, his pioneer parents having arrived in 1847. An early bicycle enthusiast, in 1899 he signed Oregon's first legislation to create a network of cycling paths.[29] Albin Walter Norblad Sr. (1881–1960), whose family emigrated from Sweden when he was twelve, served in the state senate and finished out a gubernatorial term from 1929 to 1931 when the elected governor died in office.[30]

Among the many veterans in Rose City, Alaric B. Chapin (1847–1924) won a Congressional Medal of Valor for his actions during the Civil War.[31] John Alphonsus Murphy (1881–1935) was awarded the Congressional Medal of Valor while a drummer in the Marine Corps for his service as part of the China Relief Expedition, which rescued U.S. citizens and other foreigners trapped in Peking during the Boxer Rebellion.[32]

Rose City contains many Gypsy royals, all of whom had dramatic stories of deaths, funeral processions and burials. When Gypsy king Miller Ristick (1887–1955) died in a Salem hospital, police dispersed the crowd of 150 who wailed in the street outside.[33] In 1966, as Portland king/auto wholesaler Frank Ellis lay dying in Good Samaritan Hospital, the crowd

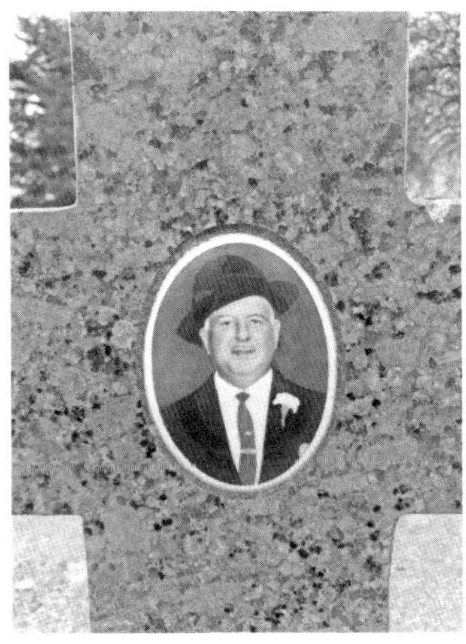

Frank Ellis, Gypsy king.

grew so large his family set up a mobile home command center nearby, and people in the hospital room communicated to the crowd via walkie-talkies.

In 1975, Steve Marks, a Gypsy king of national importance, died in Wichita, Kansas, after a twenty-two-day vigil. His family shipped his body to Portland for burial in the family mausoleum at Rose City. But more than twenty funeral homes refused to care for the body and allow the traditional ceremonies, according to family member and Gypsy senator James Marks II.[34] Funeral homes felt that a three-day wake with eating, drinking and on-site cooking would exclude or offend other customers. Eventually, the family settled on holding the wake at a North Portland meeting hall. Marks was buried at Rose City with a five-gallon Stetson on his head and a suitcase of his clothes at the ready beside his wife, Rose Catherine. While three hundred Gypsies showed up from as far away from Chicago, many boycotted the memorial because James Marks II filed bias complaints with state officials. Asking outsiders for help solving problems is not the Gypsy way. The fallout from the complaints dragged on for months. According to James Marks II, "But if we were born Gypsy, we should have the right to be buried Gypsy. We're not asking for the world, just the right to be ourselves. This is very cruel to us."[35] The Oregon Board of Funeral Directors and Embalmers eventually said Gypsies were not denied services because of religious discrimination but because of Gypsy customs. According to local morticians, those customs too often led to property damage.[36]

Notable Resident: Artie Wilson

When Arthur Lee Wilson (1920–2010) was growing up in Alabama, he taught himself to play baseball with a broomstick and golf ball wrapped in thread. He shined shoes to earn money for his first uniform. And despite losing a thumb as a teen in a work accident, he still went on to baseball glory. From 1944 to 1948, he played shortstop for the Black Barons.

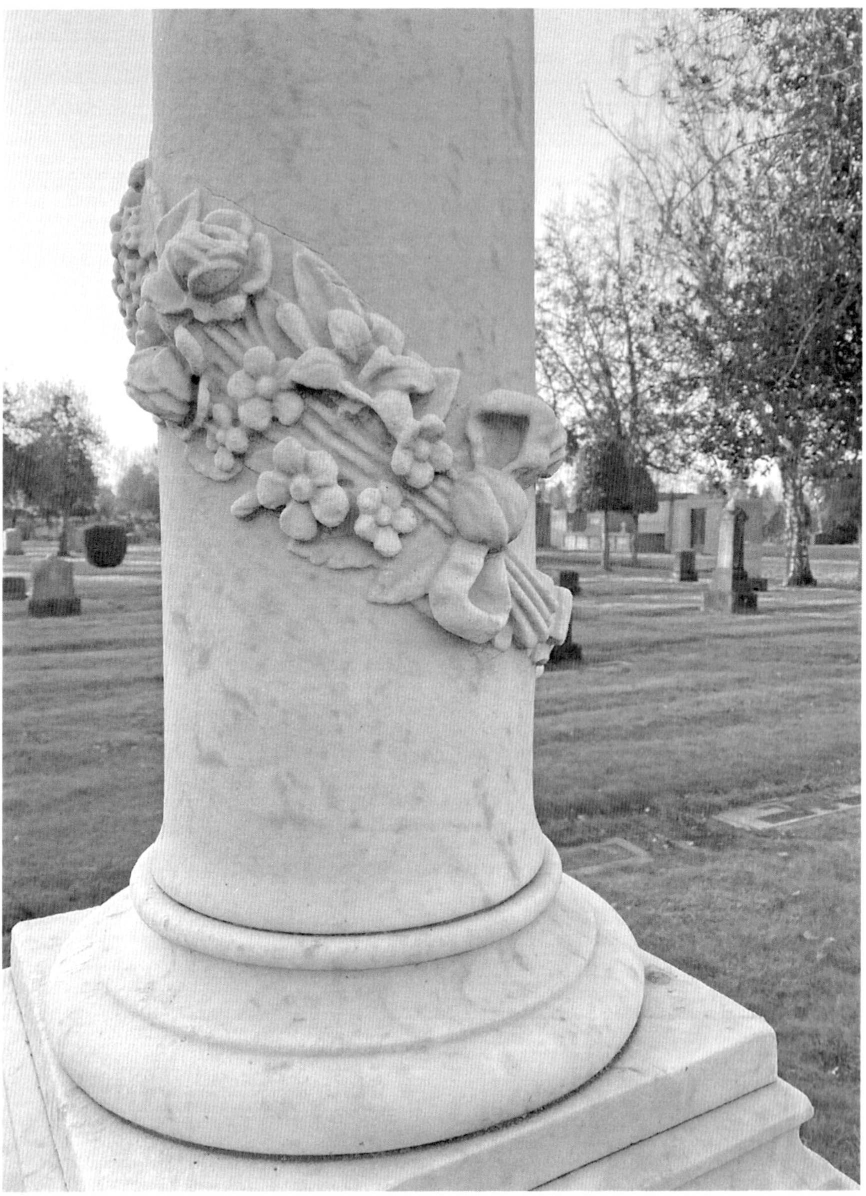

Column detail.

When the color barrier was lifted, Wilson had a brief stint in the New York Giants before settling into a minor league career. He played for Seattle, Portland, Oakland and Sacramento in the Pacific League until 1957. After retiring from baseball, he ran a Portland car dealership. In 1989, he was named to the Oregon Sports Hall of Fame and in 2003 to the Pacific Coast League Hall of Fame. His joint headstone with his wife, Dorothy Faye (1924–2012), depicts a baseball mitt and bat.

Notable Resident: Henry Shaffer

The death of twenty-five-year-old German longshoreman Henry Shaffer was a huge news story in March 1908. He was at home celebrating his wife's thirtieth birthday with twelve guests when police officers arrived, acting on a noise complaint. Shaffer, who weighed 250 pounds and had prior arrests for domestic abuse, assault and disturbing the peace, was an intimidating character. But public opinion was decidedly in Shaffer's favor when police shot him dead in his own kitchen.

The policeman, Nathan Suitter, had been sued for the nonfatal shooting of a fleeing perp the previous year.[37] Because of this, the police department issued new rules banning excessive force. At the inquest, it took the jury only ten minutes to find Suitter's shooting unjustifiable. Nobody seemed moved by Suitter's testimony that the longshoreman attacked him and he responded in self-defense. Suitter was held for second-degree murder. The *Oregonian* reported, "Not only did Suitter's testimony go to show that the shooting was altogether unnecessary, but it revealed him in the light of an unutterable coward."[38] People also blamed Shaffer's landlord, who'd called the police to complain. According to the *Oregonian*, Shaffer's union was "interested in seeing a vigorous prosecution of the case, as are many influential Germans."[39]

The Longshoreman's Union held the funeral. Six hundred men in union insignia were part of the crowd of three thousand who walked three miles from Shaffer's home in North Portland to the downtown service, then took streetcars to Rose City Cemetery.[40]

In a dramatic turnaround at the trial, a witness who attended the birthday party changed his statement and affirmed Suitter's claim that Shaffer had attacked him. Suitter was exonerated.[41]

Special Features

Rose City has an impressive veterans' memorial. The big circular area features an American Legion memorial surrounded by flags from the different military branches and a rose garden with Mr. Lincoln and Soaring to Glory varieties.

5
JAPANESE CEMETERY

3701 Northeast 50th Avenue, Portland

This separate cemetery run by the Japanese Ancestral Society is entirely enclosed within Rose City Cemetery. Wander through the compact, well-maintained grounds to get a glimpse of Japanese history in Portland.

HISTORY

The Japanese population in Oregon rose from 25 in 1890 to 3,418 in 1910, with 83 Japanese-owned farms. The Portland Japanese Benevolent Cemetery Association incorporated in 1908, soon after Rose City Cemetery opened in 1906. But some of the Japanese graves there precede the founding of Rose City, with the oldest identified marker dating back to 1899. In 1908, prosperous Portland businessman Shinzaburo Ban and his wife, Kiyo, conveyed six lots to the cemetery. Joseph B. Lee conveyed two more lots later that same year.[42]

As more Japanese established themselves in Oregon, they were met with hostility and racism by some and fascination by others. An *Oregonian* article from 1910 reported on Japanese burial customs: "The only departure from the regular American funeral is when a lock of hair and fingernail are taken from the body. These are sent home. The family and relatives in Japan hold services over them and put them away in the family tomb. This is done in lieu of transporting the body, as the Chinese do." The article also mentioned that the Japanese favored taking photographs of the casket

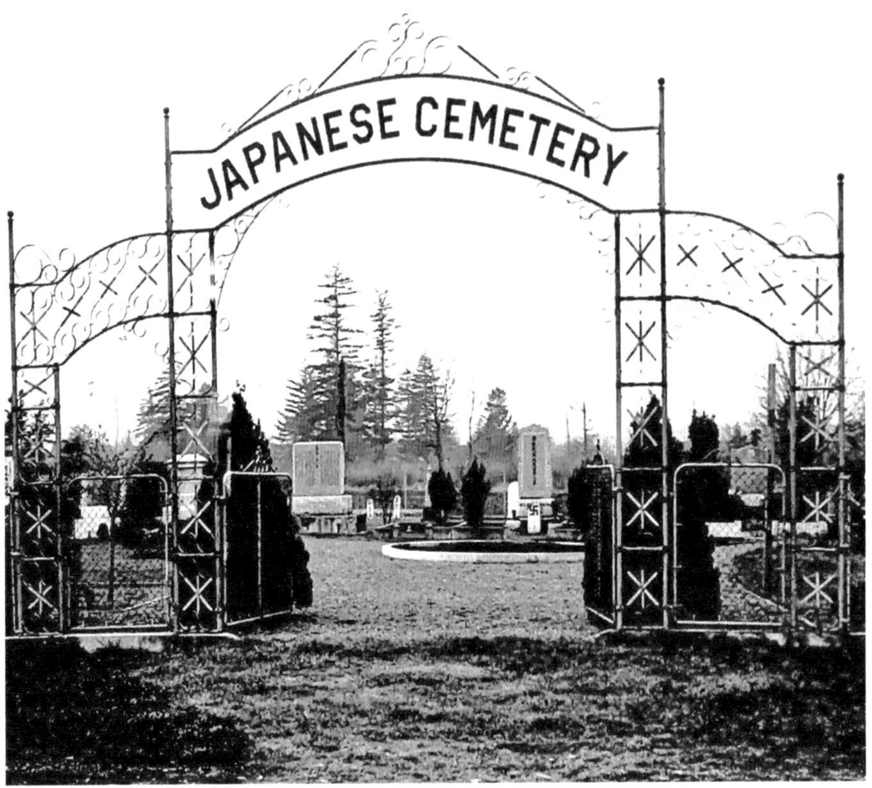

Japanese Cemetery gates. *Rose City Cemetery & Funeral Home.*

being lifted into the hearse and at the grave and that the Buddhist Japanese "have adopted a funeral song to the tune of Auld Lang Syne, which they sing at each service."[43]

In keeping with the traditions of their new country, local Japanese cleaned up the cemetery on Decoration Day, later known as Memorial Day. A 1927 *Oregonian* account describes a dual service by a Buddhist priest and a Japanese Methodist minister. But the really important days would come in July and August for Urabon, a time set aside to pray for the peace of the deceased. A man identified as "the young Portland writer named Nakazama" described Urabon traditions to a reporter. "The candles are burned to revive the fire of life. The offerings of rice, fruit and small cakes are made for the repose of departed souls, and the custom originated from the old Buddhist beliefs. The gods of the Japanese, not being far-away gods, but the souls of ancestors, who live very near, would be pleased with these gifts."[44]

Then came World War II, when things went tragically sideways for the Japanese. Families who used to be neighbors were incarcerated in concentration camps. Successful farmers, businesspeople and ordinary citizens became prisoners overnight, leaving their homes and land behind. And, of course, their cemetery. Vandals have always targeted cemeteries—who is easier to pick on than the defenseless dead? But now there was real anger behind it, fueled by fear for their own family members off fighting the Japanese. At one point, vandals overturned more than half of the approximately five hundred markers in the Japanese cemetery.[45] "People almost demolished that cemetery," said Jay Ollerenshaw, who was a little boy then and son of Jack Ollerenshaw, who managed Rose City Cemetery. "We had a very close relationship with the Japanese community. My dad helped them put things back together."[46]

Veterans' groups and many others blocked efforts to help local Japanese American families during the war. In August 1943, Reverend J.W. Reed, president of the Portland Fellowship of Reconciliation, invited volunteers to clean up Japanese graves. Japanese people had been gone an entire year by then, and weeds choked their cemetery. Portlanders incarcerated at the Minidoka camp in Idaho sent money for flowers to decorate the graves. After the cleanup, the reconciliation group planned to have speakers, a potluck and an interfaith discussion led by five youth representatives of different racial and religious backgrounds. "It is felt that this gesture of friendliness to members of a group unable to be present will not be amiss in a world too often characterized by hatred and bloodshed," Reed wrote. The group planned to send a scroll with participants' names to Minidoka, so Japanese American neighbors would know they—and their departed loved ones—hadn't been forgotten.[47]

When the *Oregonian* reported on this planned event, local officials were inundated with calls from outraged veterans' groups. About twenty law enforcement officers showed up on cleanup day, along with angry citizens. The Elks Lodge leader called reconditioning the Japanese cemetery an insult to American war dead. Joe DeBoest, commander of a Portland legion post, said, "The American Legion won't stand for this monkey business." Police prevented a riot by nixing the cleanup.

Vandalism continued throughout the war and beyond. A grassfire scorched tombstones in August 1946,[48] and that November the *Oregonian* ran a photo of the vandalized marker of a one-month-old baby.[49] After World War II, Nikkei Jin Kai, also known as the Japanese Ancestral Society, took over care of the cemetery, as well as leading many other civic and cultural programs for the community. After a question about ownership of the cemetery land, the ancestral society became the title holder in 2005. The society administers an endowment to maintain the cemetery.

Memorable Headstones and Residents

Once you enter through the Japanese Cemetery's beautiful wrought-iron gate and pass between a pair of garden pagodas, you're clearly in a separate space from the surrounding Rose City Cemetery. Stones stand close together in orderly rows. The older markers, small and elegant pillars with Japanese inscriptions, ring the edges of the cemetery.

Some larger markers in the middle stand out. Naoichi Hirofuji (1881–1938) has a huge chunk of natural rock instead of the usual polished granite. On the back of the stone is carved, "This stone shipped by his crew from Hidden Inlet Alaska."

The enormous stone of Reverend Tansai Terakawa (1893–1944) tells his story in English on the back. Born in Japan, he graduated from Buddhist University and was ordained to priesthood in 1917. He worked and studied in Hawaii, San Jose and San Francisco, earning a master's from Stanford University along the way. He served as Bishop Masuyama's assistant at the headquarters of the Buddhist Mission of North America in San Francisco before coming to Portland in 1939, where he was a priest of the Oregon Buddhist Church. He died in the Minidoka concentration camp in 1944.

In the very middle of the cemetery stands a tall monument inscribed "Dedicated to the memory of these brave men who made the supreme sacrifice in World War II." Following are the names of fifteen Japanese American men with an Oregon connection who fought and died for the United States while their relatives were incarcerated in camps. But don't look for them here. They're buried around the country, some taking their rightful places in Arlington or other national military cemeteries.

6

COLUMBIA PIONEER CEMETERY

9800 Northeast Sandy Boulevard, Portland

Once in a tranquil setting, Columbia Pioneer now sits among busy streets, its less than pristine grounds prone to litter and loitering. But the former Masonic cemetery has a nice collection of trees to provide shade on a hot day while perusing an interesting collection of stones.

History

Settlers first chose this area of Northeast Portland, now known as Parkrose, as desirable because it was close to the Columbia River. The Columbia Slough watershed covers a whopping thirty-two-thousand-plus acres and meanders for nineteen miles. This strategic location provided both a natural transportation route and plenty of water for farming. Sandy Boulevard, which runs past the cemetery, was an Indian trail long before European settlers arrived and continues to be a major thoroughfare.

Ebenezer Lane Quimby (1813–1891) traveled by ox team from New York to Oregon. He homesteaded in the Columbia Slough area, belonged to the Columbia Slough Masonic Lodge and served on the board of county commissioners from 1868 to 1869. In 1877, he donated land for Columbia Masonic Cemetery. But instead of spending eternity on his former homestead, Quimby wound up buried at Lone Fir.

Italian farmers began moving into the area near the end of the nineteenth century, buying land from original Oregon pioneers and homesteaders.

Aldo Rossi, who was born in a house close to Columbia Pioneer in 1920, recounted family stories in an oral history. His family bought land from the Pullen family—seven of whom are buried in Columbia Pioneer—in the 1880s. "When my family first farmed here they had to cut trees down, blast the stumps and there were places where there were still a little bit of woods….We cleared this land with pick and shovel and blasting powder."[50] Nowadays, cemetery visitors comment not on the number of trees but on noisy cars going by.

Responsibility for the cemetery passed between several Masonic lodges, including the Mount Tabor Masonic Lodge when it merged with the Columbia Lodge. The land was later relinquished to Elizabeth Holtgreive (1840–1928), whose late husband, Henry (1828–1906), was a trustee of Columbia Masonic Lodge. The Holtgreives are both buried in Columbia Pioneer under one of the cemetery's more impressive monuments. In 1944, Multnomah County acquired the cemetery through a state mandate. It's now one of the fourteen pioneer cemeteries operated by Metro. Also referred to as Columbia Slough Cemetery or Columbia Masonic, it is not the same as Historic Columbian Cemetery, which is in North Portland.

MEMORABLE HEADSTONES

Prominent pioneer families have impressive pillar stones here. There's the column commemorating the Zimmermans, pioneers of 1851, topped with an urn, and the even taller and more ornate urn-topped column of the Paynes. The Pullens also have a large column, but their urn or other finial has broken off. The Snovers' large column prominently displays the square and compass, the best-known Masonic symbol.

James Kintrea (1856–1903) has Columbia's lone Woodmen of the World tree stone. Alfred Baker (1858–1907) has a lovely example of the cash register–shaped headstone popular at the time. William Taylor (1789–1870), born in the Isle of Wight, and his wife, Lucina (1801–1855), lie beneath an especially beautiful weeping willow carving.

Columbia Pioneer has many recent burials marked by flat stones representing Portland's diverse modern inhabitants. A Spanish-language gravestone depicting a Jeep and the Virgin of Guadalupe lies beside an Eastern European black granite with a laser-etched babushka and a quote from Isaiah. Nearby, Mary Poppins flies across a corner of a stone in silhouette, while the marker of a four-year-old bears the Portland Trail

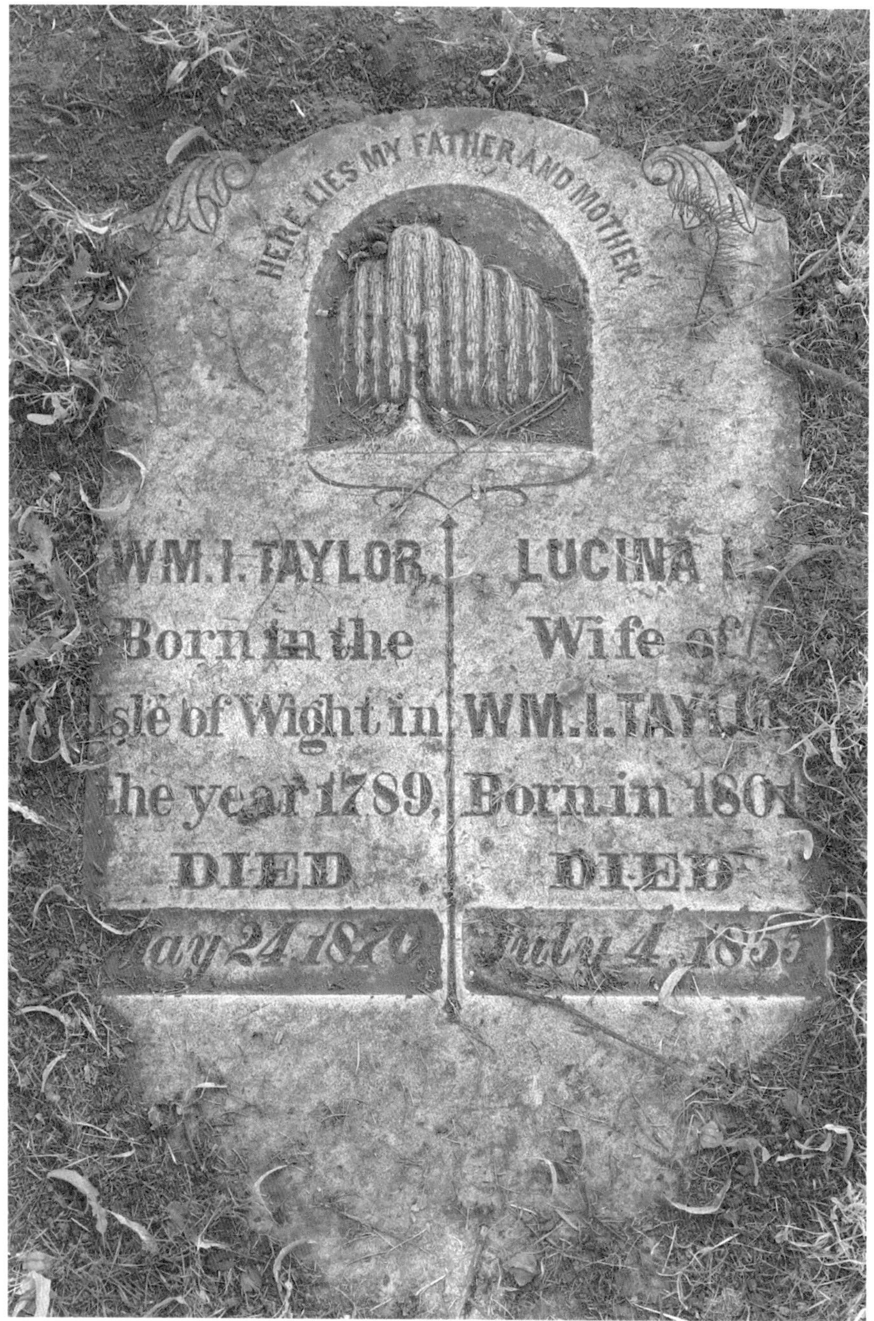

Classic weeping willow image.

Blazers basketball team logo. One stone depicts a man sitting on a cloud fishing, apparently from heaven, while his surviving loved ones wave up to him from the shore. Columbia also has some idiosyncratic markers such as a big, handmade, rusty and weathered metal cross for a woman who died in 1999.

Notable Resident: Payne Family

William H. Payne was born in West Virginia in 1824. As a teenager, he caught mining fever and went to California in search of gold. "After drifting around among the various camps he decided to cast his lot in the state of Oregon, where he hoped to find something more substantial than the ephemeral pursuit of a mining prospector," the *Sunday Oregonian* noted in his obituary.[51] Payne acquired a donation land claim on the Columbia Slough, where he and his wife, Anna Smith (1833–1898), raised a large family. He was a charter member of the Columbia Masonic Lodge.

Unfortunately, their son Kit Carson Payne (1859–1898) inherited his father's gold fever. He followed his dreams to Alaska. There, he and eight other men met their demise aboard a dangerously overloaded sloop in Turnagain Arm, a waterway in the northwestern part of the Gulf of Alaska. An 1898 *Morning Oregonian* story emphasized the perilous nature of the thirty-five-mile-long Turnagain Arm: "Through this deep and rocky gorge the wind and tide rush with terrible force. The tides rise and fall some 50 feet and run like a torrent over miles of mud flats and reefs of ragged rock….Here, when the wind is in certain directions, the waters pile up and a tidal wave sweeps in like a rushing wall of water." Broken pieces of the sloop's cabin were found, but no bodies. Only the sloop's dog survived, swimming ashore and finding its way to a mining camp.[52] Anna Smith Payne died earlier that year, after a period of being an invalid. William Payne died the following year. Both are buried in what was then still called Columbia Masonic Cemetery.

7

POWELL GROVE CEMETERY

4748 Northeast 122nd Avenue, Portland

This is Portland's most oddly located cemetery. The city grew up around it—so close around it that Powell Grove is in the middle of a traffic circle on busy Northeast Sandy Boulevard and Northeast 122nd Avenue. Visitors who dare to dash across the busy street will find old stones from local pioneer families and some recent burials as well.

History

The cemetery takes its name from the Powell family, many members of which lived in the Parkrose area. John Powell homesteaded on the west side of what's now Northeast 122nd Avenue, while David Powell homesteaded on the east side.[53] David is the one who established the cemetery in 1848, the year his first wife, Almeda Amanda Harless Powell, died. The cemetery has also been called Central Grove or Central Columbia.

This small cemetery prompted an important legal battle. After Powell Grove had been privately run for a century, descendants of those buried there asked Multnomah County to assume maintenance in 1949. This coincided with suburban development in the early 1950s. The intersection of Sandy and 122nd was a hot commodity. Fred Meyer wanted to build his first store outside of downtown there. County officials wanted to widen the intersection and run 122nd directly through the cemetery. They thought the cost-effective solution for county development would be to disinter bodies

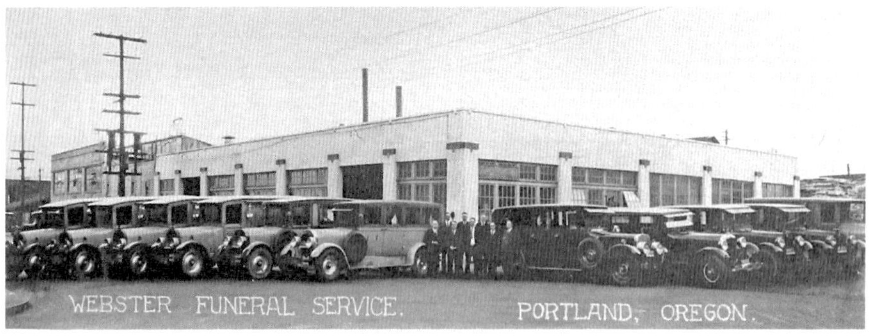

Old hearses. *Wilhelm's Portland Memorial.*

at pioneer cemeteries and rebury them at Douglass in Troutdale, which at the time had the potential to add one hundred acres onto its existing nine. A 1957 state law allowed consolidating small cemeteries.

Moving 121 bodies from Powell Grove to Douglass was a test case. "The relocation program was prompted by the probability that the county eventually will have to assume maintenance responsibility for nearly 70 small cemeteries as private maintenance funds become exhausted," said a 1959 *Oregonian* account.[54] Perhaps officials were looking south at how San Francisco had reclaimed valuable real estate by transferring 150,000 bodies from its city limits to nearby Colma from the 1920s to the 1940s.[55]

Relatives of those buried at Powell Grove resisted, and the debate dragged on for a decade. At a 1959 public hearing, only one person out of about two dozen attendees spoke in favor of moving the bodies. More typical was a woman who said that bodies "should not be shoved around just because they weren't big people. Let them rest in peace." There were also questions of legal ownership. Did plots belong to descendants who held the deeds or to the county? The legal tangle continued for a couple more years.[56] But Powell Grove remained, and the streets awkwardly went around it. New residents slowly trickled in, with more than twenty since 2000. Which might make visitors wonder: does the hearse have to double park in the traffic circle?

MEMORABLE HEADSTONES

Powell Grove has about two hundred markers. The most notable are pillars for prominent families, such as the Powells and Barkers. The Reynolds family has an especially big marker. Visitors will find a good representation

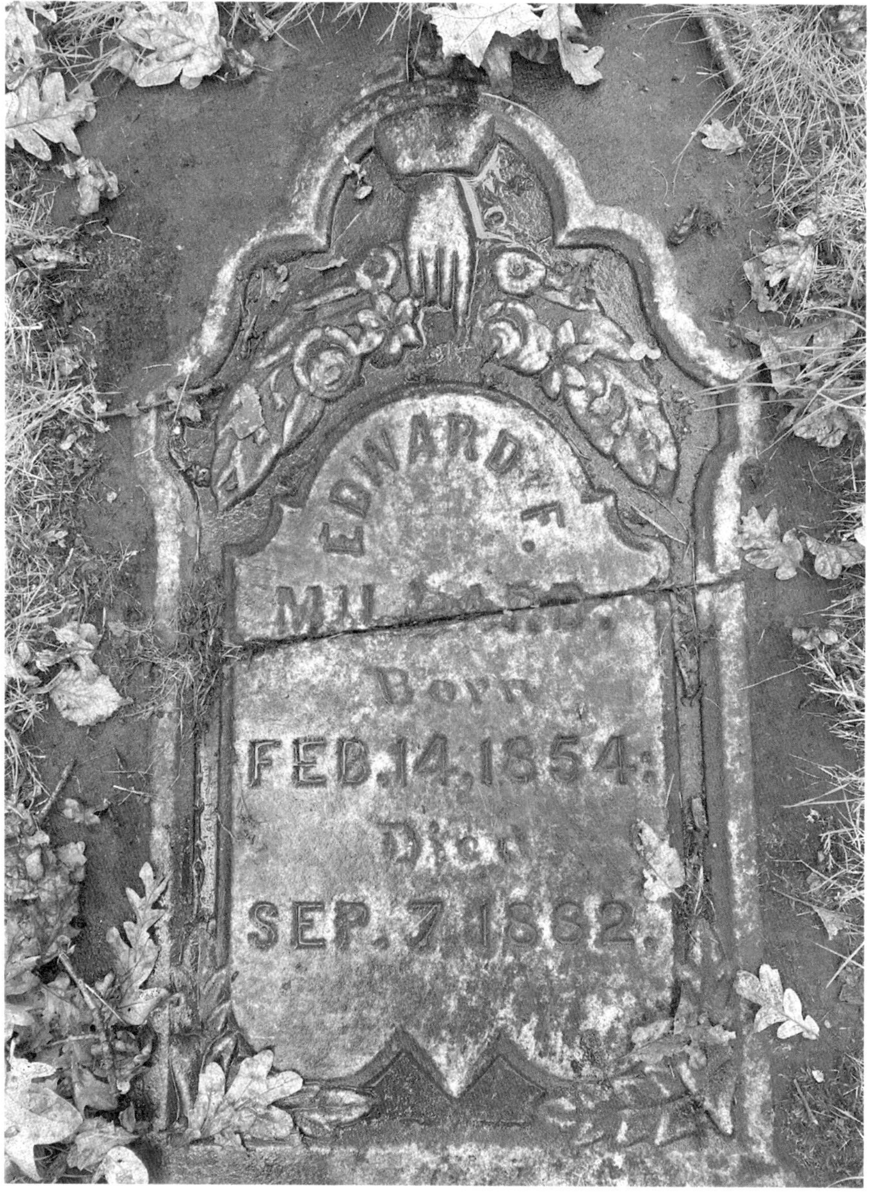

The finger pointing down represents God reaching for a soul, often used on markers for an untimely death.

of popular gravestone motifs of the late 1800s, such as clasped hands, doves, flowers and open books.

Other markers drive home the sadness of the mid-1800s infant mortality rate. The Barker family has five children buried here during the 1850s and 1860s aged between two months and three years old.

Notable Resident: David Powell

When David Powell (1814–1887) and his wife, Almeda Amanda Harless Powell (1815–1848), left Missouri for Oregon in 1847, only two other houses stood in Parkrose, where they settled. Powell had little formal education, but he worked hard to get a schoolhouse built in his district. He served in the 1865, 1868 and 1870 Oregon legislatures.[57] As the *Oregonian* summed him up in his obituary: "Mr. Powell had the true genius of a pioneer. He was steady of purpose, strong in attachments, unyielding in his positions, ready to assume responsibility, brave and fearless in his friendships as well as in his antagonisms, quite such a man in intellectual and physical hardihood as is most useful in reducing heterogeneous social and political elements into order and stability and forming them into a stable commonwealth."[58] He later married Ann Eliza Greer Powell (1834–1912). In keeping with Powell's support for education, one of his eleven children, Reverend L.J. Powell, served as president of the territorial university at Seattle and as the superintendent of schools for the state of Oregon.

Notable Residents: Barker Family

Early Oregon pioneers Hiram (1815–1893) and Susan Barker (1822–1907) are two of the many Barkers buried at Powell Grove. Hiram was born in Zanesville, Ohio, and Susan in Illinois. They lived in Illinois before setting out for Oregon with their four children in 1852. In 1853, they acquired a donation land claim nine miles east of Portland. Eventually, they had fourteen children. Hiram was a member of the Mount Tabor Masonic Lodge.[59] Susan stayed on their property for another fourteen years after Hiram's demise. In her obituary, the *Oregonian* described Susan as "a typical specimen of the pioneers who came to Oregon in the fifties—virile, full of resources, given to hospitality."[60]

GRAVE DOWSING

People have used metal or wooden rods to dowse, or "witch," for unmarked graves for more than five hundred years. "If a body is present, the two rod tips begin to swing inward and will cross in front of you, when you are over the grave. Once you step off the grave, the rods will uncross," according to dowser Linda Faye Nelson. A dowser can tell whether the person is a child or adult from the length of the grave, and determine gender by whether one rod turns clockwise (female) or counterclockwise (male). You can make your own rods out of coat hangers. Nelson emphasizes the importance of practicing on marked graves—but don't peek at the marker first.*

* Linda Faye Nelsen, "Dowsing for Unmarked Graves," http://www.jayhistoricalsociety.org/pioneerstories/Dowsing_for_Unmarked_Graves_by_Linda_Faye_Nelson.pdf.

Their daughter Lorena Barker Holcomb (1842–1907) came west with her parents. She was remembered in the *Oregonian* as "one of Oregon's best-known pioneer women." She married Samuel Holcomb in 1859 and they had two sons—Curtis, who stayed in Portland, and Cecil, who became an attorney and moved to Shanghai, China. The 1866 obituary of Samuel Holcomb allows a peek underneath the laudatory pioneer rhetoric. Once a popular figure in Portland, according to his obit, Holcomb died alone in San Francisco. "But by his course of life, after becoming addicted to the use of poisonous liquor, he was unable to attend to his own affairs, and came to an end quite unworthy of an intelligent mind....We regret the event—we regret that any man should unfit himself for the responsible duties in life by such course as that pursued by Holcomb. He very seldom refused to drink, and whiskey carried him off at last."[61]

8

HISTORIC COLUMBIAN CEMETERY

1151 North Columbia Boulevard, Portland

On busy North Columbia Boulevard with eighteen wheelers rolling by on the I-5 overpass above, the Historic Columbian is a noisy but still semi-tranquil patch of green populated with lively ground squirrels. While the pioneer influence is strong, the cemetery is looking toward the future with a dedicated green burial area.

History

Historic Columbian was originally called Love Cemetery, named for Captain Lewis Love and his family. Love (1818–1903) was born in Chautauqua County, New York. He married Nancy M. Griffiths in Illinois in 1836. In 1849, they followed the Oregon Trail to what would eventually become North Portland and took over a 635-acre donation land claim by the Columbia River. The captain became a developer and pioneer industrialist in Multnomah and Clark Counties. He also operated a gristmill, ran a ferry, farmed and manufactured lumber. Perhaps not surprisingly, considering his industriousness, Love became one of Oregon's first millionaires.[62] When he was eventually laid to rest in Love Cemetery, "The remains were contained in a magnificent black couch casket," the *Oregon Daily Journal* enthused, and thirty hacks were required to carry all of Love's bereaved friends and relatives from the chapel to the cemetery.[63]

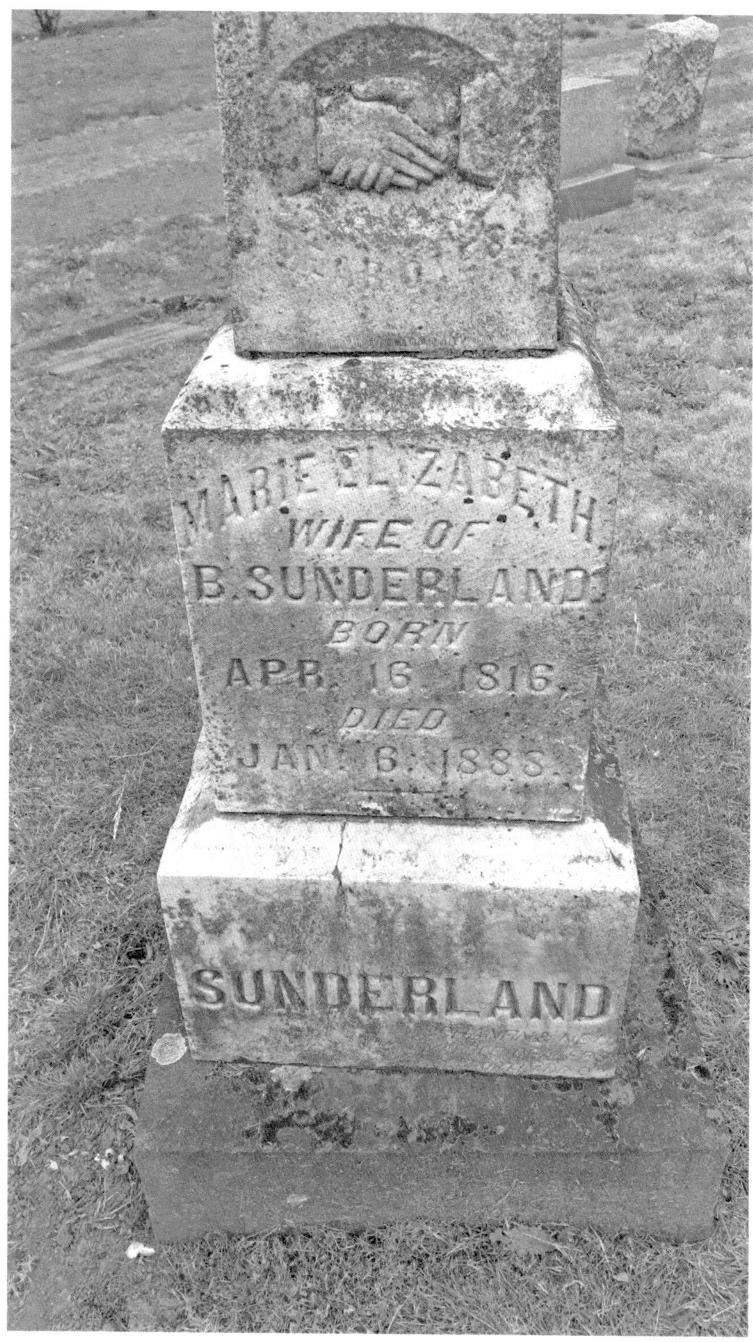

Many Sunderlands are buried in Historic Columbian.

While the family continued to bury their own there—more than thirty Loves are interred near the back of the present cemetery, some within an old iron fence—from 1857 on, other community members also buried their dearly departed in the cemetery.

Historic Columbian remained active through the entire twentieth century, while a succession of private owners ran it. The cemetery had its ups and downs as far as reputation and upkeep. By about 2012, a nonresident owner was letting things go. The grass wasn't being cut, stones were vandalized and the burial records were in disarray. A group of relatives of those buried there formed a nonprofit called, appropriately enough, Historic Columbian Cemetery. They were able to take over ownership and management of the property. They spent thousands of hours straightening out the cemetery records, identifying occupied spaces, sorting names of the cemetery's approximately 6,500 residents and storing their records at the Genealogical Forum of Oregon.

But despite their dedication, running a cemetery on volunteer power is difficult and more expensive than anticipated. Over the next decade, people stole all the maintenance equipment, desecrated stones, camped out in the cemetery and illegally dumped trash. The City of Portland demanded removal of trees with Dutch elm disease at more than $2,500 a pop. In fall of 2017, Historic Columbian lacked funds for security and decided it could open the cemetery by appointment only. The nonprofit association actively sought somebody to take the cemetery off its hands. But Metro didn't want to add Historic Columbian to its pioneer cemetery portfolio, and other community entities, local churches and nonprofits also gave it a pass.

Enter Ed Bixby, an unlikely real estate developer-cum-cemeterian who had already acquired a historic cemetery in New Jersey and two in California. A proponent of green burial, Ed Bixby saw great potential in Historic Columbian. In June 2018, the nonprofit group held a public meeting about transferring the cemetery to Bixby. Each plot owner had a vote in the transfer. Bixby acquired the cemetery for the cost of drawing up the paperwork.

Bixby and his wife, Helena, oversaw a massive cleanup, hired a caretaker and got the property on a maintenance schedule. Having a regular presence there cut down on vandalism. Once it was presentable, the Bixbys sought to raise community awareness of the cemetery as a green space to visit, enjoy and, eventually, stay for a very long while. They turned Historic Columbian into what is called, in the green burial world, a hybrid model. This means people can choose traditional burial with the works—embalming, coffin, concrete vault and headstone—or spend an eco-friendlier eternity in the green burial section in a hand-dug grave inside a simple shroud or wicker casket, marked by a natural fieldstone. The Bixbys restored the cemetery's old wrought-iron fence and repositioned it to surround the new green garden.

Bixby mapped out space for at least one thousand more burial plots, including two hundred in the green garden. "And then of course with cremation, the sky's the limit," Bixby said. The cemetery sells one-foot-by-one-foot cremation spaces for direct earth cremains burial, which means thousands more spots. Since Bixby took the cemetery over, people are starting to buy plots again. "The only way a cemetery survives is it has to produce income to take care of itself," Bixby said.[64]

Bixby's cemeteries are affiliated with Universal Life Church, a multidenominational religion founded in 1962 and best known for instant ordination of ministers. Bixby feels the inclusiveness and progressive nature of Universal Life fits well with the natural burial movement.

Memorable Headstones

Stones range from thin old uprights miraculously still standing to some homemade crosses painted in black, red and white. Historic Columbian does not have the rigid marker rules that some cemeteries have implemented, so people enjoy freer rein in personal expression.

Bion H. Darling (1857–1910) has an attractive Woodmen of the World monument with three lengths of log stacked on top of an upright marker. Gustav Adolf Hubert Jr.'s (1890–1907) heart-shaped stone is especially pretty.

Carl W. Kreeger, a German native who died at the Oregon State Tuberculosis Hospital in 1914, has one of Portland's best examples of the popular Rock of Ages headstone motif. Augustus Toplady wrote the hymn "Rock of Ages" in 1763. His song includes the lines "Rock of Ages, cleft for me, let me hide myself in thee"; and "Nothing in my hand I bring, Simply to Thy cross I cling." The lyrics inspired the 1876 painting by Johannes Adam Simon Oertel first titled *Saved, or an Emblematic Representation of Christian Faith,* later reproduced as *Rock of Ages*. The image of a woman clinging to a cross, usually surrounded by angry ocean waves, was destined to be a huge hit for both headstones and tattoos, with many variations.

John Zeids (1882–1919), a Russian native who died of influenza, has the Workers of the World insignia on his marker and the inscription: "From the vast world above my grave, I hear the tread of marching men, the patient

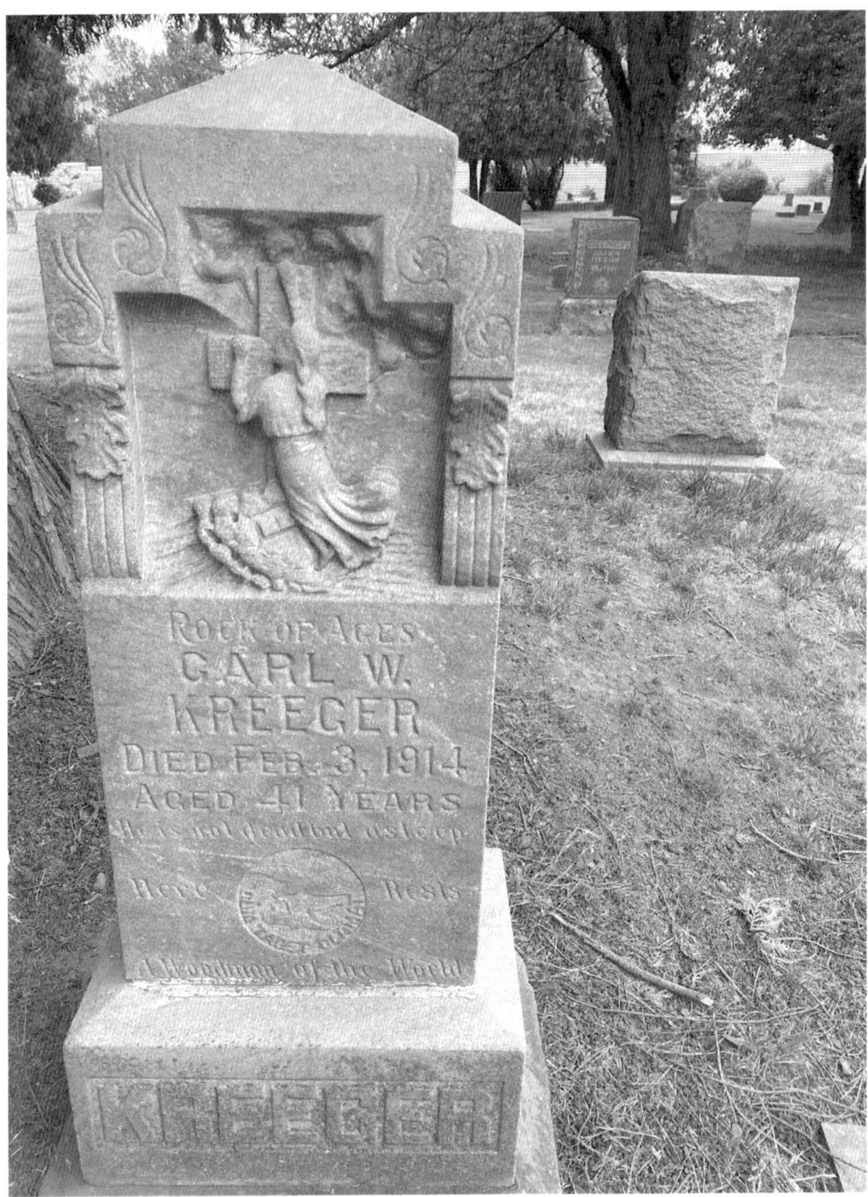

The popular Rock of Ages motif.

armies of the soviet." This is a paraphrase of a classic Socialist poem by Thomas Wentworth Higginson called "Heirs of Time" that reads: "Of this vast world before my door, I hear the tread of marching men, The patient armies of the poor."[65]

Historic Columbian has several baby sections. The older is on the north side of the cemetery, containing perhaps fifty babies who died in the 1940s and 1950s. On the west side are rows of 1970s babies. Most remarkable, in the cemetery's northeast corner, baby graves and a few adult markers are interspersed within mazelike hedges.

A pretty, white gazebo offers visitors a place to sit and also contains clearly labeled bowls of water left for resident squirrels and rabbits. The green burial ground is a plain strip of grass in the very back of the cemetery, set off by the historic fence.

NOTABLE RESIDENT: JAMES "JIMMIE" JOHN (1809–1886)

Twenty-two-year-old Ohio native James John left Westport, Missouri, in May 1841 with the party of General John Bidwell following the California Trail. A year later, John joined a Hudson Bay Company party at Sacramento, bound for Vancouver, British Columbia. John stopped in the Tualatin Plains, where he began his life as an Oregonian. He settled in Linnton for a couple of years before moving east of the Willamette River in 1846 and taking on a 320-acre donation land claim. His homestead covered the whole area of present-day downtown St. Johns. In 1852, he was operating a ferry where the St. Johns Bridge now stands. He platted an eight-block town site in 1865. The town of St. Johns was incorporated in 1894, several years after John's death, and annexed by Portland in 1915.

People described John as reticent, noncommittal and disinclined to talk about his pre-Oregon life. Because he was reclusive, people called him "The Saint." This morphed into St. John, and eventually St. Johns was used to describe the neighborhood. "The final 's' attached itself to the name through usage, and no amount of petitioning before state and national geographic boards has succeeded in correcting it," the *Oregonian* grumbled. John was thought to be a lifelong bachelor but once told a friend that his wife and child had died before he left home at age twenty-two. He also told people he came from Indiana, but an entry in his family Bible found after his death revealed Ohio as his home.[66]

John's grave was unmarked for many years. But in 1909, Multnomah County officials honored John's donation of land for the town library and James John Elementary School with a stone describing him as a "friend of education."

Notable Resident: Reverend Daniel Drew (1843–1923)

Daniel Drew was born enslaved in Virginia in 1843. During the Civil War, Union troops in Missouri freed him. Drew enlisted in Company F, Fifty-Sixth U.S. Colored Troops, joining 180,000 African American Union soldiers. Sometime after the war, he moved to Oregon and became a Quaker minister. He was involved with both his church and with the Grand Army of the Republic, Ben Butler Post No. 57, named for the major general who formed the first African American regiment in the U.S. Army.

Drew was a public figure in Portland, a deep thinker and a man of conscience. In 1902, he lectured on the "Condition of the Colored Race Before, During and Since the War" as part of a fundraiser for the soldiers' monument in Lone Fir Cemetery.[67] But the following year, he publicly resigned from his role as chaplain of the GAR post, saying that his Quaker faith would no longer let him participate in an organization that "fosters the spirit of war," an allegation hotly contested by other members. "I honor the veterans for all they have done for my race," he said at the time of his resignation. "While it is true that the Union soldiers did not fight to give us our freedom, that was one of the results of the war, and we might have remained in bondage but for the war."[68]

He and his wife, Laura Ann, both later converted to the African Methodist Episcopal Church. One of their children, William S. Drew, married Alice M. Bills (1886–1949), a Wisconsin native who played the organ at the AME Zion Church for many years. Alice is also buried at Historic Columbian.[69]

Eerie Tales

A ghostly hostess named Lydia whispers in visitors' ears and sometimes appears, according to ghost hunter Jeff Dwyer. When he visited the cemetery, he "heard the muted tones of musical instruments, horse's hooves on the muddy ground and a gunshot that echoed off the wall of a warehouse that stands adjacent to the east border of the cemetery."[70]

Bixby hasn't experienced any unexplained phenomena but has heard accounts from others. "I think the biggest thing is people claim that they feel dizzy or out of sorts back by the babies. I've had lots of people say the same exact thing, that when they get back there, they just start feeling like their equilibrium is off. Like they started feeling sick. A little nauseous and a little out of sorts."

Thelma Taylor (1933–1949), who's buried at Historic Columbian, has an especially tragic tale. The fifteen-year-old was waiting for a bus in St. Johns to take her to Hillsboro to pick beans when an ex-convict kidnapped her. He held her overnight on the east bank of the Willamette and then beat and stabbed her to death about eight blocks north of the St. Johns Bridge. People say they hear her ghost screaming for help at night under the bridge in Cathedral Park.[71]

9

HUMANE SOCIETY ANIMAL CEMETERY

1067 Northeast Columbia Boulevard, Portland

The West Coast's oldest animal cemetery clings to a steep hill near the Columbia River in North Portland. It's a moving testament to people's love for their furry, feathered and even scaly companions.

History

Ella Leota Smith Swanton (1868–1933), longtime general manager of the Oregon Humane Society, founded the animal cemetery. She and her husband, Frank W. Swanton, buried the beloved pets of many friends and acquaintances in their orchard on Palatine Hill. But once the orchard was full, Leota chose a grassy knoll overlooking a little lake behind the humane society headquarters. When it was dedicated in 1918, the land was adjacent to a meadow where the humane society's goat and two cows grazed.

Animals were first buried in what's now a large rose garden outside the cemetery gates. Many of those bodies were later exhumed and replaced inside the current official confines of the cemetery. Some of the bodies, including that of a horse, still lay beneath the roses.

The original plots filled up quickly. By 1931, the humane society had enlarged the area and hired a landscape architect to develop more pathways through the grounds and provide more parking. "In addition to the graves of average-sized animal pets, there is a row of tiny, tiny plots where pet canaries are buried," reported a 1931 *Oregonian* article. "For the many to whom a

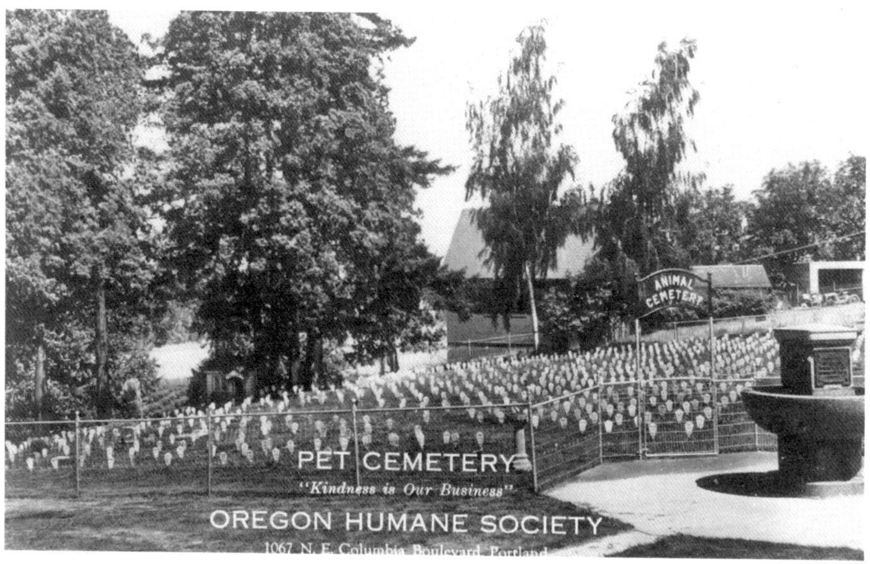

The Humane Society Pet Cemetery, circa 1950. *Oregon Humane Society.*

grave seems to be 'overdoing it,' there is the incinerator."[72] By 1940, the cemetery had doubled in size.

By 1961, the graveyard was so full at 1,200 burials that some people who already had a pet buried there added the remains of subsequent pets in the same grave. So the humane society built mausoleums and columbariums to make more space. Amazingly, Oregon's famous future governor Tom McCall spoke at the dedication of the animal mausoleum and columbarium.

In 1966, a third mausoleum was added, paid for by an anonymous donor whose only condition was that it be built to the same standards as a human mausoleum. Indeed, they look just like human mausoleums in miniature, right down to the little vases on their fronts. Two more mausoleums were dedicated in 1973 on the second Sunday in June, which is Pet Memorial Day.

More than six thousand animals were interred by 1982, including crows, rabbits, pigeons, canaries, parrots, monkeys, goldfish, a tarantula and a bantam rooster named Cluck. Alan Thomas, manager of operations, told an *Oregonian* reporter, "I wake up at night with nightmares about our cemetery—the upkeep is so expensive."[73] To help remedy this, they did what lots of cemeteries do: replaced upright monuments with flat ones to save time and money maintaining what was by then a three-acre area.

The on-premises crematorium has two incinerators, small and large. The largest pet to be cremated in recent years was a three-hundred-pound potbelly pig. While pet owners aren't allowed to attend the cremation, they often attend interments and sometimes hold memorial services. "You're like a funeral worker, knowing when to step up and talk and when to give them space," said Kaylee Guerrero, a facilities tech whose job includes cemetery work.[74]

In 1993, the animal cemetery was the site of a wedding instead of a funeral. Retired OHS adoption counselor Ruthye Dennis got married in the rose garden. Kaiser and Berlin, a pair of Rottweilers, pulled the newlyweds in a ribbon and balloon-bedecked cart, and staff dogs served as attendants.

The humane society now has four mausoleums and two columbariums. The society stopped burying pets in the mid-2010s, and the last mausoleum space filled up in 2020. At press time, only about twenty columbarium niches remain unoccupied.

Memorable Headstones

While the plots came with standard small plaques, quite a few mourners contracted with monument makers for something special. Some of these reflect the culture of the pet's family. A pet named Mary has her name written in Japanese as well. Bijlee Shirish Patel's large granite marker features an om symbol and the epitaph "Hari Om Byoo Beta, May you spread the same joy wherever you go." Tasha (1975–1989), a beloved black Lab who somehow managed to score a rare upright stone, got a Bible quote.

Several stones have full-color portraits inset behind glass. Orange and white cat Buddy (1991–2004) has his portrait near the bottom tip of a heart-shaped stone. Triskell Haggerty-Demuth (1982–2002), "Our Beloved Siamese Friend," lounges in front of a fireplace in his portrait. Most impressively, the portrait of Devil (1930–1941), "My pal for 11 years," is still holding up, despite a crack and some fading. The lawnmower has not been so kind to many other stones, which have craters where glass-encased photos used to be.

The devotion of some of these animals' human companions is touching. One family has nine burial plots for their Scotties and bull terriers with death dates ranging from 1959 to 1998. Four days before Christmas in 2020, each grave was meticulously tended and topped with fresh pine wreaths, pinecones and red bows.

The names are more unusual than at your average human cemetery, including Queenie Weed, Poo Choo Kie, Monkey Boy, Baby Dolly, Princess

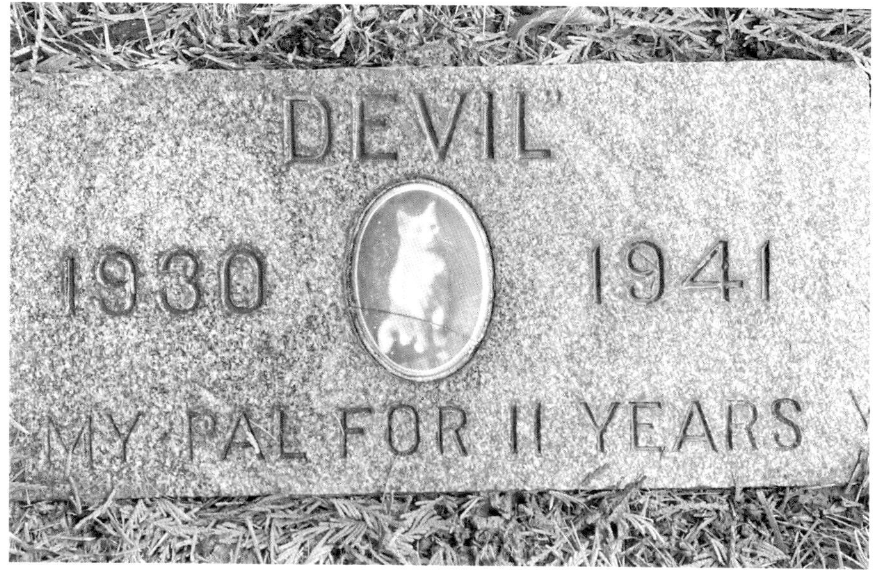

Devil's photo marker from 1941.

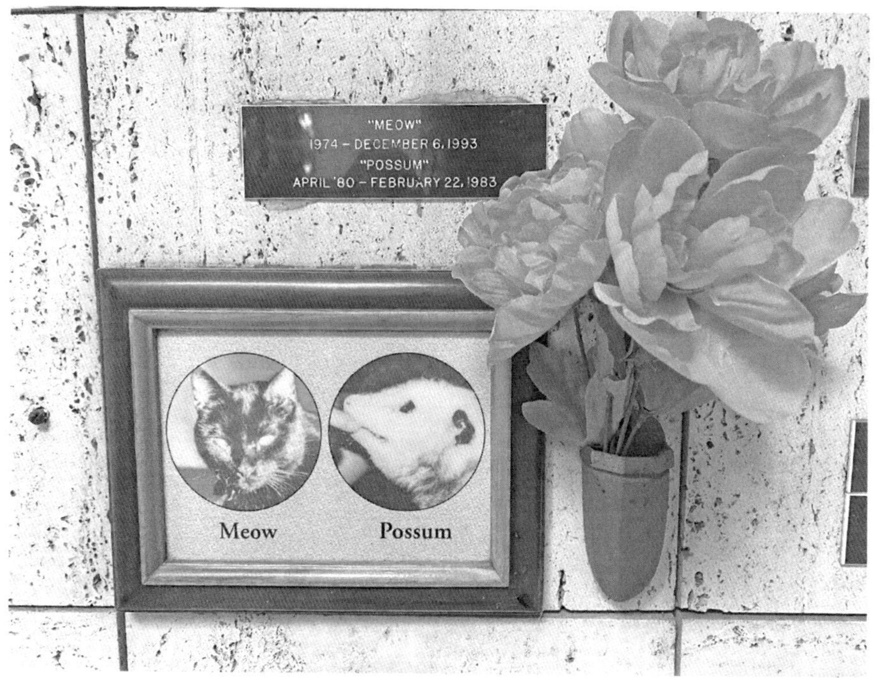

Interspecies friendship.

Tinky Poo, Pee Pee Le Pugh, Fifi Babydoll Smileyee and Poody Baby. The epitaphs are evocative: Komur, the "Black Queen who lived nine lives"; Mojo, "Black knight shining silver heart"; "Calico, 23 years old, she loved birds"; Smokey 1973–1989, "He will always have a whisker wrapped around my heart"; and Punkin, 1975–1990, "She will be purring wherever she is."

And like any cemetery worth visiting, the personalities and relationships of the interred and their survivors are often thought-provoking. What was the relationship between Meow (1974–1993) and Possum (1980–1983, yes, a real opossum), which were interred together? How did Trudee (1974–1986) demonstrate that "She was half human"? And why were Art and Betty Dickson so attached to the name that their three dachshunds were Tookie (1951–1966), Tookie-Too (1966–1980) and Tookie Three (1980–1990)?

Just outside the cemetery gates is a sad and moving memorial to a human. Aimee Wood lost her life in 1992 while trying to rescue an injured dog from a freeway.

Local Celebrities

Most of the animals in the pet cemetery were the ordinary beloved pets of Portlanders. But some made the news. Dolly was a war mascot that J.A. Kraft brought back from the infamous Flanders Fields of World War I.[75] Brownie, a cocker spaniel, was also a military mascot. He lived at Hill Military Academy, the school that sat atop Rocky Butte before closing in 1959. When Brownie died, he got a soldier's funeral. Two young military men carried his casket while others stood at attention graveside as the casket was lowered.[76]

Jiggs's human was of a much different character, but Jiggs didn't care. When Charles McPool got taken to jail for bootlegging in 1923, his Boston brindle bulldog went on a sixteen-day hunger strike. The Oregon Humane Society tried to take care of Jiggs, even arranging a jailhouse visit with McPool. Several people offered to adopt Jiggs.[77] But sadly, the dog was too devoted. Jiggs died of a broken heart while his master was serving a ninety-day sentence.

Notable Resident: Bobbie

Bobbie the Wonder Dog is undoubtedly the most famous resident of the animal cemetery. In the summer of 1923, the two-year-old collie mix got

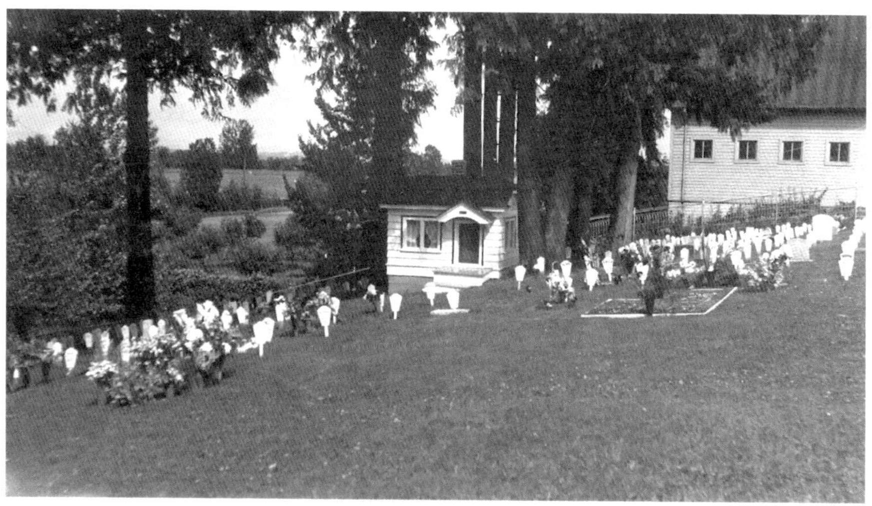

The view of the pet cemetery with Bobbie's doghouse/grave marker. *Oregon Humane Society.*

lost in Iowa while on a cross-country road trip with his owner, G.F. Brazier. Despite searching and placing ads, Brazier couldn't find his dog. Eventually, he went home to Silverton, Oregon, without him.

Six months later, a skinny, haggard dog with his feet worn to the bone walked into Brazier's Silverton restaurant. The humane society launched an investigation and determined that Bobbie had indeed traveled 2,800 miles, much of it in winter, to come home.

Bobbie's incredible journey became a huge media story. Soon Bobbie was receiving fan mail, keys to cities, medals and a jeweled harness. More than forty thousand people came to see him at the Portland Home Show, where the organizers presented him with a special white doghouse with red trim. Charles Alexander wrote a book about him, *Bobbie, a Great Collie.* Bobbie even appeared in the silent film *The Call of the West*, in which he plays himself.[78]

Bobbie died too young, in 1927. He was buried at the Humane Society Cemetery with his doghouse atop his grave. Portland mayor George Baker delivered the eulogy at his memorial service. Later, Hollywood canine star Rin Tin Tin laid a wreath on Bobbie's grave.

Notable Resident: Peggy Borneo

Around 1920, Portlander Mrs. Hauber was traveling in Singapore when she met and adopted a baby orangutan. She brought the new baby home and named her Peggy Borneo. Peggy became a hit with the society ladies in her Laurelhurst neighborhood and was sometimes written about in the newspaper. "She is somewhat of a tomboy and as strong as a man, although she weighs less than a hundred pounds," said one account.[79] Peggy wore rompers, slept in a bed, ate with a fork and spoon and kissed people's hands when she met them. If she took a dislike to a person, she'd toss their hand aside with a show of repugnance. Hauber claimed that Peggy understood English. She enjoyed swinging from trees and riding in automobiles. In fact, she even made the automotive section of the *Oregonian* one week in 1923, sitting in the driver's seat of Mrs. Hauber's new Hudson.[80]

Hauber was grooming Peggy to be a film star. "Her admirers say that Miss Peggy knows by intuition that she is destined to be a moving picture actress," according to the *Oregonian*. But when Peggy was about seven, soon after Hauber signed a film contract for her, the orangutan died suddenly.

Peggy Borneo was buried at the Humane Society Cemetery. She had a grand funeral and a white, satin-lined casket.

10

DOUGLASS CEMETERY

1408 Southwest Hensley Road, Troutdale

Douglass Cemetery sits on 9.1 acres in a peaceful, quiet residential Troutdale neighborhood with plenty of memorial benches for contemplation. Douglass is one of the larger pioneer cemeteries in the greater Portland area.

History

Troutdale is a small town of about sixteen thousand in Multnomah County, seventeen miles east of Portland. American settlers began filing land claims in the area in the early 1850s, attracted by commercial opportunities at the confluence of the Columbia and Sandy Rivers. In 1882, the area got a railroad stop and depot, and in 1907 it was incorporated as a town.

Pioneer and shipbuilder John Douglass donated part of his land claim for use as a cemetery in 1866. He lived to be eighty-seven and was buried in his eponymous cemetery in 1881. In 1957, Multnomah County acquired the cemetery, and it's now one of the fourteen run by Metro.

Like many cemeteries in the twentieth century, Douglass gravitated toward a flatter look. In 1958, Irene Douglass Waldo, great-granddaughter of the original donor of the land, sent an angry letter to the editor of the *Sunday Oregonian*. "How far must being modern go?" she asked. "Cemeteries must now cease being graveyards and be massive lawns." Cemetery officials no longer welcomed plants on graves, such as the roses and lilac brought across the plains by the Douglasses, or flags marking the resting places of veterans, as they slowed down lawn mowers. Irene also mentioned a grudge she'd been nursing for a long time, which showed how tightly her family had been tied to the cemetery that bore their name: "My father had dug most of the graves, free, until his sickness interfered. Then mother paid for this burial lot; and cash for the man who dug the grave, although my father had dug the graves of all his relatives, free."[81]

While many of the Metro cemeteries are full or nearly so, Douglass has lots of room to grow. Whole expanses of grass await new residents. One section is the Eastside Jewish Cemetery, consecrated in 2003 for Jewish burials with several hundred sites available.

Memorable Headstones

The older upright stones tend to be closer to the cemetery entrance and around the edges. Douglass has two handsome Woodmen of the World tree stones, one for Bruno Loeffler, born 1875 in Reichenbach, Germany, who died in 1900, the other for Adolphus Jackson Vandever, who died in 1907, aged forty-seven. All the tree stumps are a little different, and Vandever's has some lovely calla lilies carved around its base. A standout modern headstone for Zachary Allen Shelton Wilson (1993–2018) shows a full-color photo of the man, plus a line drawing of him playing his flying V guitar.

A black and red speckled granite columbarium stands strangely blocky and isolated on an empty stretch of grass. While a couple of niches depict traditional crosses, most are marked by art showing the person's preferences and quirks, such as a frothing mug of beer or a school bus. The most memorable epitaph belongs to Kathleen L. Walker (1955–2019): "Does this niche make my ash look big?"

Local Celebrities

At least five former Troutdale mayors are spending eternity in Douglass. Clara Latourell Larsson (1875–1939) became the town's first female mayor in 1914, two years after Oregon women won the right to vote. It was a busy time for the town's development, as construction started on the Columbia River Highway in 1913 and local residents were opening new businesses at a rapid rate to serve the motorists. Larsson continued

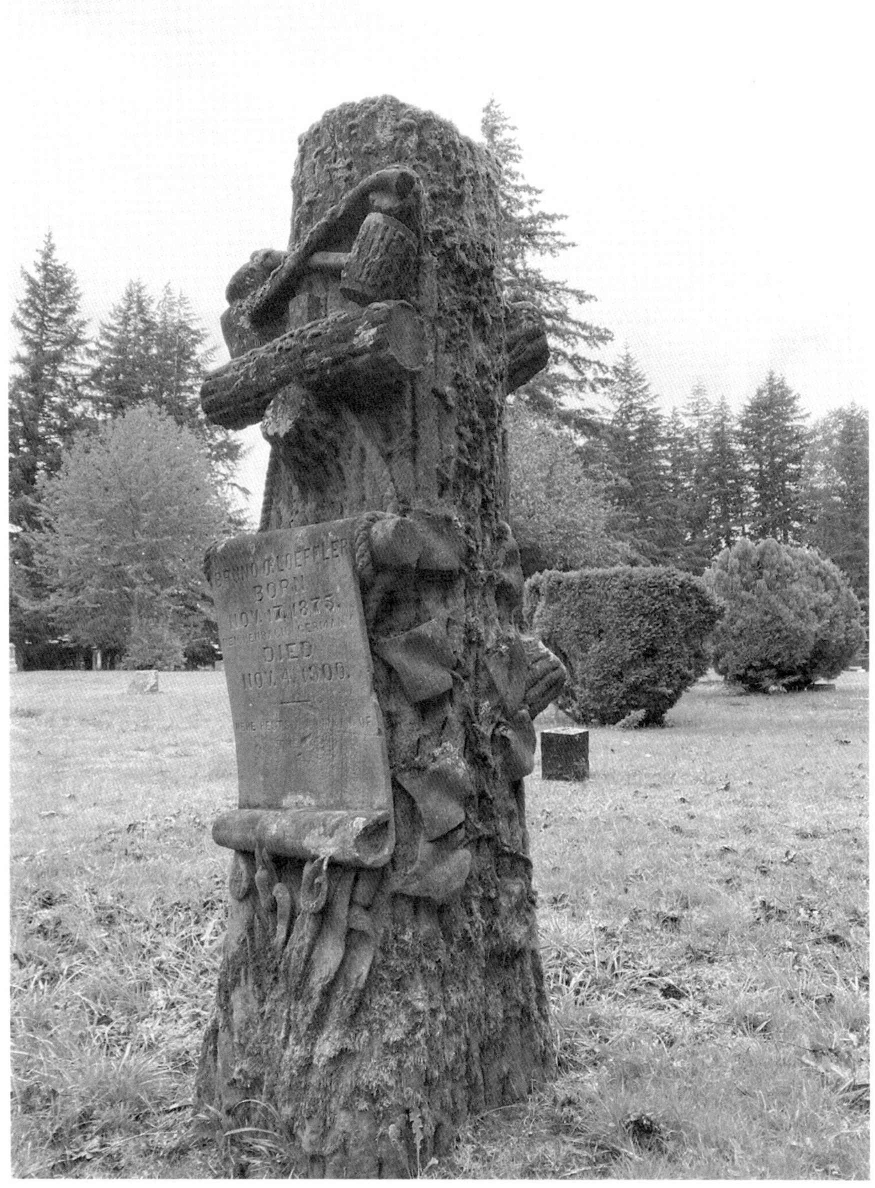

A tree stone, one of the death benefits from the Woodmen of the World insurance company.

working in city government up to her death in 1939. A life-size statue of her stands downtown.

In 1925, Larsson's good friend Laura Bullock Harlow was the town's second elected female mayor. During her term, she started a dog tax, policed Troutdale's rowdy dances and saw a new school built. She and her husband, Louis Harlow—Troutdale's second mayor, who is also buried at Douglass—lived in what's now the city's Harlow House Museum.

Charles Richard Knarr served in World War I, founded a sand and gravel business and helped establish a bank before becoming Troutdale's mayor in the 1950s. He was unquestionably a hard worker, as he started his business shoveling sand by hand from the Sandy River into an old truck.[82] Among his claims to fame were having a wonky thumb from trying to throw a pro boxer out of one of Troutdale's aforementioned rowdy dances and, in 1953, passing a law banning outdoor privies from being built within the city limits.[83]

Troutdale might not have had a real royal family, but Erick Rolf Enquist was nicknamed the Fish King. Born in Sweden, he arrived in the United States in 1902 and allegedly taught himself English by comparing verses in English and Swedish Bibles. He made his fortune in fish wheels on the Columbia River. These contraptions were like a windmill crossed with fish nets, plucking salmon from the river 24/7. An early threat to salmon survival, a single fish wheel could pull half a ton of salmon from the river per day. In 1906, more than seventy-five such wheels were deployed along the Columbia. Later, voters passed laws prohibiting fish wheels. Oregon banned them in 1928 and Washington in 1935. Enquist then worked as a builder and became mayor of Troutdale in 1944.[84]

Garth Sterling Nelson (1943–2000) became famous for being Oregon's first successful liver transplant recipient. Nelson was teaching at Mt. Hood Community College when he contracted a rare liver disease at the age of forty-two. Since his medical insurance didn't cover transplants, the community stepped in, dubbing March 1, 1985, as "Garth Nelson Day" and raising more than $100,000. In June that year, he flew to Texas for the transplant.[85]

NOTABLE RESIDENT: KENT HENRY

The ashes of Henry Plischke, who went down in music history under his stage name Kent Henry, are in Douglass's columbarium. Henry was born in Hollywood in 1948 and joined his first band, the Lost Souls, at age fourteen.

By the time Henry was twenty-one, he was already esteemed enough that Jimmy Page of Led Zeppelin fame asked him to perform on an album he was producing for Screaming Lord Sutch. Sutch was a British musician known for his outrageous clothes and behavior and for repeatedly being the parliamentary candidate for the Monster Raving Loony Party.[86] The most famous bands Henry played with were Blues Image, known for its hit "Ride Captain Ride," and Steppenwolf. In the 1980s, Henry settled in Portland, where he played with the bluesy Paul deLay Band and worked as a technician at Apple Music. He developed Alzheimer's and died at the age of sixty. His spot in the Douglass columbarium gives his name as "Kent Henry (Plischke)." Below a drawing of an electric guitar, his epitaph says, "'The Wizard' played with Steppenwolf & Blues Image. Keep Rocking!"[87]

NOTABLE RESIDENT: EUNICE DOUGLASS

Eunice Douglass didn't get a headstone in the cemetery, as her ashes were interred with her husband, James, a storekeeper and grandson of the man who donated the cemetery land. Born Eunice Meserve, she was a music teacher who married Douglass in 1887. After he died of tuberculosis in 1905, Eunice ran the store, as well as collecting dolls and organizing the Troutdale chapter of the Woman's Christian Temperance Union. She was especially well known for her unusual pet. Bob, the Auto Rider was a goose who rode on the hood of her car, sometimes as far as Astoria or Seattle.

11

MOUNTAIN VIEW STARK CEMETERY

25899 Southeast Stark Street, Troutdale

Take a practically invisible road off busy Stark Street across from Mount Hood Community College and you'll find this small, parklike pioneer cemetery.

History

When the Menzies family established this cemetery in 1886, it was fourteen miles up the old Base Line Road from downtown Portland and must have felt remote. The dirt road, which was later named Stark Street, was used as a baseline for surveying—all Oregon land was measured from this road, which shows up on an 1852 survey map as an original street to downtown Portland.[88] Sometime after 1854, road builders marked Base Line with stone obelisk markers every mile or so from the Willamette River's east bank all the way east to the Sandy River. That way, travelers could estimate how many more bumpy, dusty miles they had to travel to reach their destination.[89]

The cemetery was used by surrounding farming families to bury their dead. According to the *Oregonian*, it was always an obscure cemetery, seldom visited aside from funerals and Decoration Day. But the cemetery had its moment of fame in 1910 as a mystery unfolded around it. First came the disappearance of Hannah Smith on May 8. She withdrew $600 from her bank and was seen visiting an undertaker's office before falling off the radar. Detectives came up with the idea that the undertaker, Eric E. Ericson,

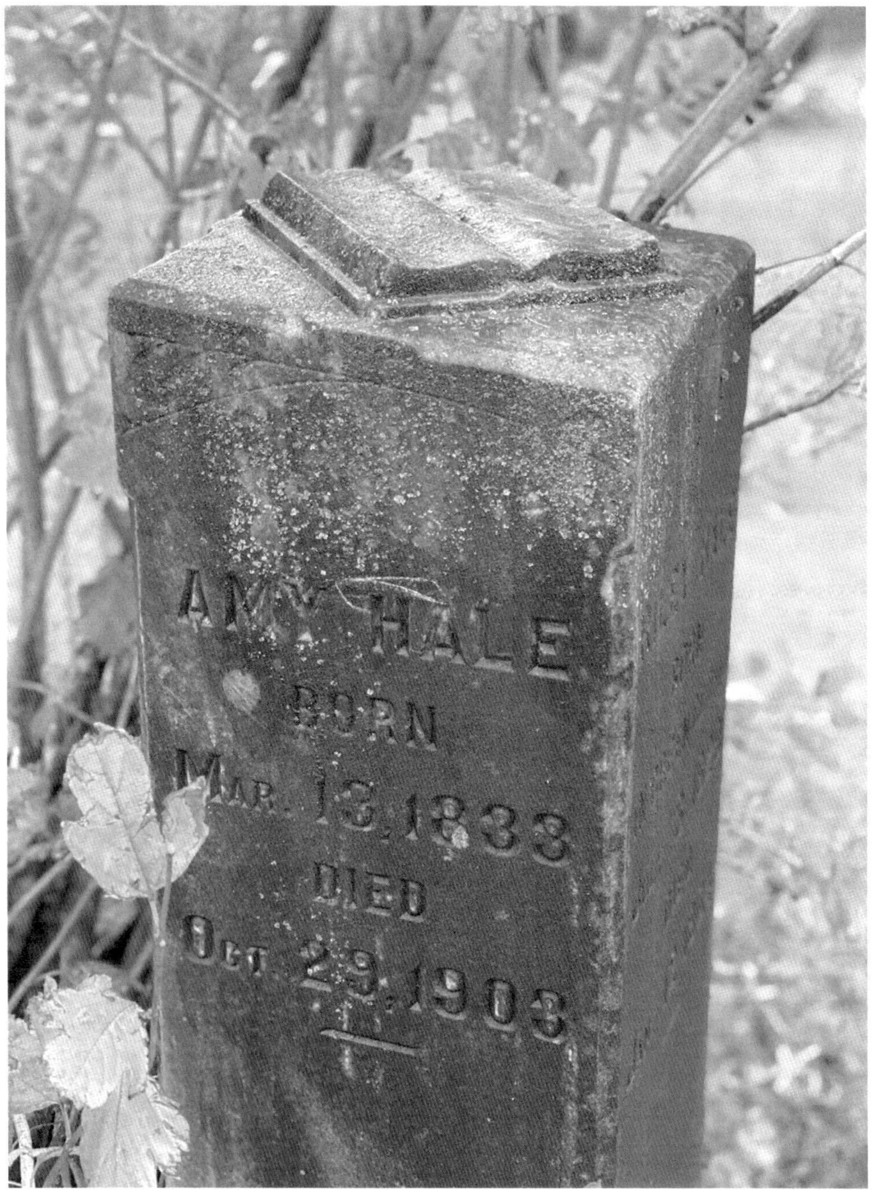

The popular open book motif often represents the Book of Life, in which God records who is heaven bound.

murdered her and buried her in a cemetery. They searched all the local cemeteries for suspicious new graves.[90]

On May 29, 1910, when Mrs. O. Jenkins of Fairview went to tidy up for Decoration Day, she found a fresh new grave in the family plot at Baker Cemetery, an earlier name for Mountain View Stark. A wooden cross marker read, "Byron T. Vincent, Died 1905." The sexton had no record of such a burial. People speculated that the mysterious Mr. Vincent was really the murdered Hannah Smith. A rumor went around the farmers on Base Line Road that a hearse or "dead wagon" had been seen headed toward the cemetery at dawn a couple of weeks ago. "It would be possible for persons to dig a grave in the cemetery in broad daylight and not be seen," said sexton D.W. McKay. "The cemetery is on a hill and the road passes through a deep cut, so that no one could be seen in the graveyard, even by persons in vehicles."[91]

The mystery was partially solved when Dr. A.W. Vincent came forward and explained that when his son died five years earlier, he couldn't find the sexton and just looked for a vacant spot in the cemetery to bury his son. "He said that the grave had been partially obliterated by earth from other graves, and when he renewed the mound for Memorial day it had all the appearance of a new grave." The disappearance of Hannah Smith remained unsolved.[92]

This story illustrates how loose recordkeeping was back in the day and helps explain why there's still confusion in many pioneer cemeteries about which graves are occupied and exactly who is buried where.

Multnomah County took over care of the cemetery in 1957. There have been about twenty burials since 2000, but Mountain View Stark is closed to new sales.

Memorable Headstones

Mountain View Stark has some nice old headstones, including pioneers, but nothing too flashy. Hester A. Bolton (1832–1909) and William M. Bolton (1828–1923) have an attractive, lichen-spotted double stone with an urn and floral carvings and the inscription "Lived together 60 years, 6 days." A stone for Amy Hale (1833–1903) and Riley Hale (1829–1904) is an impressive square pillar topped by a carving of an open book. The marker of Lavina Williams (1849–1926) points out that she was a (young) pioneer of 1851. She married Peer Corwin Williams (1843–1904), a pioneer of 1852, according to his headstone. Susannah Keasling Sherwood (1849–

Odd Fellows

The Independent Order of Odd Fellows (IOOF) is a fraternal organization whose membership hit a peak of 3.4 million in 1914.* The IOOF ran cemeteries around the country and provided death benefits at a time when few people had life insurance.

IOOF members' headstones often display a three-link chain and the letters FLT, which stand for friendship, love and truth. Fellow IOOF members would conduct a graveside ritual including special readings, poems, and dropping sprigs of evergreen into the grave as a sign of rebirth. Many people belonged to multiple lodges to get multiple benefits. Often the Odd Fellows would conduct the funeral and the Masons would buy the headstone. This is why one usually sees more Masonic symbols in cemeteries than IOOF symbols, according to David Scheer, secretary of Peninsula Lodge No. 128 in North Portland and a fourth generation Odd Fellow.

Over the years, some IOOF cemeteries were integrated into larger cemeteries—like River View in Portland—and others were taken over by counties as membership declined and aged. "The cemetery business model is not very sustainable," said Scheer. "People pay for their plot. And once plots are taken, you have an obligation to keep taking care of them but there's no more money coming in."

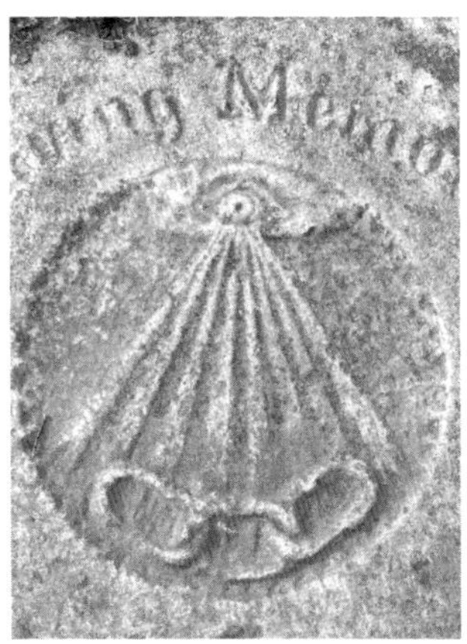

The eye and three-link chain are Odd Fellows symbols.

Odd Fellows also buried indigent nonmembers, including Chinese railroad workers. "They would get worked to death," said Scheer. "The railroad wasn't going to pay for their funeral. They often had no idea who their contacts were back in China." The Odd Fellows intervened to prevent the Chinese from being sent to medical schools for dissection and then sold in catalogues as skeletons.†

* Grand Lodge of Oregon, "Units of IOOF," http://www.oregonioof.org/whats-an-odd-fellow.html.

† Interview with David Scheer, November 3, 2020.

1932) was also presumably a young pioneer, judging from the covered wagon carving that adorns her marker. Her children Sarah Sherwood and William Sherwood tragically died about four months apart in 1895, at ages twenty-two and twenty, respectively. They have matching stones with a few lines of rhymed verse at the bottom. William's reads, "He has gone to live with Jesus, In that land so pure and bright, He is with the happy angels, Robed forevermore in white."

12

PLEASANT HOME CEMETERY

31698 Southeast Bluff Road, Gresham

The small cemetery is bordered on one side by a historic church and on another by a house and yard full of farm equipment, a mountain of chopped wood and about twenty chickens. At twenty-four miles southeast of downtown Portland, just past Gresham, Pleasant Home is a quiet community with a rural feel, which the cemetery reflects.

History

Kelly is the big name in this cemetery. Pioneer Clinton Kelly and his three brothers came to Oregon with their families in covered wagons in the late 1840s.[93] Archon Kelly, one of Clinton's sons, established the cemetery in 1884. Many Kelly descendants have since been buried there. The large Kelly family plot in the center is reserved for family members, although Clinton and some other family members wound up buried at Lincoln Memorial Park or other area cemeteries instead.

Both Clinton and Archon were itinerant ministers. So it makes sense that building a church would be a priority. Archon and his son John Bunyan Kelly built the adjacent church in 1884, the same year they established the cemetery. Archon planned to sell the church to whichever established denomination made him an offer. However, nobody wanted to buy it. So Kelly gave the building to the Methodist Episcopal Church, the denomination with which his family had ties back home in Kentucky.[94]

Despite the cemetery being so identified with the family that it was sometimes called the Kelly cemetery, the first few people buried there—two infants and a veteran—bear different surnames. The first Kelly buried in Pleasant Home was Sarah Elizabeth Roark Kelly (1835–1889), Archon's wife. He would join her the following year.

Multnomah County acquired Pleasant Home Cemetery in 1960, and it is now one of the fourteen pioneer cemeteries run by Metro.

Memorable Headstones

This is not a showy cemetery. Visitors won't find private family vaults or other big displays of wealth here. Aside from one Woodmen of the World tree stump, most of the stones are fairly simple, many flat to the ground. Gerald Cutler (1799–1890) has a notable stone in that eighteenth-century birthdates are uncommon in Portland-area cemeteries. A few markers show more personalization, notably the joyous carving on Lorena Mary Anderson Hanson's (1929–2001) stone, which depicts her dressed in winter hiking gear, standing before a snowy mountain, smiling at two birds on her outstretched hand.

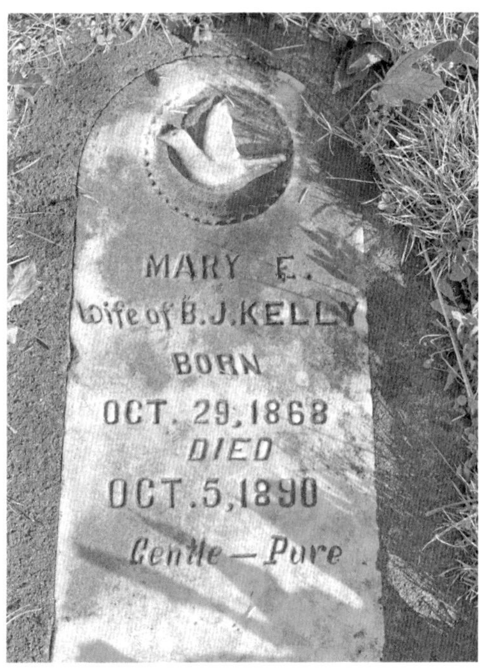

Doves represent peace and purity and are often used on children's headstones.

A rose garden beside Pleasant Home United Methodist Church provides an alternative type of memorial. A metal stake beside each rose bush bears a tag telling the name of the rose and who it commemorates.

LOCAL CELEBRITIES

Daniel (1832–1897) and Caroline Welch (1838–1929) were pioneer settlers in Powell Valley, as is proudly stated on their tombstone. Four members of the Lusted family are buried in Pleasant Home, including William Lusted (1824–1914) and Elizabeth Humphrey Lusted (1825–1917), both of whom were born in England. Locals will recognize the name from nearby Southeast Lusted Road.

Lena M. Collins (1912–1998) was known as the "glad lady" because of the beautiful gladiolas she and her husband, Freelin E. Collins, raised and sold on their property in East Multnomah County for over thirty years.

NOTABLE RESIDENT: J.B. KELLY

Coming from such religious stock as father Archon and grandfather Clinton, John Bunyan Kelly (1863–1939) was probably named after the famous preacher and author of *The Pilgrim's Progress*. He went by J.B. His first wife, Martha Kelly (1868–1890), died young. His second marriage was to Ada Angelia Russell Kelly (1870–1942).

J.B. went into the machine and early automotive business. He tried to gain the Republican state senator nomination in 1908, describing himself as a "Native of Multnomah County, Member of the Kelly Clan Pioneers of '49"[95] but ultimately didn't win. Around 1910, J.B. donated a lot at Southeast 42nd Avenue and Southeast Powell Boulevard, part of his grandfather's original massive 640-acre donation land claim, for a church to be built. The Clinton Kelly Memorial Methodist Church stood for about fifty years until it was demolished. Currently, a large Natural Grocers store stands in its place.

Cars were still new when J.B. got involved in the auto business, and they would prove a source of success, pride and pain. In 1907, J.B. visited California for three weeks as part of his work as the local agent for White Motor Company. An *Oregonian* account of his visit to Los Angeles relates how Kelly visited an auto factory with the then mind-boggling output of eight hundred cars per year.[96]

But cars were also responsible for the worst tragedies in his life. In 1904, his brother Bengal Joy Kelly (1865–1904) died in an explosion at J.B.'s garage. J.B. then wrote a letter to the *Oregonian* explaining the accident and attempting to allay public fears that cars were dangerous and would explode, stressing that the auto igniter his brother was testing was not connected to an automobile at the time.[97]

So it was cruelly ironic that in 1911, while driving on the Crescent City stage road near Kerby in southern Oregon, the gas tank on the back of Kelly's car hit a projecting rock and exploded. His fourteen-year-old daughter Myrnie was killed. Daughter Angela was able to jump from the car but rolled underneath it and was run over, breaking several ribs. J.B. and his two small sons were severely burned. At that time, the family was living in San Francisco.[98] They took Myrna to Pleasant Home to be buried in the family plot, where J.B. and his wife eventually wound up as well.

13

MOUNTAIN VIEW CORBETT CEMETERY

35300 Southeast Smith Road, Corbett

This small cemetery on a hill in the Columbia River Gorge has the most stunning setting of any cemetery in the Portland area. Its name really delivers on its promise: On a clear day, visitors have a perfect view of white-capped Mount Hood. Several memorial benches make this a nice spot for contemplation. Mountain View makes you feel far from the city.

History

Thomas Evans, a farmer who grew vegetables and had a prune orchard, established the cemetery on his land in 1880. Multnomah County acquired it in 1949, and it's now one of the fourteen pioneer cemeteries managed by Metro. Mountain View Corbett has also been known as the Evans Cemetery or Cemetery Hill. Once surrounded by fields of daffodils, visitors now see vineyards, orchards and vegetable and tree farms.

Memorable Headstones

The new headstones are more interesting than the old ones, which are unremarkable in shape, weathered and hard to read. Sitting exposed on a windy hill doesn't help one age well. The most memorable stone belongs to a little three-year-old girl and incorporates tiny bare footprints and a

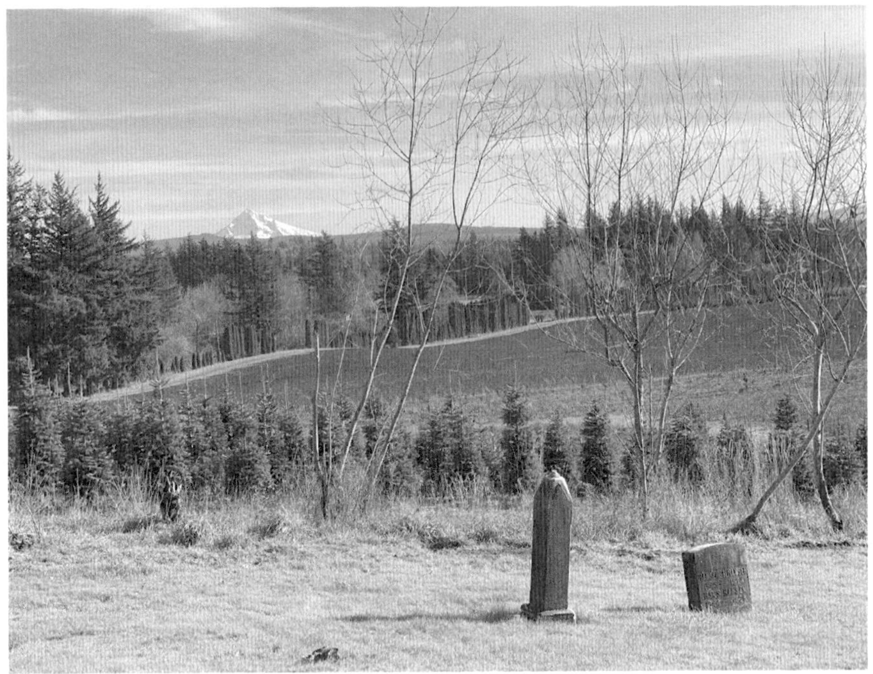

Can't beat the view.

sculpture of red and black ladybug–spotted rainboots that serve as twin vases. Carvings on some of the new stones reflect the person's personality and interests, including whales, a World War II pilot's airplane, a young man jogging with his dog, a sweet couple sitting on a log and a full-color cartoon flying unicorn. The headstone of one tractor-driving man includes pieces of machinery welded onto its base. Nature scenes prevail here—especially mountains and trees—fitting in well with the cemetery's abundant trees, mushrooms and views.

NOTABLE RESIDENTS: JOEL BRONSON AND MARY SALOME BATES

Joel Bronson Bates (1844–1929) grew up in Stevens Point, Wisconsin. "Practically uneventful was his youth and early manhood," reads a 1903 biographical entry about Bates, "and the breaking out of the Civil War found him ready and anxious to serve the cause of the Union as his country should direct." Bates enlisted in the Third Wisconsin Battery, driving ammunition-hauling mules to the front lines and accompanying Sherman on his march to the sea.

In 1865, a couple of months after he mustered out of his unit, Bates married Mary Rowley (1842–1914) of Meadville, Pennsylvania. They lived and farmed several places in the next two decades, including Wisconsin, Nebraska and Iowa. After a couple of years of crop-destroying Nebraska hailstorms, the Bateses and their five children moved to Oregon in 1877.

In 1889, they bought forty acres of farmland in what's now called Springdale, between Troutdale and Corbett, and began clearing it for crops and livestock. Mary served as a midwife and was the closest thing to a doctor available for many nearby farmers. During one of her most memorable trips to deliver a baby, the snow was so bad she doubted her horse could make it, so she went on foot. "It was quite dark and a cougar was following her from tree to tree with terrifying screams," reads an account of her journey.[99] The couple built a seven-room house, planted an orchard and flower garden and later ran a small dairy.[100]

NOTABLE RESIDENT: SHIO UYETAKE

Shio Uyetake (1915–2009) was a lifelong Corbett resident. A second-generation Japanese American, he was the oldest of five children born to a farming couple, Juichi "Harry" and Chise (Nakahara) Uyetake. In 1923, 60 percent of Oregon's Japanese population worked in agriculture. Families like the Uyetakes in eastern Multnomah County grew vegetables and berries.[101]

In addition to his public schooling, Shio attended a small Japanese school on the Uyetake land where children learned to read, write and speak Japanese. These schools were common in areas with large Japanese populations. In the 1920s, Portland had two Japanese schools, and others were located in Gresham, Hood River, Milwaukie, Salem and Banks. Uyetake attended Columbian (now Corbett) High School and then graduated from the University of Washington with a degree in business administration in 1937. He made his first of two trips to Japan during high school, traveling on his own by ship.

Although the Uyetakes seem to have had good relations with their non-Japanese neighbors, groups like Hood River's Anti-Asiatic Association were already stirring up trouble, unnerved by agricultural competition. Then on April 28, 1942, came the exclusion order requiring all Portland residents of Japanese descent to report to the assembly center in North Portland.

Shio Uyetake was incarcerated at Tule Lake Camp in California. Some internees had the option of taking jobs instead of staying in the camps. Shio Uyetake went to Michigan, where he drove a large gasoline tanker, delivering gas to farmers. After the war, he came home to Corbett and was able to resume living on his family land. His sisters had taken jobs in Chicago during the war, during which they met Nobuko "Nobi" Mukai (1921–2016), who became Uyetake's wife. They married in 1950 at the Portland Buddhist Center. Eventually, they had four children.

Uyetake farmed strawberries, raspberries, cauliflower, lettuce, cabbage and broccoli. In 1961, he took a better-paying job at a frozen vegetable company, Kubla Khan, where he worked for twenty years. He and his wife continued growing flowers and vegetables. Despite the bitterness of the war years, he managed to live in both the Japanese and non-Japanese communities, serving as president of the Japanese American Citizens League but also participating in the Oregon Farm Bureau and the East Multnomah Pioneer Association, which one year even honored him as a "pioneer king."[102] Shio lived to be ninety-four, and Nobuko lived to be ninety-five. On their joint tombstone, one of their beloved cats lounges above his name, and flowers adorn her side.

14

GRESHAM PIONEER, ESCOBAR AND WHITE BIRCH CEMETERIES

100 Southwest Walters Road, Gresham

Officially, these are three different cemeteries. But it's hard to tell where Escobar ends and Gresham Pioneer starts, and White Birch is right across the street. So if you visit one, you'll probably visit them all.

History

This area twelve miles east of Portland was known as Powell's Valley in the 1850s, thanks to pioneer Jackson Powell, who arrived in 1847, and his brothers who followed. His big marker in Gresham Pioneer says, "Settled Powell Valley, 1848." But a religious camp that set up here in the 1870s gave the town's first post office its original name: Camp Ground. In 1884, merchant Benjamin Franklin Rollins opened a new post office in a local store and petitioned for it to be named after the postmaster general and Civil War veteran Walter Quentin Gresham.[103] This was a smart move, as the postmaster was responsible for approving the application. The name stuck, and Powell Valley is now a neighborhood within the city of Gresham. Rollins wasn't the only one with the clever idea, as several U.S. towns are named after the postmaster, who never set foot in Gresham, Oregon.[104]

Gresham Pioneer is the largest of the three cemeteries at two acres, with White Birch and Escobar each measuring a half acre. Gresham Pioneer is also the oldest. Dates on the markers go back to the 1850s, and it was officially established in the 1860s. However, the dates can be deceiving. James Powell's baby has the death date of 1851 inscribed on a family headstone but probably died somewhere along the Oregon Trail and is only commemorated here. James was one of Jackson Powell's brothers.

Dr. John Powell, unrelated to the brothers, buried his infant son in Gresham Pioneer in 1863, the first recorded burial. Tragically, a few weeks later, he buried another young child there. Dr. Powell is credited with discovering the cause and prevention of cholera—bad water and boiling it, respectively—but historic reports conflict about whether or not this knowledge saved members of his wagon train.[105] White Birch was established in about 1888 and Escobar in 1907. All three are now run by Metro and closed to new sales.

The land that Gresham Pioneer occupies was originally part of the 1850 land claim of Jake J. Moore. Later, Frank Metzger, who purchased Moore's land, donated a larger section for the cemetery.[106] The cemetery contains almost thirty Metzgers, but no Moores.

White Birch was once part of Reverend Alfred Cornutt's donation land claim during the 1850s. He also donated adjoining land for a school. Many Gresham residents remember eating their lunch and playing among the gravestones during their school days.[107] Historical records sometimes refer to White Birch as an indigent cemetery, and its four unmarked graves of unknown people could attest to that. But several leading local families, including the Beers, Stokers and Palmquists, are buried in White Birch, so it might have served different purposes at different times. White Birch includes Japanese settlers with surnames such as Kinoshita, Hatori and Morishita.[108]

Sometime around the 1950s, Gresham resident Sarah E. Harrison (1888–1964) learned that White Birch was going to be sold. Several of her family members and friends were buried in the cemetery. She purchased the cemetery and organized other descendants of people buried there to form an organization to care for White Birch, which had fallen into neglect.[109] She died in 1964 and is buried in White Birch. Multnomah County took over the care of the cemetery the following year.[110]

While the layout of Gresham Pioneer is a bit erratic, Escobar Cemetery is a neat strip, two lots deep, sandwiched between Gresham Pioneer and the Springwater Corridor Trail. Each lot could contain ten or twelve people. There's no sign to tell you that you've left Pioneer and entered Escobar; you have to check a cemetery map. The cemetery is named for Frank Escobar (1860–1946), the area's first known Hispanic resident, whose forebears came

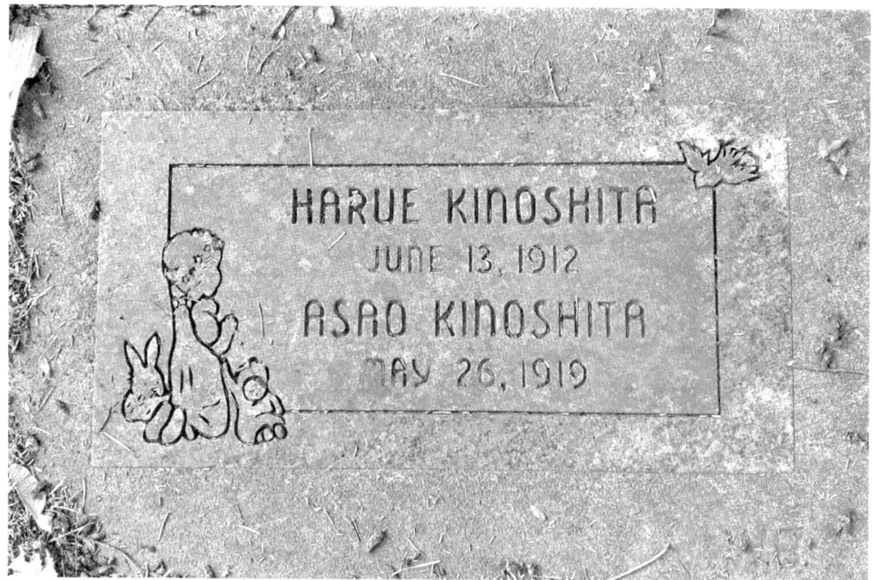

A marker in White Birch.

from Mexico. In 1902, Escobar took a job caring for the horses of Joseph Short, a local doctor who served as Gresham's second mayor in 1907–8. Escobar was a versatile worker who rigged a water tank in Short's attic, connecting pipes to the kitchen so that the doctor's house was the first in Gresham to have running water. He also worked as a gardener, a foreman on the Bull Run pipeline project and a cemetery caretaker. He was selling lots in Escobar and Gresham Pioneer in the early 1900s. Escobar was known as a kind eccentric who grew beautiful roses and sweet peas, supplied neighbor children with watermelons and ice cream and helped widows and the poor.[111] He is buried in neighboring Forest Lawn Cemetery.

Memorable Headstones

Gresham Pioneer has lots of big old pillars and generally more impressive headstones than White Birch or Escobar. The Kenney family buried seven family members in Gresham Pioneer, mostly in the late 1800s. They went in for poetic inscriptions on their large pillar monuments. The stone of James P. Kenney (1829–1887) reads, "Sweet may he rest from toil and care, Laid low beneath the sod, His body mouldering back to dust, His spirit dwell with God." The marker for young James Kenney (1882–1898) bears this poem:

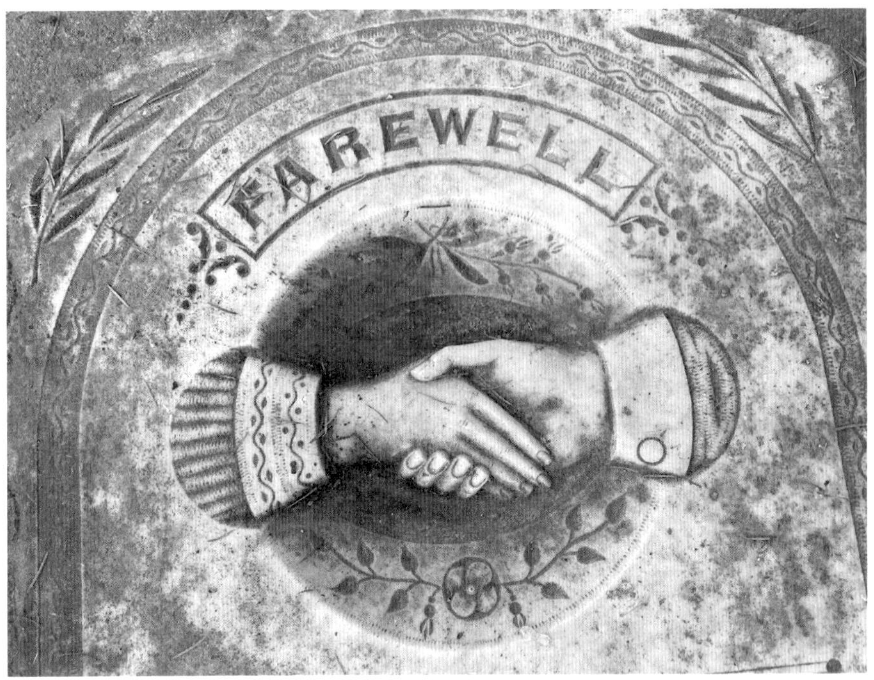

Above: Farewell handshakes became popular in Victorian times. The deceased is saying goodbye to earthly life and loved ones. Note the woman's hand on the left and man's on the right.

Opposite: Jane Fancher's grand stone in White Birch.

"Lonely the house and sad the hours, since our dear ones have gone, but oh! a brighter house than ours, In Heaven is their own."

If you visit enough cemeteries, you'll notice repetition. The Gresham cemeteries have well executed examples of all the classic carvings—weeping willows, doves, clasped hands, calla lilies and the less usual hand holding a flag. Markers with the same design as Jane Stoker's (1850–1925)—a tall pillar that depicts a hand holding an open book with "At Rest" written across the pages, flowers and impressive draperies topped with a large draped urn, and the most outstanding in White Birch—can be spotted in other area pioneer cemeteries. Isabel Giese's (1840–1909) book-topped podium with the illustration of gates ajar in Gresham Pioneer is the same as Herman Werner's of Oregon City, who died in 1915.

Epitaphs also repeat. Well over a century past the demise of Fleetwood F. Powell (1855–1882), his epitaph is still a standard offering on the websites

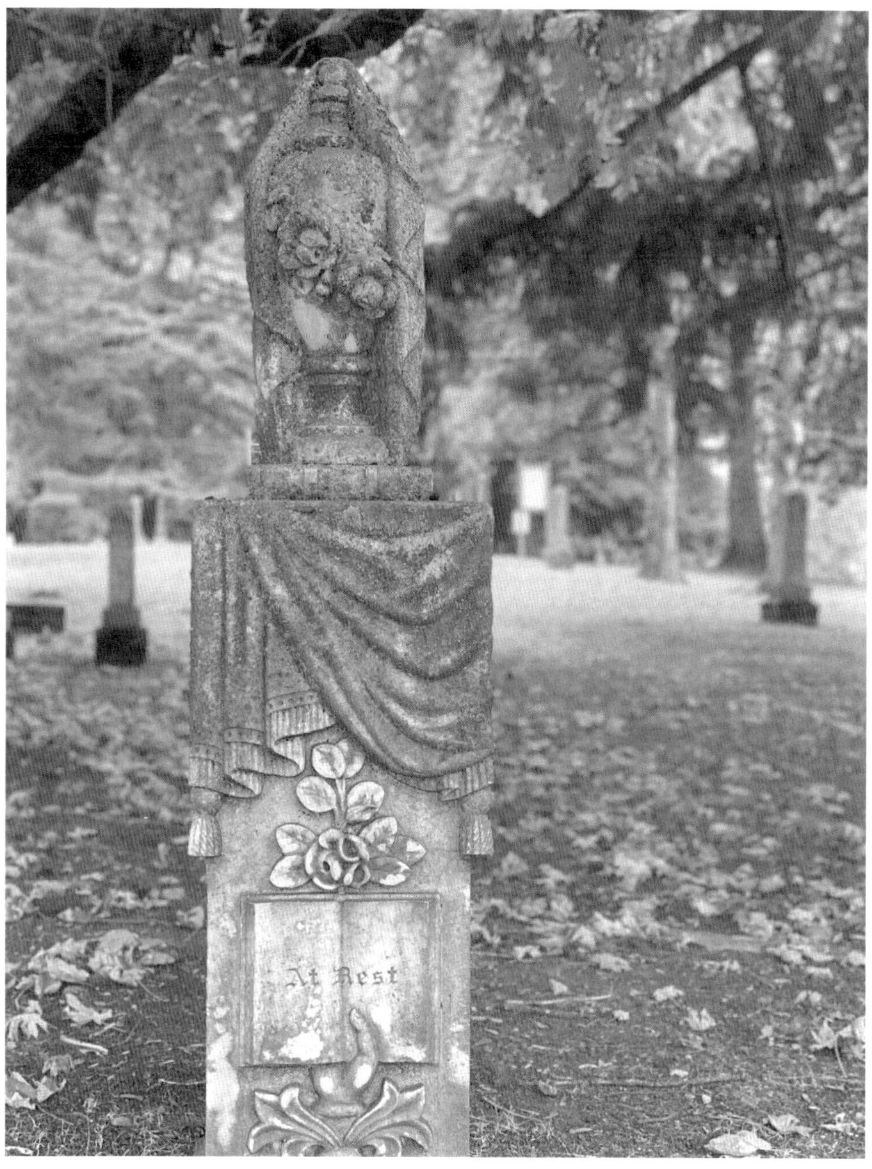

of headstone makers: "No pain, no grief, no anxious fear, can reach the peaceful sleeper here."

White Birch is known for having quite a few older Japanese markers. Gresham Pioneer contains newer markers of people from American Samoa, Micronesia and other Pacific Islands. A couple of these have metal lockets attached to the front of the stones with photos inside. With the help of

Google Translate, visitors can quickly decipher Samoan sentiments, such as "You are always remembered as the beloved mother by your children and family. Have a nice trip."

One Gresham Pioneer resident has a billiards-themed stone, with "8 ball Anyone?" written on one side and an illustration of racked up pool balls on the other.

Notable Resident: Miyo Iwakoshi (1852–1931)

Miyo Iwakoshi came to Oregon from Japan with her Scottish husband and their adopted daughter in 1880. She's considered the first Japanese woman to settle in Oregon. She and her husband, Andrew MacKinnon (1822–1886), built a steam sawmill on land outside Gresham, which they dubbed Orient. The small unincorporated community of Orient still exists today. When their daughter Tama married Shintaro Takaki in 1891, theirs was Oregon's first Japanese wedding.[112]

More than 2,500 Japanese people were living in Oregon by 1900. Most worked as contract laborers in logging camps and fish canneries and on railroads. This soon shifted to agriculture, with many eventually managing to buy land and own their own farms. Gresham, Salem and Hood River all had sizable Japanese farming communities. Iwakoshi was known for helping hundreds of Japanese settlers in the Gresham area.

But when Iwakoshi died in 1931, her burial sparked controversy. There was already strong anti-Japanese sentiment on the West Coast. The following decade, some white Gresham landowners would form the Japanese Exclusion League, a name toned down from the originally proposed Oregon Anti-Japanese, Incorporated.[113] Such people didn't want a Japanese woman buried in Gresham Pioneer. Instead, they suggested she be buried in White Birch.

"But a deal must have been struck," the *Outlook* surmised, "as she was buried next to her husband Andrew MacKinnon (born in Scotland) in the Pioneer Cemetery." However, her grave bore no official marking. Later researchers discovered that somebody had planted a Japanese cedar tree beside MacKinnon's headstone to mark Iwakoshi's grave at the time of her death. In 1988, the Japanese American Citizens League and other donors installed a granite marker for Iwakoshi.[114] Ironically, the tree of the "Western Empress," as she was sometimes known, has grown to an impressive height and towers over all the stones in the graveyard.

Notable Resident: Dinger Family

Gresham Pioneer holds the remains of three family members killed in the infamous July 4, 1900 Tacoma trolley tragedy. It was a drizzly morning as the overcrowded train made its way along slippery tracks toward downtown's Independence Day Parade. Passengers stood on running boards and on the front and rear platforms, clinging to railings, and one little boy even climbed onto the cowcatcher. As the train went downhill, it had to take a left curve onto the "C" Street Trestle, which bridged a one-hundred-foot ravine. But on its way there, the wheels slid. The streetcar operator's efforts to brake and apply sand to the tracks failed. Passengers realized they were on a runaway trolley and started jumping off the front and rear platforms. The train busted through the guardrails and plunged one hundred feet into the ravine, landing upside down and leaving a three-hundred-foot trail of injured passengers who'd managed to get off. Of the more than one hundred passengers, forty-three were killed and about sixty-five maimed or injured. Rescuers had to use ropes to hoist bodies out of the ravine.[115]

A jury blamed both the motorman, F.L. Boehm, for his handling of the trolley, and Tacoma Railway and Power Company for safety violations and gross negligence. The ensuing lawsuits nearly bankrupted the company.

Among those dead were Louis Dinger, who was born in Germany in 1866. His six-month-old baby Floyd and four-year-old daughter Dorothy were also among the victims. His remaining daughter, Viola Ruth Dinger Bacon (1897–1997), lived to be one hundred.

Notable Resident: Benjamin Claggett

Benjamin Mason Claggett (1811–1859) was a hardworking pioneer from Kentucky who made newspaper headlines long after he died. In 1900, the *Oregonian* reported on a mysterious box of bones two laborers found buried partly in the street and partly in a private Gresham Pioneer lot. "The bones were not all there, but the skull and nearly all the larger bones of the body were found," the paper reported. "The lower bones of the legs were missing, and showed signs of having been burnt, and all of them were without flesh." The workers gave the bones a decent burial in another part of the cemetery, "but retained a part of one of the jaws which held a gold-filled tooth." The *Oregonian* speculated the mystery bones might belong to a man who had disappeared from a local hotel a few years earlier.[116]

Fortunately, the mystery was cleared up the following week. The *Oregonian* reported that "Grandfather Claggett" had been originally buried on his farm in Powell's Valley. After his son Charles (1836–1899) was buried in Gresham Pioneer, relatives decided it would be nice if Benjamin's remains could keep him company. Apparently, the family employed some shoddy workers to move Benjamin, and his box of bones didn't quite make it to the proper grave.[117]

Recreational Activities

The Gresham cemeteries are located right on the popular twenty-one-mile Springwater Corridor multiuse trail, so consider combining cemetery sleuthing with a bike ride. Check with the Gresham Historical Society about its fascinating walking tours.

15

LINCOLN MEMORIAL PARK

11801 Southeast Mt. Scott Boulevard, Portland

Portlanders who visit Lincoln for the first time will be amazed to find so much land in the city not built up beyond headstone height. This enormous, hilly property ranges from early twentieth-century pioneer graves to some of Portland's swankiest real estate for the posthumous set, with sweeping views of the city.

History

The cemetery now known as Lincoln Memorial Park was built as Mount Scott Cemetery in 1906. In 1909, H.R. Reynolds, M.K. Reynolds and Roscoe E. Nelson filed articles of incorporation with a capitalization of $500,000.[118] They bought 335 acres of land on the 1,089-foot butte from longtime *Oregonian* editor Harvey Scott, for whom Mount Scott was named.[119]

The idea was to create an upscale burial ground for Portland's east side. In 1910, J.P. Finley, one of the cemetery directors, traveled to San Francisco and Los Angeles to check out their leading cemeteries and get cutting-edge ideas for Mount Scott, particularly about landscaping.[120] The plan worked. "That's where wealthy East Portlanders went to be buried," said Eric Cordingley. "They called it the River View of the east." Cordingley co-founded Friends of Multnomah Park Cemetery, which lost a few residents in the early 1900s as survivors decided to reinter them in the pricier cemetery up the hill.[121]

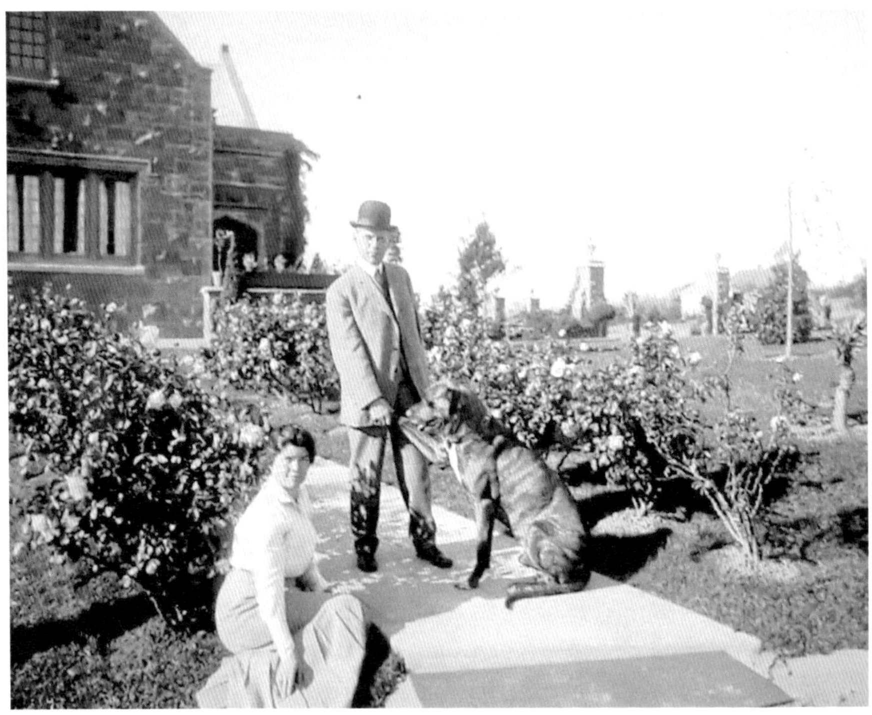

Man shaking hands with large dog, woman seated on ground, in front of building at Mt. Scott Park Cemetery, Portland. *Angelus Studio photographs, PH037_b047_CE00051, Special Collections and University Archives, University of Oregon Libraries, Eugene, Oregon.*

Mount Scott was formally dedicated on Memorial Day in 1912. Ten thousand people visited the new cemetery that day, strolling the grounds and listening to speakers and musical entertainment.[122] Most people took the streetcar to the Lents neighborhood, then rode the cemetery shuttle up the hill, a service Mount Scott provided from 1911 to 1950. In 1913, fifteen thousand people visited on Memorial Day, despite there only being six hundred graves at that time.[123]

In 1914, the *Oregonian* reported on Mount Scott's stunning new crematorium, "said to be one of the finest and most modern mortuary incinerating plants in the country." The paper praised the facility's art glass windows, glazed tile and white enamel, "the aim being to get away from the factory-like appearance of the old-style crematorium."[124] Mount Scott featured the new crematorium in its ads, which boasted of the overall setting "where nature's peaceful quietude lends an influence to soften sorrow."[125]

Mount Scott had a Chinese section almost from the beginning. In 1912, an advertisement signed On Hing & Co appeared in the *Oregonian*, declaring,

"The services of [cemetery superintendent] Wilson Benefield are not wanted at the Chinese cemetery anymore." The ad claimed the cemetery had failed to fulfill grave cleaning work the Chinese community had contracted for. But the relationship improved over the years. Before his death in 1927, pioneer Chinese resident Long Hong donated a burial plot for use by his country people.[126] Another private donor may have supplemented this contribution, and by 1931 there were two thousand burial sites on the slope facing Johnson Creek, initially providing free burials for Chinese people.[127] Today, the Imperial Garden, dedicated to Portland's Chinese and Vietnamese, has some of the best views on the grounds.

Mount Scott straddles the county line, with the older part technically in Multnomah and the newer part in Clackamas. In its early days, the cemetery sat in the midst of farmland. Ads offered the adjacent land for pasturing cows. In 1915, the *Oregonian* ran a story about Mr. J. Lewis reporting his horse stolen and later realizing it broke out of the stable at night and wandered over to Mount Scott Cemetery to die.[128]

Because the cemetery was so large and far removed, it was the scene for some unfortunate and unlawful events. When a fire started in the chapel in 1914, no local fire departments could arrive in time to stem the $27,000 worth of damage, mostly not covered by insurance.[129] In 1928, a stolen safe was found discarded in the cemetery,[130] and in 1929, George Walmsley was robbed of $80 by an elderly man in a stocking cap who carried a blue gun.[131] William L. Hoff was fined $50 for hunting pheasants in the cemetery in 1930.[132]

But the most egregious thing to happen in the cemetery was on June 11, 1923, when two thousand people were initiated into the Ku Klux Klan in a nighttime ritual. Twelve thousand robed members attended the event—according to the klan, which may have exaggerated its numbers—which featured two thirty-foot-tall burning crosses.[133] Lot holders were upset to have their departed desecrated by the klan initiation. W.E. Pearson, president of the Mount Scott Cemetery Association, stated that he knew nothing about the initiation and that "the board of directors of the cemetery association is in no way connected with the klan."[134] Mounts Scott and Tabor were favorite cross-burning spots for the klan, since the fiery displays could be seen for miles.

The American Legion, Veterans of Foreign Wars and United Spanish-American War Veterans organized a cemetery association and acquired five acres at Mount Scott for interring deceased veterans free of charge. The state appropriated funds for improvements.[135] On Memorial Day 1922,

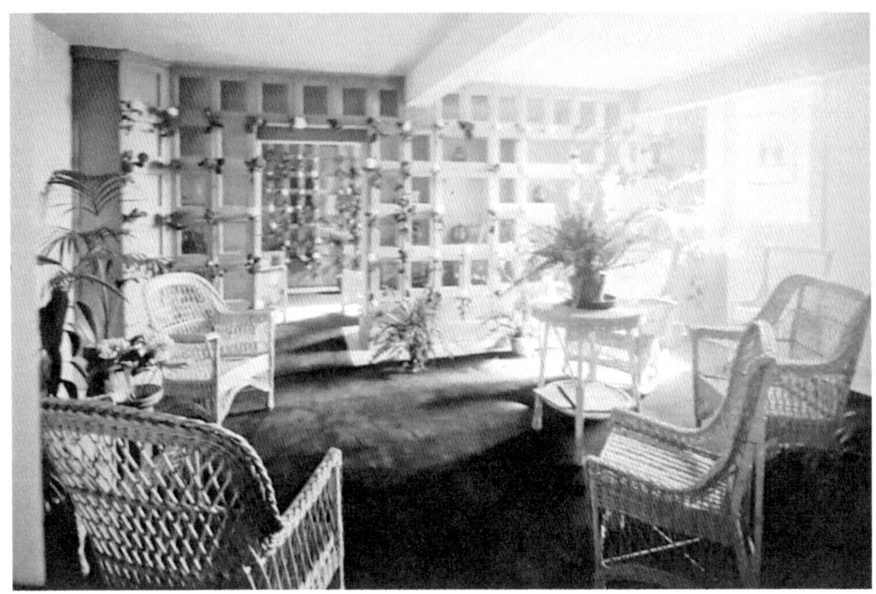

Interior of rose chamber in columbarium, Mt. Scott Park Cemetery, Portland. Wicker furniture in room, niches for urns along wall. *Angelus Studio photographs, PH037_b047_CE00063, Special Collections and University Archives, University of Oregon Libraries, Eugene, Oregon.*

soldiers, sailors and marines gathered to dedicate the new veterans plot. In 1923, President and Mrs. Warren G. Harding laid a wreath on a soldier's grave while visiting Portland.[136] In 1950, the enormous Willamette National Cemetery opened right across the street. But Mount Scott still supports veterans, with its Homeless Veterans Burial Program providing proper military burials for indigent veterans with no family to claim them.

In 1926, Mount Scott changed its name to Lincoln Memorial Park in honor of President Abraham Lincoln.[137] The old indoor mausoleum features a large stained-glass portrait of Lincoln.

As the twentieth century progressed, Portland's ethnic makeup changed, and Lincoln reflects that. When Randal Houle sold plots at Lincoln during the early 2000s, he estimated about 30 percent of his clients were Chinese. He also helped many Romanian, Ukrainian and Romani families.[138]

Now Lincoln Memorial covers 430 acres and is part of Dignity Memorial, North America's largest provider of cemetery and funeral services. Dignity Memorial is one of Service Corporation International's (SCI) brands. Houston-based SCI is the leader in the American death business. Lincoln itself plays the Hills & Mazy Cemetery in season six of the TV series *Grimm*, and one of its mausoleums appears in the Nicholas Cage movie *Pig*.

Memorable Headstones

Mount Scott was founded as a modern cemetery after the Victorian era, perhaps accounting for the plainness of its early memorials in contrast to some of Portland's pioneer cemeteries. The older parts are mostly at the bottom of the hill. Lincoln has an especially large area called Baby Land, where hundreds of babies were buried starting in the 1940s. Lambs, angels and birds adorn the babies' flat stones. There's an old Chinese section with graves from the 1920s and an old Masonic area.

But even pioneer cemetery enthusiasts might find the new areas of Lincoln most fascinating because of the variety of ethnic groups, the high degree of marker personalization and the cemetery's liberal attitude toward grave offerings. Personal tributes include a convertible etched on a young man's marker; a single marker featuring a color portrait of a woman with big '80s hair, an electric guitar, a muscle car, an elk, a dachshund, a mountain and the message "We Love You Mom"; and a Laotian woman with calla lilies, bamboo, dragons, a portrait of herself in hill tribe garb and a cartoonish bald eagle with the American flag.

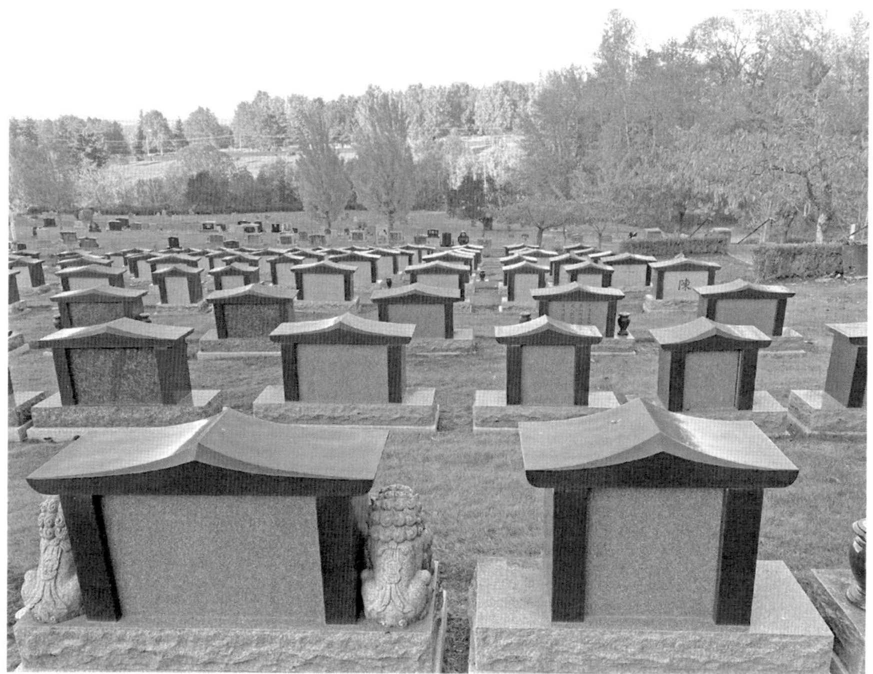

Asian-style monuments with a fabulous view.

Many visitors at Lincoln leave offerings to their people, ranging from sticks of incense burning at Chinese graves to Batman action figures to full-blown Halloween decorations. The dead also enjoy a drink at Lincoln, be it a beer, soda or carton of soymilk, and one grave even welcomes the occasional fresh corndog and fries.

Several special monuments are dotted around Lincoln's grounds, notably the Darcelle XV AIDS Memorial. Named in honor of Darcelle XV, legendary Portland drag queen and cabaret owner and a tireless advocate for people with HIV/AIDS, the memorial commemorates both those who have died from AIDS and those who cared for them.

On a clear day, visitors can see Mounts Hood, Saint Helens and Rainier. The best real estate is huge plots surrounded with low walls and metal gates with incredible city views. Up by the office at the top of the cemetery, the flashiest memorials are the private Romani family mausoleums, which have been built since about 2010. Rose City still has more Romani graves, but Lincoln is becoming a popular afterlife address as well. While the Gypsy markers may look ostentatious to outsiders, in their culture, giving a lavish funeral and providing the largest marker possible are signs of love and respect.[139] Monument aficionados will find these impressive displays the perfect antidote to the move toward bland, flat headstones designed for easy mowing.

LOCAL CELEBRITIES

With more than sixty thousand people interred at Lincoln, there are tons of notables. Among them rest Henry Waldo Coe (1857–1927), state senator, bank president, friend of President Theodore Roosevelt and founder of Morningside Hospital. While modern Portlanders may not know Coe's name, they've passed the statues he brought to the city: Joan of Arc in Southeast Portland's Coe Circle, plus likenesses of Presidents Washington, Lincoln and Teddy Roosevelt.

Lincoln is the forever home to Jay Bowerman (1876–1957), who finished out a deceased governor's term from 1910 to 1911, and two former U.S. congressmen: David Emmons Johnston (1845–1917), who represented West Virginia from 1899 to 1901, and William Wallace McCredie (1862–1935), who represented Washington from 1909 to 1911. Oregon poet laureate Ben Hur Lampman (1886–1954) is buried here, as is Detroit Lion Ray "Butch" Morse (1910–1995).

DESIGNING MARKERS

Sometimes the signature of the stone carver is visible on the bases of old markers. Portland's top early carvers were John Gruber, Alvin B. Roberts and Jacob Shartle and brothers Thomas and William Young. Signing their best work was a means of advertising.

Nowadays, marker design is largely computerized. Jason Pope, co-owner of Affordable Family Memorials (AFM) in Portland, says the most important part is sitting down with the family, finding out what they need and figuring out how to convert that into a stone. While religion is still popular, more personalization is in, and nature images are huge. Pope especially enjoys drawing portraits to incorporate on markers.

Co-owner Angie Pope says the biggest changes she's seen are a move toward smaller, more affordable monuments, and less emphasis on Memorial Day. "Memorial Day used to be a time when folks would take the whole family to the cemetery."*

Many of AFM's clients require a different writing system, such as Chinese, Japanese, Arabic, Persian, Vietnamese or Hebrew. Pope has to be extra careful that he doesn't inadvertently alter the language. He also touches up old stones in cemeteries to make them more legible.

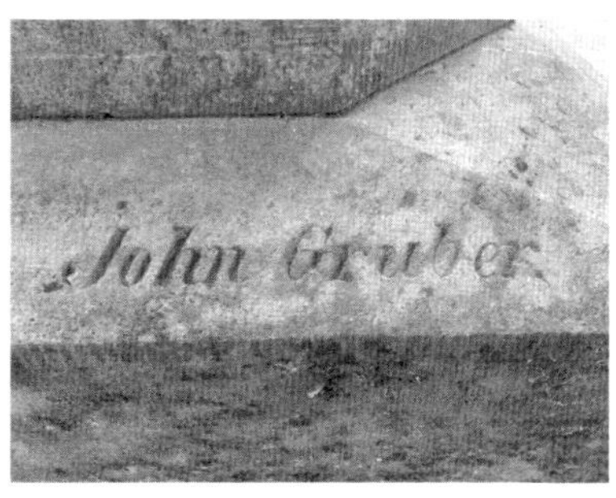

John Gruber's signature on a monument at Lone Fir.

Granite is the usual choice of material now for longevity. Many cemeteries require flat stones to be four inches thick so they can take the pressure of a riding lawnmower. The Popes caution that purchasers should always check the cemetery rules first. They've seen people economize by buying too-thin stones online. "And they just bought a huge paperweight. It's a bummer."†

---

* Author correspondence with Angie Pope, May 2, 2021.

† Author interview with Jason Pope, November 24, 2020.

Notable Resident: Emory Parady

Civil War veteran Emory Parady served with the Sixteenth New York Volunteer Cavalry, which was called upon in 1865 to help capture John Wilkes Booth, President Lincoln's assassin. Parady and twenty-five other cavalry members tracked Booth and an accomplice to a Virginia barn. Booth refused to surrender, so the soldiers set the barn on fire. When Booth came out, they shot him. The government paid Parady and each of the other cavalry soldiers $1,658.18 as a reward. This was a fortune, about ten years' worth of army wages. Parady and his family settled in Michigan for many years before moving out to Portland, where Parady—nicknamed "Emory the Avenger"—owned a shoemaking shop. Parady's tombstone tells a short version of Booth's comeuppance.

Notable Resident: Charlee Lucille Coote Moore

Charlee Lucille Coote Moore (1928–2018) was born in Colorado but grew up in southern California, where she met her husband, Bob Moore. Charlee's dedication to feeding her family an organic diet full of whole-grain foods sparked an interest in milling. After starting their business in California, the couple moved to Milwaukie in 1978 and turned an abandoned mill into the internationally successful business Bob's Red Mill. They introduced amaranth and farro to the masses, manufactured one of the first gluten-free product lines and made enough money to become philanthropists. Nutrition research centers are named for them at both Oregon Health & Sciences University and Oregon State University.[140]

Recreation

The large and hilly space is good for jogging, biking and leashed dog walking. Keep an eye on small dogs and children, as coyotes prowl the cemetery. Lincoln occasionally offers spiritual events aimed at uplifting people healing from recent loss.

16

WILHELM'S PORTLAND MEMORIAL FUNERAL HOME, MAUSOLEUM AND CREMATORY

6705 Southeast 14th Avenue, Portland

You could spend an entire day wandering the corridors of this ridiculously huge mausoleum, which feels like a chilly, quiet library full of cremains instead of books—if you can get in. Unless you have a loved one interred here, the mausoleum is open only on Memorial Day and for official walking tours. It's worth planning ahead to see the exquisite stained-glass windows and beautiful urns.

History

In 1900, the only crematorium west of the Mississippi River was located in San Francisco. If people opted to cremate their dearly departed, the cost and logistics of transporting the remains to California was considerable. In February 1900, some prominent Portland businessmen invited Frank B. Gibson, secretary of the San Francisco Cremation Company, to visit and explore the possibility of building a crematory in Portland. An *Oregonian* editorial presented cremation as modern, and those insistent on earth burial as practically superstitious: "The belief still perhaps unconsciously entertained of the literal resurrection of the body and a shrinking, which is difficult to reason away, from committing anything greatly prized to what seems utter destruction by fire." Cremation solved both the space constraints of a growing city and sanitary concerns about buried bodies spreading disease. "The arguments in support of cremation are familiar to all thoughtful, observant people. They are those of purity, which shrinks from the subjection of the tenantless clay of a beloved one to the revolting process of decay."[141] One reader brought up an equally modern reason against cremation, a full century before *CSI*, worrying that murderers would get away with their crimes when incinerators burned evidence.[142]

By the time Gibson gave his public lecture on cremation, city leaders Judge C.B. Bellinger, J. Couch Flanders and Emmett B. Williams had already drawn up articles of incorporation for a Portland crematorium and were selling $25,000 worth of stock.[143]

The Portland Cremation Association was in business the following year. As it was the Pacific Northwest's first crematorium, people shipped their loved ones from as far away as northern California and the Canadian border.[144] The new enterprise was built in a Spanish mission style with whitewashed stucco walls, a tile roof and mosaic tile floors.

Cremation caught on in Portland, and the business expanded both its buildings and its services. Soon it was a major place of interment in addition

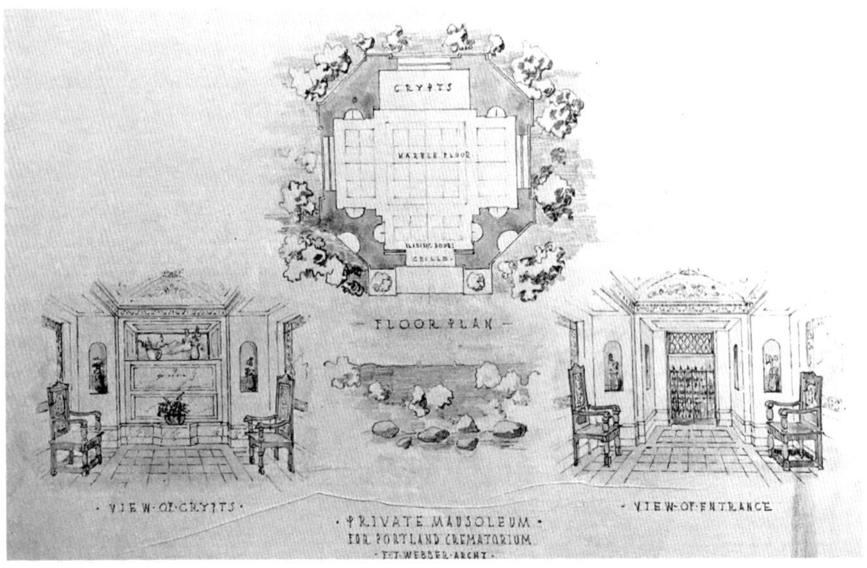

An early mausoleum plan. *Wilhelm's Portland Memorial Funeral Home, Mausoleum and Crematory.*

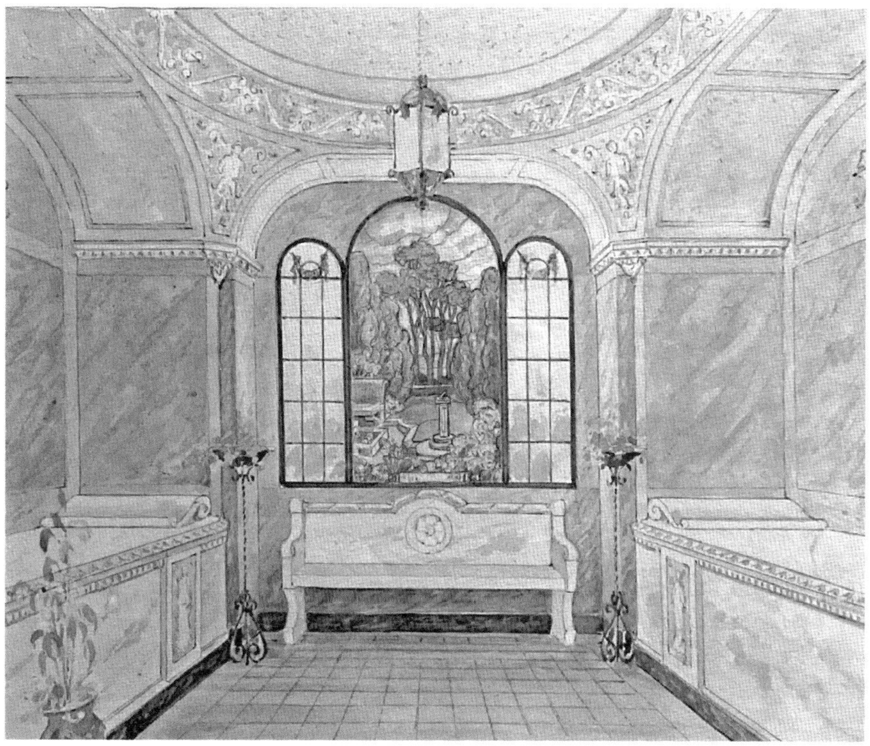

Early sketch for a private alcove. *Wilhelm's Portland Memorial.*

to a crematorium. Many people even had their relatives disinterred from ramshackle cemeteries and inurned at the mausoleum. The Eastside Streetcar installed a track extension along 14th Avenue. Families could rent funeral cars to transport caskets and mourners right to the chapel.

The mausoleum amassed an incredible collection of artwork, from the marble fronts of crypts—quarried in Italy—to intricate stained-glass windows made by big names: Povey brothers, Albert A. Gerlach, Louis C. Tiffany. Many of the stained-glass windows depict regional themes, such as Multnomah Falls, the Columbia River and Pacific Northwest woods. The building itself looks out over Oaks Bottom Nature Reserve and the Willamette River, with countless opportunities for visitors to gaze at the river through urn-framed windows. The statues placed throughout the massive mausoleum are mostly of a religious theme and were made in Italy by Taverelli Studios. Most notable is one of three exact recreations of *La Pieta*. The seven-thousand-pound statue was carved in 1969 of marble from the same quarry Michelangelo himself used.[145] Phil Rogers, who was superintendent

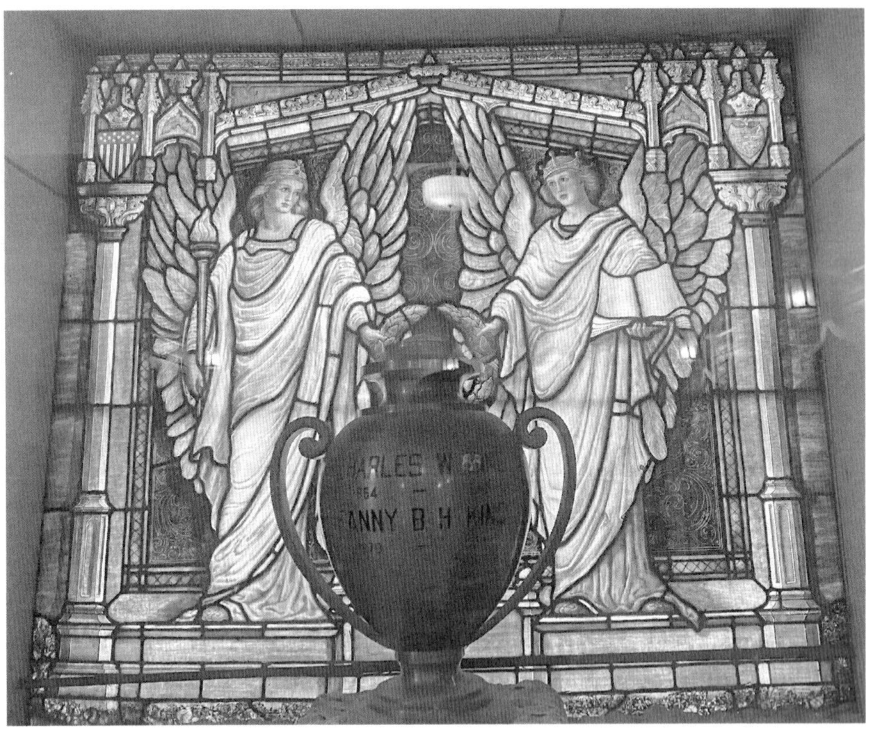

Urn and angels.

of Wilhelm's for half a century, crafted much of the decorative woodwork throughout the corridors. But it's not just pretty; during World War II, the mausoleum was designated a bomb shelter because of its formidable granite, steel and concrete construction.

The mausoleum has gone through several changes of ownership, including stints with Loewen Group, the Alderwoods Group and funerary giants Service Corporation International. But in 2008, the mausoleum came back into local hands when Sellwood's Wilhelm Funeral Home bought the property and renamed it Wilhelm's Portland Memorial Funeral Home, Mausoleum and Crematory. The new owners were well situated to serve the rise in demand for cremations, while casketed burials were waning. But with ownership comes great responsibility—in this case, reroofing and addressing extensive water damage caused by years of deferred maintenance.[146]

The current operation covers two and a half city blocks, eight floors and about seven miles of indoor corridors. Those who don't want to spend eternity indoors can be placed in the rose garden. Altogether, Wilhelm's holds the inurned or interred remains of more than 100,000 people.

Wilhelm's is still on the cutting edge. It now contracts out for alkaline hydrolysis, also known as aqua cremation. In four hours, the machine uses water, potassium hydroxide, heat and pressure to dissolve a human body to white powder with 90 percent less of a carbon footprint than flame-based cremation. Aqua cremation allows metal implants like pacemakers to be recycled and gold dental fillings to be reclaimed.[147]

Notable Crypts

Just when you think you must have reached the end of the mausoleum, you turn a corner and there's more. Some people are interred behind marble fronts; others are in urns visible in niches behind glass doors. Many of the more recent interments feature photos, flowers or mementos of the deceased. A printed sign in the niche of Margaret "Rachel" Bailey Godfrey (1844–1930) says, "Inurned 1930 Oregon State Hospital, claimed 2017 by her great grandchildren." A happy fate for one canister of the thousands of cremains warehoused and forgotten for decades at the mental hospital.

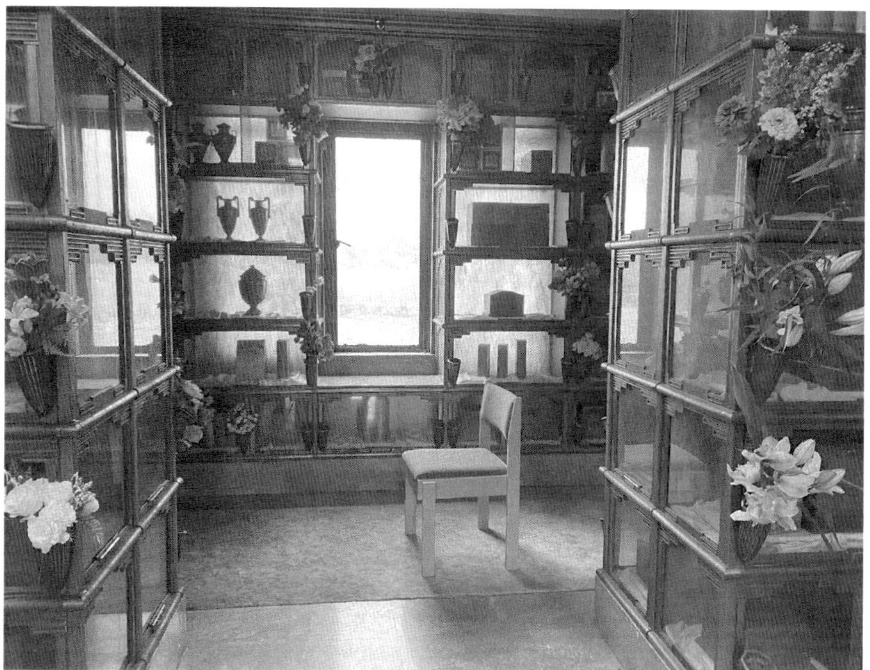

A chance to sit and contemplate.

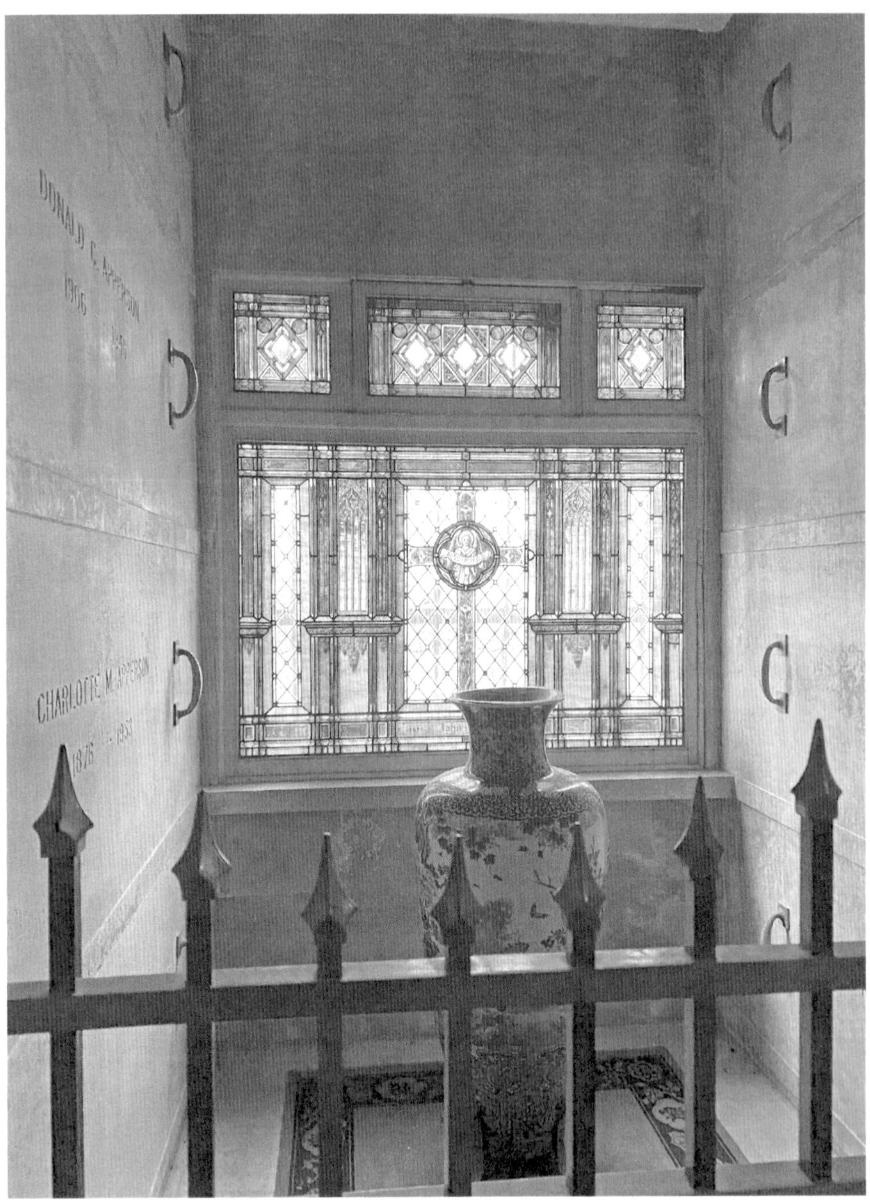

Above: A private family alcove.

Opposite: Last horse-drawn funeral in Portland, February 13, 1918, from the funeral parlor of Walter C. Kenworthy Company on Southeast 13th and Bidwell Streets, predecessor of Wilhelm Funeral Home. *Wilhelm's Portland Memorial.*

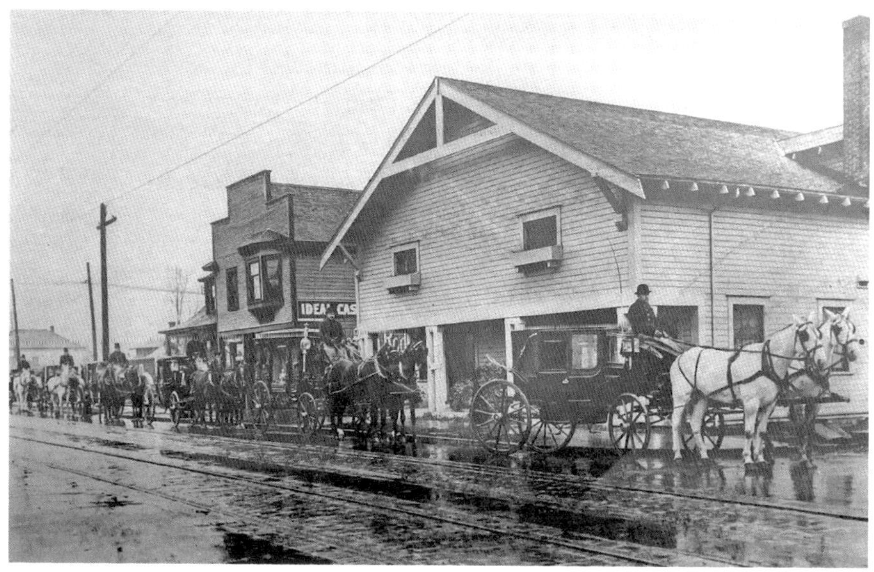

The oldest rooms are underneath the chapel, the foyer of which has a breathtaking stained-glass dome. Go down the stairs and you'll find a series of rooms named for flowers. The rooms toward the front are grander, with big glass-fronted niches, impressive urns, attractive molding and stained-glass accents. Toward the back are lower-rent districts, looking a bit more like post office boxes and less like showcases. Some of these niches have cremains dating from the 1930s and '40s, still in the original crematorium box. Tags dangle from the boxes, "This is to certify that __________age ___ yrs __ months was incinerated on ___________ at the Portland Crematorium."

Some families have private mausoleum alcoves big enough to sit in a chair and commune with their departed. These are where you'll find the largest, most beautiful stained-glass windows, and marble fronts shield the interred from public view. Some alcoves have intricate wrought-iron gates for added privacy.

Grandest of all is the Rae Room, Portland's own little Taj Mahal, a fifteen-by-fifteen-foot marble testament to love. Inside, wealthy Portlander George Rae (1843–1918) lies in a sarcophagus beside his second wife, Elizabeth, who is in her own, like solemn marble twin beds. Rae, who was born in Scotland, co-owned the Inman-Poulsen Lumber Company, located about where OMSI is now, which supplied much of the lumber for old Portland houses. The mill also provided lumber to help San Francisco rebuild following the 1906 quake and fire. After his first wife died in the state mental hospital in 1914, Rae married his housekeeper ten months later. Elizabeth Maxwell (1869–1942) was twenty-six years younger. The couple was happy. The public was scandalized. When George died four years later, Elizabeth entered into a sensational legal battle with Rae's estranged adopted daughter. The judge eventually ruled in Elizabeth's favor. George was initially buried at River View. But Elizabeth used some of his fortune to create the exquisite room for them at the mausoleum and had him disinterred and moved to their tomb. Now they lie side by side under an enormous stained-glass window depicting woods and a mountain, which bears the inscription, "The end of a perfect day."[148]

Notable Residents: Povey Brothers

Some of the most beautiful stained-glass work in the mausoleum—and the Northwest—is the work of the Povey brothers, who are inurned there. Brothers David (1865–1924) and John (1867–1917) were born in New Jersey and raised in a stained glass–making family. They arrived in Portland and set up a stained-glass studio in 1888 at Northwest Fifth and Flanders in what is now Chinatown. Povey Brothers Studio became known as "Tiffany of the Northwest."

David was the artistic leader who designed the pieces, having studied art in New York and Europe before settling in Portland. John was in charge of glazing and assembling the windows. They were successful from their first commission, a high-profile job for the First Presbyterian Church. Soon they were creating both religious and secular windows for churches, public buildings and private homes.[149]

More than forty buildings now listed in the National Register of Historic Places boast Povey brothers windows. When designing for private homes, the brothers favored roses, lilies, grape clusters, dogwoods and birds, and they often incorporated clear glass to let more light pass through on gray Portland days. At the height of its production, the studio employed twenty-five workers.[150]

You can still see Povey windows around the area, including at the Atkinson Memorial Unitarian Church in Oregon City, the Pittock Mansion and, of course, the Portland Mausoleum. The Architectural Heritage Foundation in Portland rescued some Povey windows from demolished buildings.

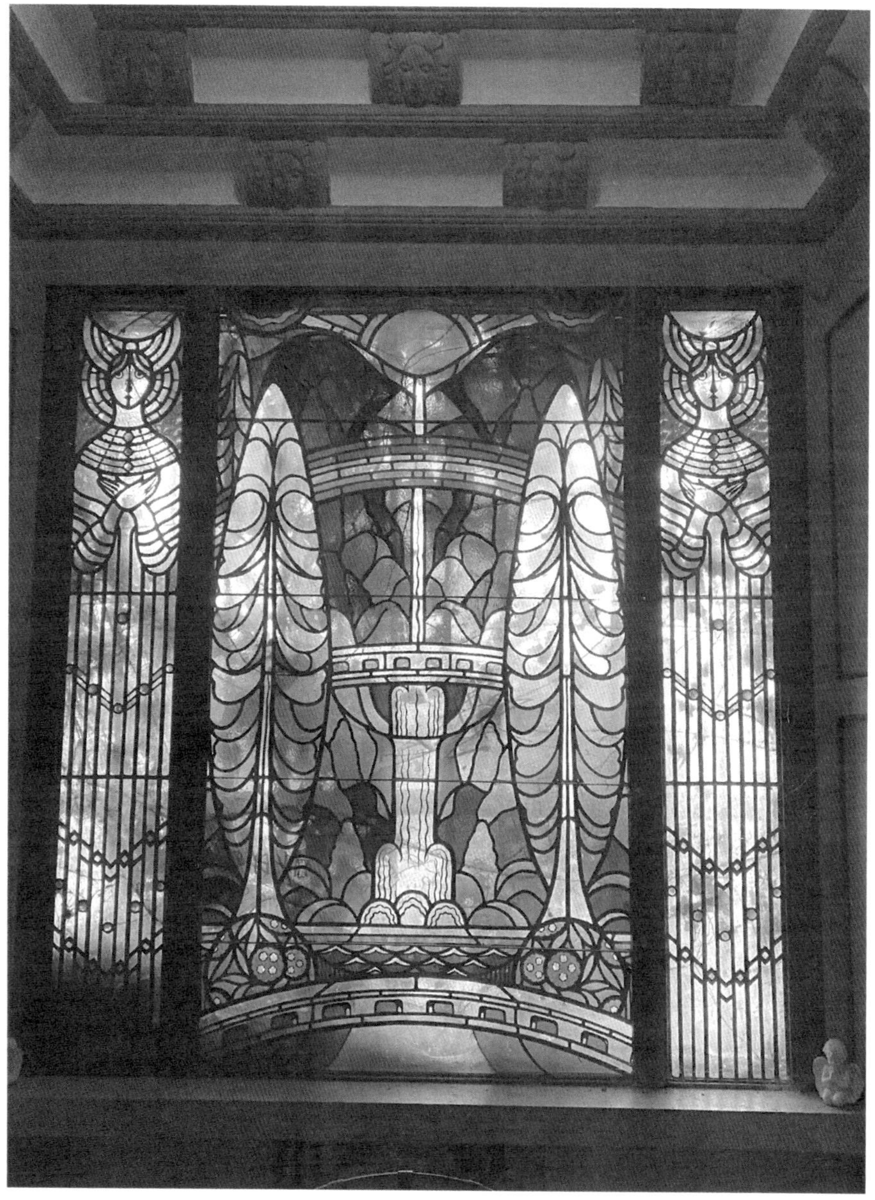

Stained-glass window depicting Multnomah Falls.

Notable Resident: Lucy Rose Mallory

One of Portland's most fascinating and ahead-of-her-time characters, Lucy Rose Mallory (1843–1920) was the daughter of Minerva Kellogg, part of the famous Seventh-Day Adventist family known for early nutritious breakfast cereal. Lucy's mother died in childbirth. Her father, Aaron Rose, quickly remarried an evil stepmother who did such awful deeds as beating Lucy when she fed a pie to a starving cow. Lucy, her sister, father and stepmother left their Michigan home in 1851 to settle in a town her father named Roseburg, Oregon.

Lucy's friendship with an Umpqua Indian boy named Solomon was one of her formative frontier experiences. She later described him as a mystic and a philosopher who taught her about connecting with animals and plants. She was given to psychic experiences and astral projection from a young age.

At seventeen, she married Rufus Mallory, a Roseburg schoolteacher. He soon became a successful attorney and was elected to the Oregon House of Representatives. At nineteen, Lucy found herself the wife of a state congressman. After a two-year term in Salem, they moved to Portland, where Rufus became a millionaire. Among other business dealings, he built the Hotel Mallory (now Hotel deLuxe).

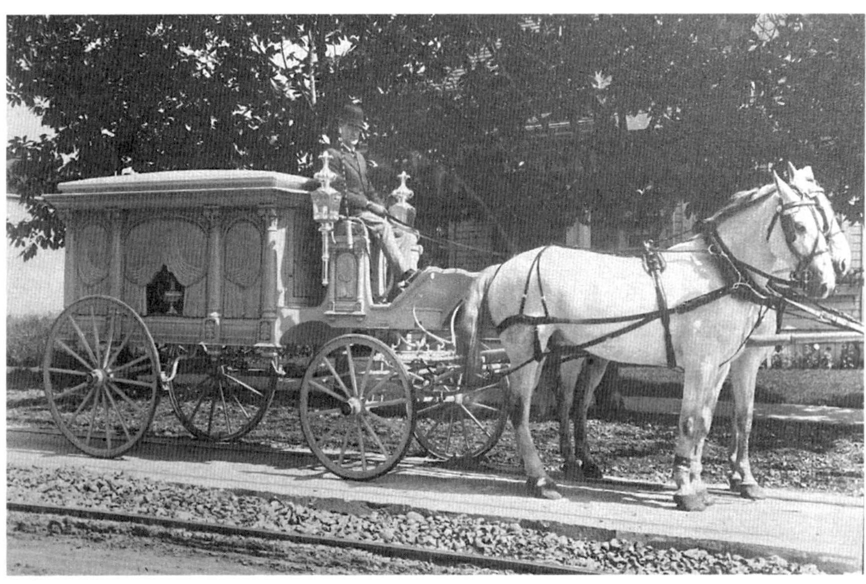

Horse-drawn hearse serving Sellwood. *Wilhelm's Portland Memorial.*

Lucy's interests were of a more esoteric bent. She was famous for gathering vegetarians, spiritualists and freethinkers in their Hawthorne home. Lucy founded a journal called *The World's Advance-Thought*, most of which she wrote herself. Thousands of people around the world subscribed, reading Lucy's thoughts on animal welfare, spiritualism and feminism—such as corsets being a "woman's prison-house" and "badge of slavery." Leo Tolstoy was a subscriber and quoted her hundreds of times in his books.

Lucy lost heart and ceased publishing a few months after her son Elmer Ellsworth Mallory (1862–1917) succumbed to an illness. She died two years later and is now inurned in the Lilac Room.[151]

Special Features

While the front entrance of Wilhelm's looks like an attractive villa and the inside is endlessly intriguing, the back of the mausoleum was a mammoth neighborhood eyesore for many years. In 1991, after an informal opinion poll with families of those interred in the mausoleum, Mark Bennett of Portland-based ArtFX Murals got the go-ahead to paint a 70-foot-high, 50-foot-wide heron on the building. The neighborhood response was enthusiastic. But it wasn't until 2009 that Bennett, his son Shane and artist Dan Cohen painted the current expanded mural depicting hooded mergansers, an osprey, red-tailed hawk and other local birds.[152] At 43,485 square feet and covering eight surfaces of the building, this might well be the largest mural you ever see.[153]

17

MILWAUKIE PIONEER CEMETERY

9515 Southeast 17th Avenue, Portland

This historic cemetery in Milwaukie, seven miles south of Portland, is tucked between a busy thoroughfare and historic Waverley Country Club's golf course. The approximately 2,150 burials include many leading Milwaukie citizens.

History

Oregon pioneer Lot Whitcomb acquired a nearly six-hundred-acre land claim after arriving in 1847 and named it Milwaukie after the Wisconsin town he admired, a spelling that has confused people for at least one hundred years. Back then, Democrats mostly spelled the city's name with an *ie*, while Republicans and Whigs favored the double *e*.[154]

By 1850, the population had grown to almost five hundred. Two of them died that December and became the first two occupants of Milwaukie Pioneer Cemetery. Seventeen-year-old Mary Luelling Meek—already a wife and mother—was the first to be buried. Then on Christmas Day, Frederick Morse was killed setting off a cannon to celebrate the launch of Lot Whitcomb's eponymous steamboat. As the *Western Star* graphically reported, "Captain Frederick Morse of the schooner 'Merchantman', while in the act of touching fire to a cannon, was instantly killed by the bursting of the fuse, which was blown into atoms and its fragments scattered about

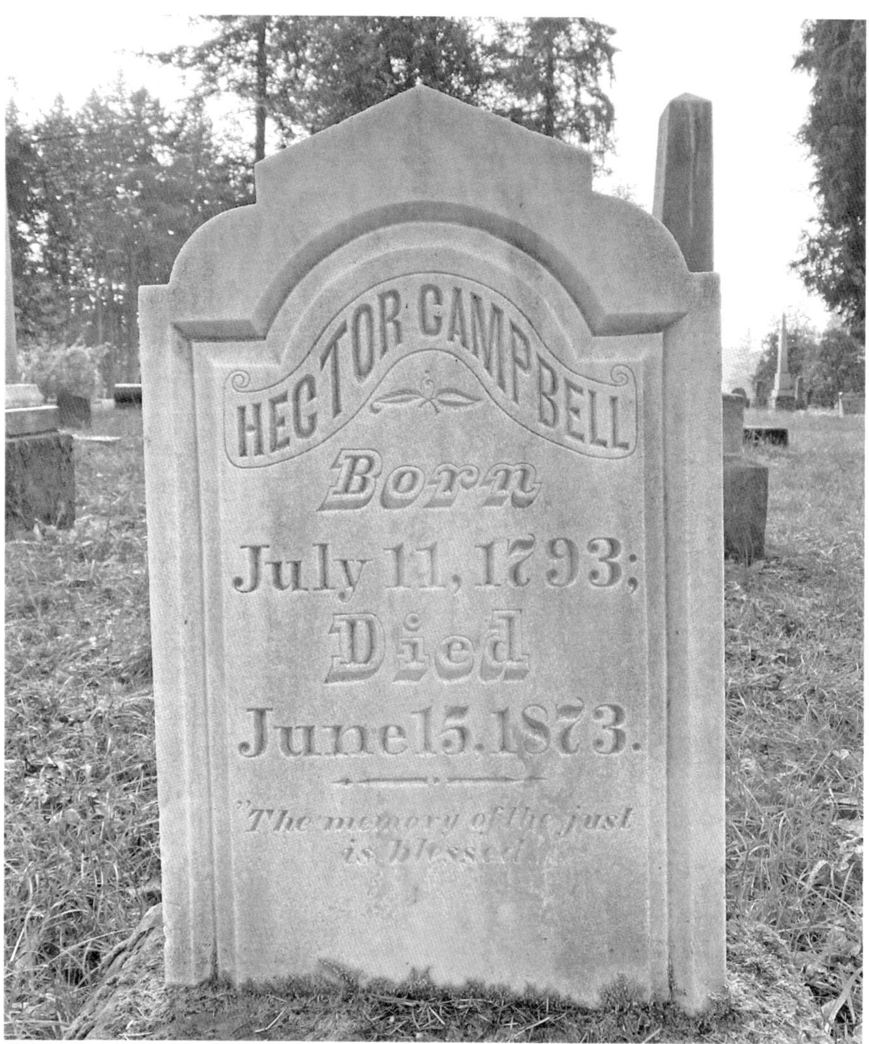

A rare pre-1800 birthdate in an Oregon cemetery.

for some distance, injuring no one, however, but Capt. Morse. A fragment of the gun struck him in the neck, below the jaw, carrying away one-half the contents of the neck, breaking the vertebra of the neck and lower jaw."[155]

In 1869, Mr. and Mrs. William Meeks and Mr. and Mrs. H.W. Eddy deeded the property to "the public of Milwaukie" for continued use as a cemetery. The first trustees were appointed, with new trustees continually appointed as needed until the 1980s, when the city took over care of Milwaukie Pioneer Cemetery.

Fallen branches and untrimmed shrubbery quickly overtake old cemeteries, outraging relatives of the interred, and Milwaukie Pioneer is no exception. Back in 1899, Sellwood residents were already griping. "The manner in which it has been cared for, or, rather neglected, has caused considerable discontent," said a *Morning Oregonian* article. "The sum of $5 is charged for a burial lot, and the money is to be used to keep the grounds in repair, but, as far as known, the cash received has not been applied for that purpose."[156] Even in 1899, five bucks stretched only so far. And many cemeteries failed to factor in inflation and long-term care when setting prices.

Milwaukie declared the cemetery full in the 1950s, at which time its profitability further plummeted. In the 1990s, the cemetery was included in an intergovernmental agreement with North Clackamas Parks District. By 2003, citizens were again unhappy about the cemetery's unkempt state and a group of citizens formed the Milwaukie Pioneer Cemetery Association. They petitioned the Oregon Circuit Court to appoint trustees.

The association quickly got to work on multiple fronts, including addressing legal aspects, maintenance, restoration, fundraising and PR. Funds were mostly limited to membership fees and donations, and the occasional miniscule grant. Fortunately, the trustees and members excelled at getting the community involved and local businesses to donate everything from portable toilets for volunteer cleanup days to a safe deposit box for cemetery records. At least, for what records they could find. An ongoing search for the official burial record, supposedly loaned to a teacher and not seen since, went on for years. The reward climbed to $650 before volunteers finally gave up on finding it.[157] Some receipts for burial plots from the 1920s to 1940s eventually turned up in the basement of city hall. Like many pioneer cemeteries, endless hours of diligent volunteer effort still result in a best-guess list of who's buried there.

As open-air historical locations, pioneer cemeteries are liable to find surprising things left on their grounds. The strangest for Milwaukie Pioneer was in August 2007, when volunteers found 240 pounds of frozen chicken hidden in the cemetery. Volunteers delivered it to a local charity before it thawed.[158]

Memorable Headstones

At the entrance to the cemetery stands one of the larger monuments, which commemorates "our unknown dead of the Civil War." The Blackmar Circle

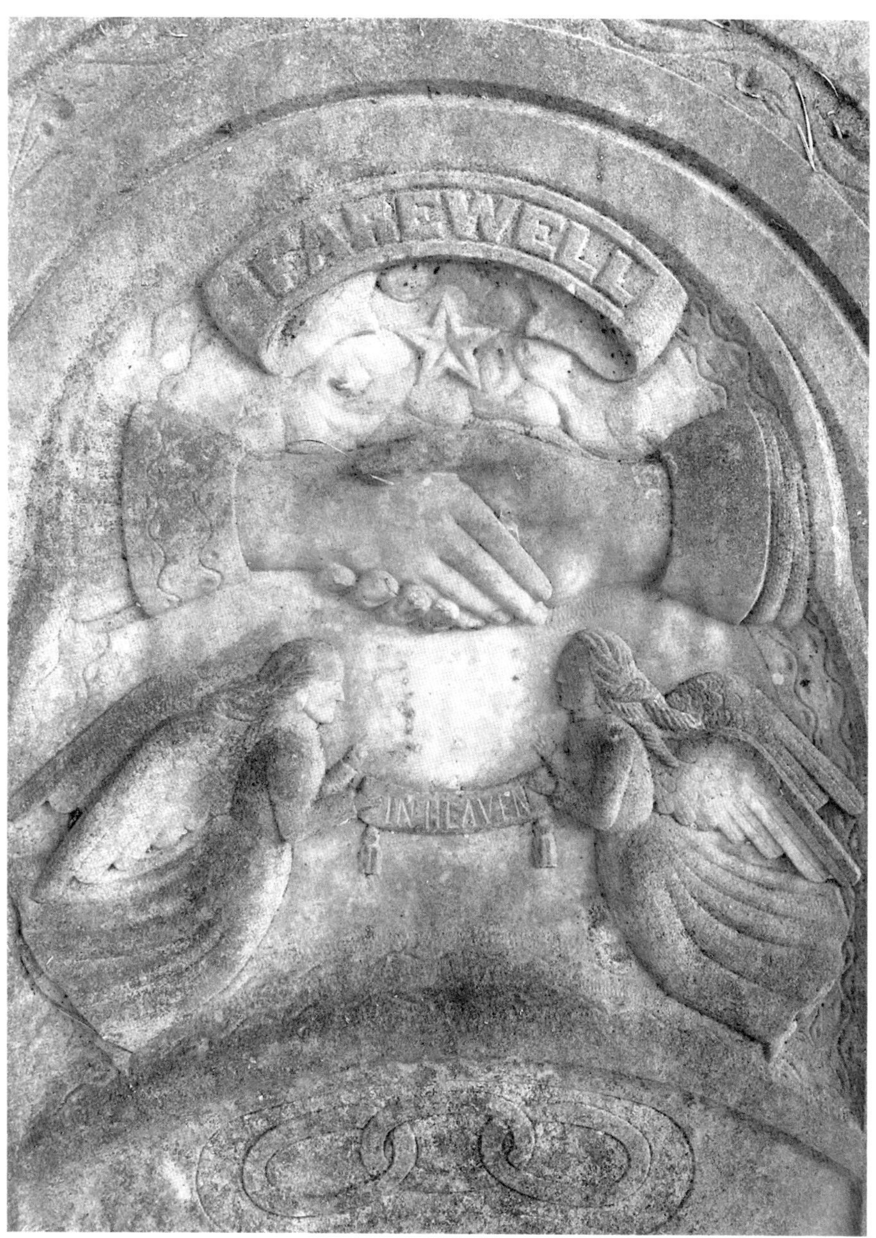

A farewell handshake.

Ladies of the GAR and A.J Smith Post No. 26 dedicated this monument to celebrate Memorial Day in 1911. This women's auxiliary for Civil War veterans had more than sixty thousand members in twenty-nine states in 1910. As well as raising money for veterans' homes and hospitals, the ladies erected scores of monuments.[159]

Knee-high fences enclose many family and individual lots. The fences around the small graves of infants and young children are especially poignant, as they resemble cribs.

Attractive gravestone carvings include a wreath for Elva, wife of W.J. Bradbury, who died in 1862 at the age of seventeen. Ernst Strauss's (1857–1914) stone depicts a friendship handshake under the word "farewell" and two angels holding a banner proclaiming "In heaven." Hector Campbell (1793–1873), has an eighteenth-century birthdate, unusually early for Oregon cemeteries.

The strangest memorial looks handmade and is entirely covered with stone tiles the size of Scrabble squares, even the base. Unfortunately, most have fallen off one side, revealing the concrete beneath. Any inscription is no longer visible.

Visitors might notice some shiny new stones for old burials. Cemetery volunteers successfully lobbied the U.S. Department of Veterans Affairs for stones to place on formerly unmarked graves.

NOTABLE RESIDENT: NANINE JONES

Nanine Jones (1842–1915) was born enslaved in Louisiana, speaking only French. According to a 1913 *Sunday Oregonian* article, "She was paying her master $15 a month for the privilege of working out at cutting wood and washing to secure money with which to buy her freedom, until after the war was over." In 1894, Jones, her daughter Mary and her granddaughter Pauline all set out for Oregon. The state passed women's suffrage in 1912, and the family wound up in the 1913 newspaper under the headline "Ex-Slave to Vote." Officials brought the roster to Jones's home on Harold Street because she was too ill to go to the courthouse. The three generations of women registered together.[160] Nanine Jones and her daughter Mary Dupuy are buried in Milwaukie Pioneer. Pauline Young and her son Cornelius are buried at Lincoln Memorial Park.[161]

Notable Resident: Seth Lewelling

In 1847, Henderson Luelling left Iowa with an oxcart full of cherries. He hauled them to the Willamette Valley and established a commercial fruit nursery close to Milwaukie. His brother Seth Lewelling (Seth changed his surname's spelling) joined him soon after. In 1875, Lewelling crossed a Black Republican cherry with a Napoleon and created a new type of cherry. He named it Bing after Ah Bing, his foreman, who came from the Manchurian part of China. Since then, the Bing has become the most widely planted type of sweet cherry in the United States and perhaps the most famous in the world.

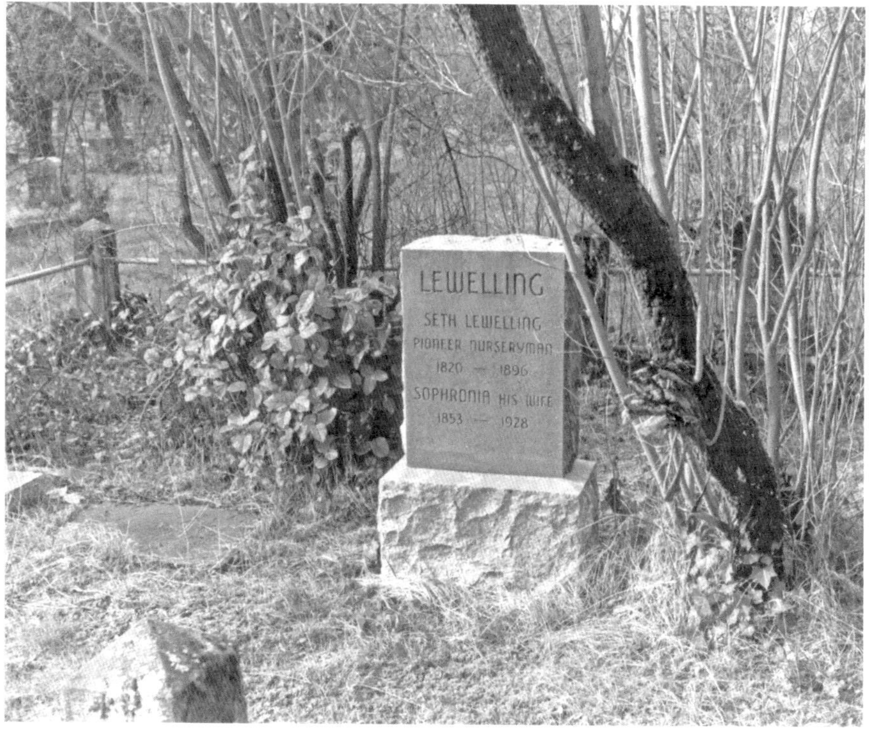

Lewelling marker. *Milwaukie Museum.*

Notable Resident: Denzell George Arthur Venville

Denzell Venville grew up in a shack in Sellwood with seven siblings and an illiterate, hardworking mother. He was a sickly child whose doctor recommended he join the navy for healthful sea air and to toughen him up. So he did, at age sixteen. Once aboard the gunboat USS *Yorktown*, peers mocked his effeminate gestures and called him a "girl sailor."

In April 1899, during the Philippine-American War, the *Yorktown* was captured by insurgents. Venville took four gunshots to his ear, throat, armpit and ankle. He couldn't keep up with the rest of the prisoners of war when the Filipinos marched them into the interior. Instead, he spent ten months around the remote coastal town of Baler, where the locals nicknamed him Bembio. At 119 pounds and walking with a cane after his crippling injuries, he posed no threat. Local fishermen taught him to fish with the casting nets they used.

Ten months into his captivity, unbeknownst to Venville, about six hundred American troops had entered the Baler Valley. His guards were getting worried. One morning, he was invited to join a fishing expedition on the Diatt River. At some point, the four men accompanying him dropped back. A band of Ilongots laid in wait. This tribal group, who carried machetes called "head knives," probably started by shooting barbed, leaf-shaped arrows into his back. Taking a head was a prerequisite for manhood and marriage, so the chosen Ilongot stepped forward and sliced off Venville's head. His hands and feet were also cut off and the remains left in a shallow grave for wild animals to find.

Meanwhile, the Americans were searching for Venville and other sailors from the *Yorktown*. Most were rescued. Of Venville—after many months of searching and investigation—Americans eventually recovered thirteen bone fragments. Part of the reason for their perseverance were the letters Venville's mother dictated, begging for help from presidents and generals. American soldiers and his Filipino friends attended a religious service for Venville in September 1901 at the church in Baler before sending his remains home to Oregon. In December, all of Milwaukie and Sellwood turned out for a funeral that starred a petite metal box rather than a casket. Venville's remains were small, but his monument at Milwaukie Pioneer is enormous, complete with an inscribed summary of his dreadful story.[162]

EERIE TALES

An alleged ghost sighting at Milwaukie Pioneer made the *Morning Oregonian* in 1910. Matto Ignato, an Italian gardener, was walking on a path one misty January morning. "As he glanced at one of the graves he was surprised to see a form rise from the ground and, with a yell, he started on a cross-country sprint which had no letup till the runner had reached another county." It turned out not to be a ghost, but gravedigger Thomas Neal, who had gone to the cemetery early that morning to prepare a grave for a funeral. "Feeling certain that it was a real live phantom, the foreigner emitted a yell of terror, hurdled the fence and started on a run toward the Scott farm, where he excitedly told the story of the ghost which came from the spirit land."[163] Sounds spooky enough to send anybody running.

RECREATIONAL OPPORTUNITIES

Milwaukie Pioneer is right on a major bike path, so it's a perfect outing to combine with a bike ride. If you're on foot, leashed dogs are welcome.

The cemetery has partnered with the Audubon Society in the past, both on its Headstone and Habitat tours and for bird counting events. So it's a promising place for birders.

For people who'd like to appreciate the cemetery from home, the Milwaukie Historical Society published the book *Milwaukie Pioneer Cemetery Comes to Life*. Or watch the movie *Way to Heaven*, a comedy about an angel filling in while the Grim Reaper is on vacation, which was partly shot at Milwaukie Pioneer Cemetery.

18

RIVER VIEW CEMETERY

300 South Taylors Ferry Road, Portland

Arriving at River View, the cemetery sleuth's heart quickens at the first view of grand monuments and the forest of obelisks. This is Portland's largest and fanciest cemetery, set on a hill overlooking the Willamette River and filled with names visitors will recognize from local streets and businesses. The cemetery's trees have grown tall in the century plus since its founding, but in certain places you can still glimpse the river below, making this a stunning setting for eternal rest for the seventy-five-thousand-plus people interred there.

History

While Lone Fir is probably Oregon's best-known historic cemetery today, back in 1879, about twenty-five years after Mount Crawford (later Lone Fir) was founded, upscale Portlanders were looking for something more in a cemetery. A reporter described the older cemetery's drawbacks, including its "flat and barren surface" and "the tameness and dullness of the view on every side."[164] Leading lights W.S. Ladd, H.W. Corbett and Henry Failing—names still familiar to Portlanders due to streets and neighborhoods that share their surnames—formed the River View Cemetery Association. Corbett bought 286 acres of land three miles south of the city and then sold it to the association for $10,000. A mountain stream could be directed into fountains and artificial lakes, and it commanded an amazing view of Mounts Hood and Saint Helens and miles of forest.

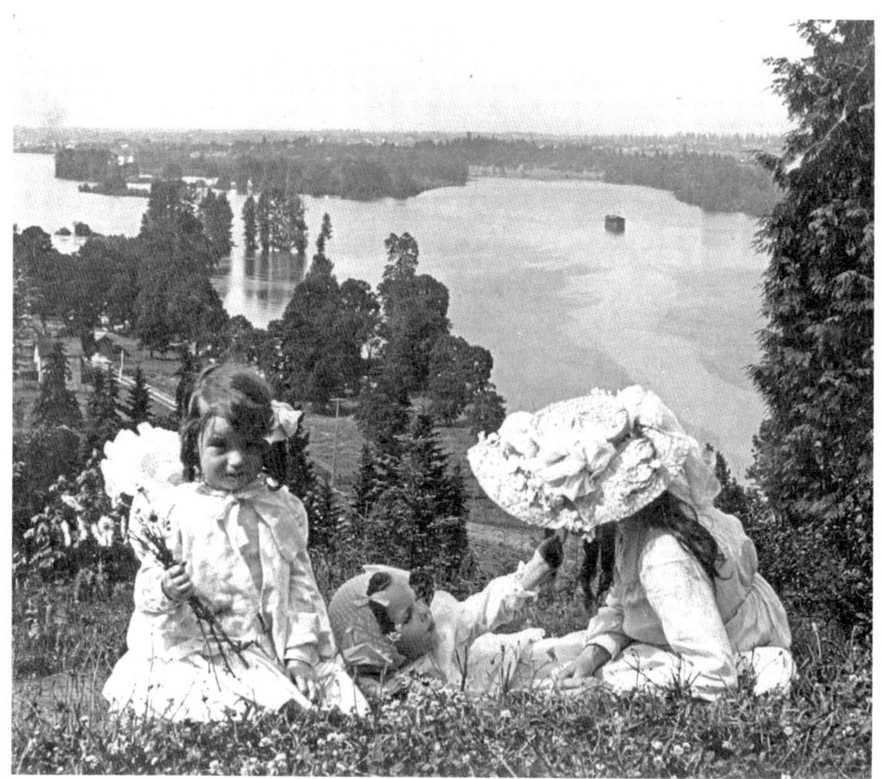

A 1903 view from River View. *Photo by Benjamin Lloyd Singley, City of Portland (OR) Archives, A2004-002.792.*

River View was modeled after the East Coast rural garden cemeteries, which stressed walking paths and aesthetics nearly as much as a place to put the bodies. But Ladd, Corbett and Failing set up the cemetery as a nonprofit, unlike most East Coast cemeteries of the time. They raised $130,000 to start the cemetery[165] and commissioned German-born landscape architect Edward Otto Schwagerl (1842–1910) to design the grounds.[166] Thirty percent of burial receipts went into an endowment that would be worth over $2 million a century after the cemetery's founding.[167]

River View enraptured publisher Harvey Scott from the get-go—and a good thing, because he would wind up spending eternity there. "By special provision the grounds are to be tastefully and even elaborately improved," he wrote. "Nothing unsightly or uncouth to be allowed, and the graves of those whose friends are absent still to be kept green and adorned with flowers. It is a graceful feeling of the human heart that would make a little border land between this world and the unseen."[168]

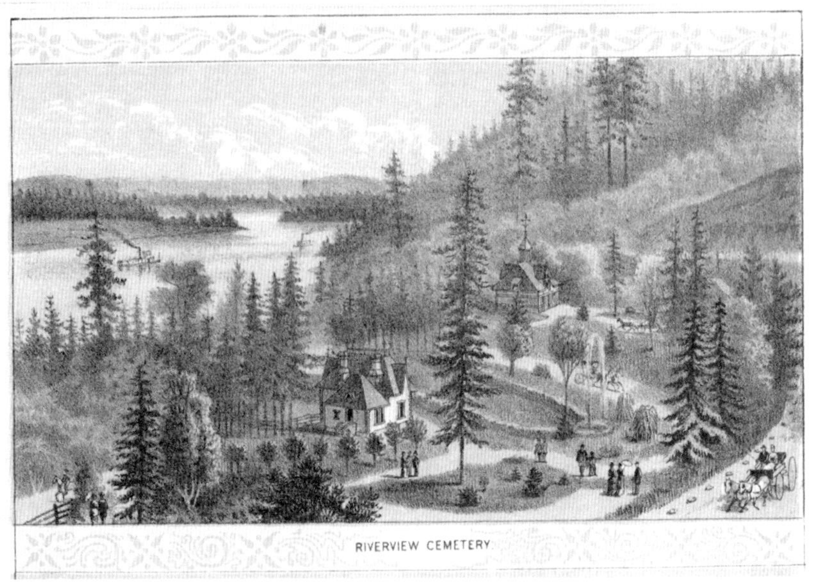

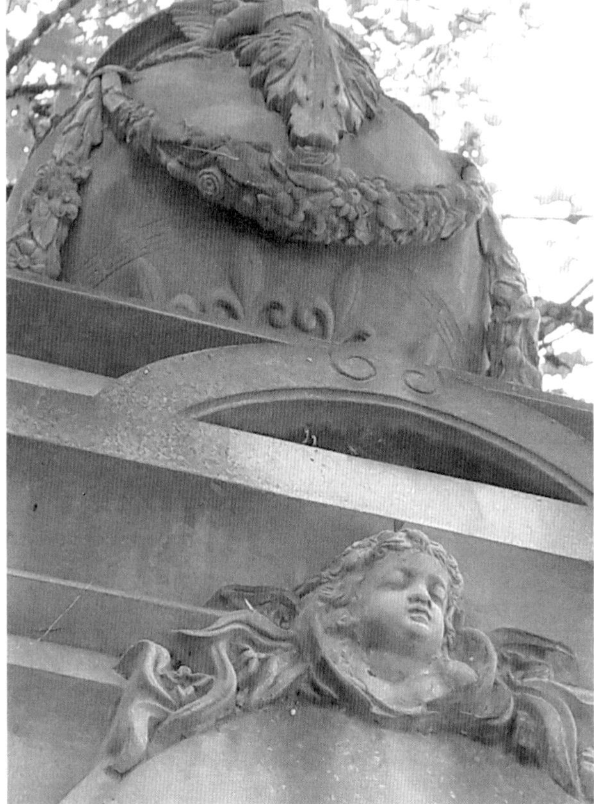

Above: Drawing of River View from the May 1, 1888 issue of *West Shore* magazine. *Architectural Heritage Center Library.*

Left: Details on private mausoleum.

The new cemetery on a hill was stiff competition for Lone Fir, which required funeral parties to cross the Willamette on a ferry and slog up a muddy road. Many early Portlanders decided that their dearly departed deserved a better eternal view; by 1900, more than sixty pioneers had been exhumed from Lone Fir and transferred to River View.[169] One of Portland's first trolley lines, operated by Metropolitan Railway Company, began running an electric streetcar to the cemetery in late 1888 or early 1889.

The cemetery served as a final resting place, a park for the living and a backdrop to some colorful stories. In 1904, Italian florists saw a streaker about seventy years ahead of his time. "Just before dark they were in the extreme western end of the graveyard when a goblin-like person, naked as Adam, appeared on the skyline on the top of the rise, rushing over graves, gravestones and shrubbery, headed south,"[170] the *Morning Oregonian* reported. In May 1906, one of the biggest stories was a missing girl, Bessie Bauer, who disappeared from her home in Sellwood. Five days later, the girl was found "through the sagacity of a dog belonging to the sexton of River View Cemetery." Apparently suffering from a mental disturbance, Bauer had been hiding out in the cemetery for days. "Exposed to rains, which drenched her to the skin, and suffering from cold, Miss Bauer slept in the brush and under logs for five nights, with wild beasts, birds and the tombstones for her only company."[171] The following month, she again disappeared, this time for three nights, and was found in the woods around the cemetery.[172]

More Oregonians began to choose cremation over burial as the twentieth century progressed. River View still had a lot of undeveloped areas and began exploring other uses, such as developing apartments or housing.[173] After a series of land-use battles with the city, the City of Portland Parks & Recreation Bureau, Bureau of Environmental Services, Trust for Public Land and Metro jointly bought a 146-acre parcel and turned it into River View Natural Area.[174] The cemetery still has about 200 acres left over.

River View was on the forefront of green burials in Portland. In 2010, the cemetery announced that anyone wanting a natural burial—sans embalming, casket and concrete vault—could do so anywhere on the grounds. This differed from most other cemeteries around the country, which allowed green burials only in designated areas.[175]

Memorable Headstones

At River View, families made their last stand to show their power and prestige. Some monuments are beautiful, some impressive, some are just really big. Wander around for five minutes and you'll encounter cemetery art's greatest hits—obelisks, sarcophagi, statues, private mausoleums, many with names familiar from streets, neighborhoods and longtime Portland businesses. This cemetery needs its own guidebook.

The Terwilligers' white bronze monument is especially tall and manages to incorporate an impressive number of funerary tropes: cherub heads, floral wreaths and inverted torches, topped with an urn. George Carleton Sears has one of the biggest statues, a towering woman with one hand raised, a book in the other, dressed in draped classical garb. A spectacular Celtic cross covered with carved ivy commemorates Emma Bartholf (1834–1884). She was born in Switzerland and died in the Vancouver Barracks, married to a doctor serving there. As for obelisks, the Green family might have the tallest, but there's a lot of competition, including from the Burrell, Dolph and Corbett families.

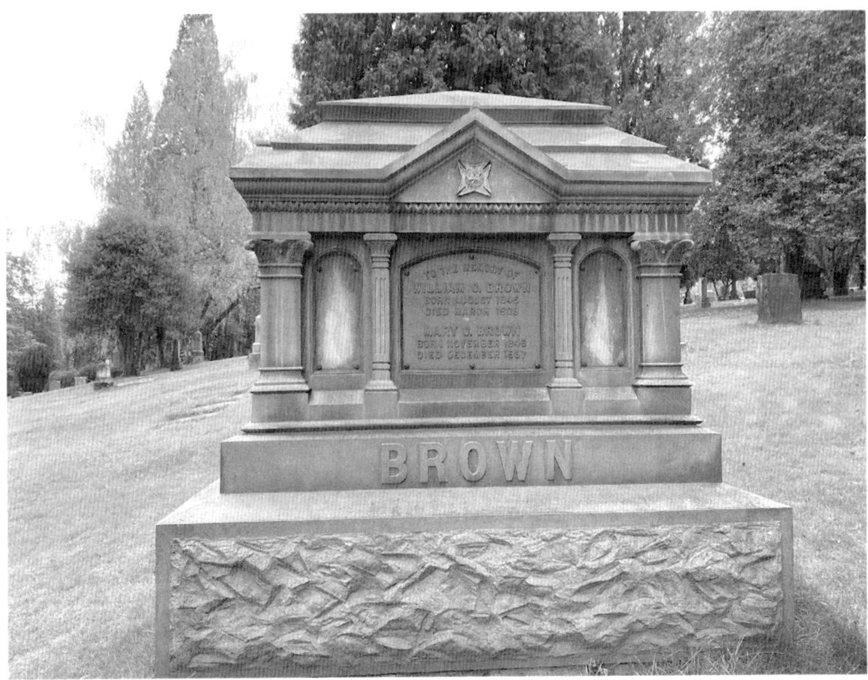

A grand sarcophagus.

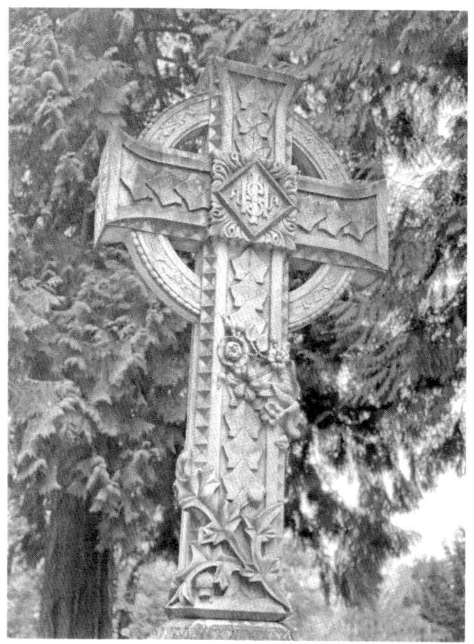

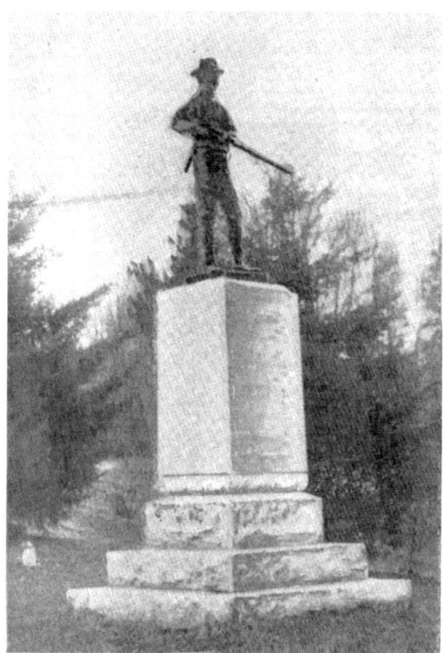

Left: Emma Bartholf's cross.

Right: A 1907 drawing of the soldiers' monument. *City of Portland (OR) Archives, A2004-002.9701.*

While River View has a large indoor mausoleum, families who wanted to make an even bigger splash opted for private mausoleums. Some, like the Pamplins, have small chapel areas inside with wee benches and stained-glass windows. Oregon-born actress and costume director Corinne Riely Barker (1865–1928) came back home from New York to be buried in her own private mausoleum.

But the less showy monuments are also fascinating. Markers often raise questions. George H. Fairchild's (1855–1896) marker says, "Erected by passengers to the memory of engineer Geo. H. Fairchild," and mentions his affiliation with the BLE, or Brotherhood of Locomotive Engineers, a labor union founded in 1863. Some monuments make you wonder by their understatement, such as that of Roscoe Knapp (1882–1906), whose grave is marked with a red granite oval with simply "Roscoe" carved in all caps.

The Spanish-American War (1898–1899) was the United States' first overseas conflict and is prominently remembered at River View. At the beginning of the twentieth century, River View set aside part of its grounds to bury war veterans. About 430 Spanish-American War vets fill the plots, many of them in a circle around a statue of a soldier. Thomas Canning

(1861–1906), also buried here, served as the model for the statue. William M. Green (1878–1969) was the last Spanish-American veteran buried at River View.[176]

LOCAL CELEBRITIES

River View has an astounding number of locally famous residents and many that were known nationally or even internationally. There's a long list of politicians alone—governors, Congress members and other high officials.

Lawman Virgil Earp (1843–1905) is one of River View's most visited occupants. The older brother of Wyatt Earp served with the Union army during the Civil War. In 1881, as city marshal of Tombstone, Arizona, he, his brothers and other lawmen went up against a group of outlaws known as the Cowboys. The shootout near the OK Corral lasted only thirty seconds but became the most famous in western history. Virgil moved to Southern California and became city marshal of Colton. Meanwhile, Earp's first wife, Ellen, believed Virgil had been killed in the Civil War. She remarried and moved to Portland with Nellie Jane, Virgil's daughter. When Earp died of pneumonia in 1905, his daughter buried him at River View.

Henry Weinhard (1830–1904) was raised in Germany and immigrated to the United States in 1851. He worked for others in the beer business, refining his brewing skills in Philadelphia, Cincinnati and St. Louis before opening his own brewery in downtown Portland. Longtime Portland residents remember the smell of hops hanging like a thick cloud over downtown before the brewery closed in 1999. Visitors to Weinhard's grave often leave beer cans and bottlecaps.

Salmon cannery millionaire Frank Manley Warren Sr. (1848–1912) and Anna Sophia Warren (1851–1925) were first-class passengers on the *Titanic*. With lifeboat space limited, Mr. Warren helped his wife aboard and then stepped back.

Ella Leota Smith Swanton (1868–1933), longtime general manager of the Oregon Humane Society, organized Alaska's first humane society in Nome during the gold rush. She allowed a World War I vet's seeing-eye dog to be buried on the grounds, perhaps foreshadowing her founding of the West's first animal cemetery at Portland's OHS in 1918.

Abigail Scott Dunaway (1834–1915) and Harvey Scott (1838–1910) were siblings and publishing rivals. He was an editor and part owner of the *Oregonian*. She founded the more progressive *New Northwest Newspaper*, advocated for women's rights and was the first woman registered to vote in Multnomah County.

In 1908, Lola Greene Baldwin (1860–1957) became the first woman in the country to be sworn in as a detective. She worked her whole life for the public good, especially of women, filling roles in social work, travelers' aid, juvenile justice, suffrage and pay equity for women. After retiring from the police, she served on the Oregon Parole Board and the National Board of Prisons and Prison Labor.

Simon Benson (1851–1942) was born Simon Berger Iversen in Norway, but changed his name after immigrating to the United States at age sixteen. He made a fortune in lumber, building railroads into forests to haul logs to the Columbia River and developing enormous oceangoing log rafts. He built the Benson Hotel and donated money to build the Benson Polytechnic School. But he's best known for the Benson Bubblers, the twenty bronze drinking fountains he donated to the city in 1912, hoping people would quench their thirst with water rather than frequenting taverns.

Seid Back (1851–1916), born San Way Chung Sar in China, came to the United States at age seventeen. Like many early Chinese residents, he worked on railroads. However, his cooking skills helped him advance beyond manual labor. He worked in private homes, saving his money until he could open his first store in downtown Portland at 3rd Avenue and Washington Street. He married Chong Quey Choy in 1875, and their only child, Seid Gain, was born in 1878. Seid Back's fortunes grew as he began importing Chinese goods and then supplying workers for salmon canneries on the Columbia River and in Alaska. He and his second wife, Ching Won, adopted two white boys from orphanages. Seid Back skillfully navigated both the white and Chinese communities, and his ability to foster intercommunity dialog may have made Portland a less violent place for Chinese people than some other West Coast cities. He was known for his philanthropy both in Portland and China, for supplying local children with Independence Day fireworks and hosting businessmen and government officials at an extravagant annual buffet featuring Chinese dishes and rare wines. When he died in 1916, an astonishing number of both Chinese and Caucasians attended his funeral at First Baptist Church in Portland.[177] In 1907, his son Seid Gain was the first person of Chinese descent to graduate from University of Oregon Law School and the first to practice law in the United States.[178]

Charles Piggott (1855–1924) made his fortune in bricks but is most remembered for his eccentricities. In 1892, he built his dream home—a three-story Romanesque Revival brick castle in the West Hills. When the

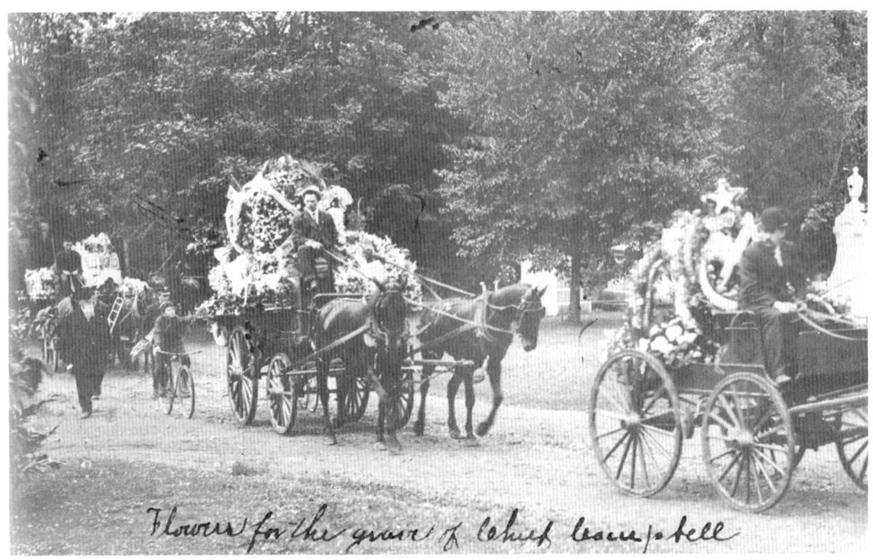

Flower-laden carriages bound for Portland Fire Chief David Campbell's 1911 burial. *Oregon Historical Society.*

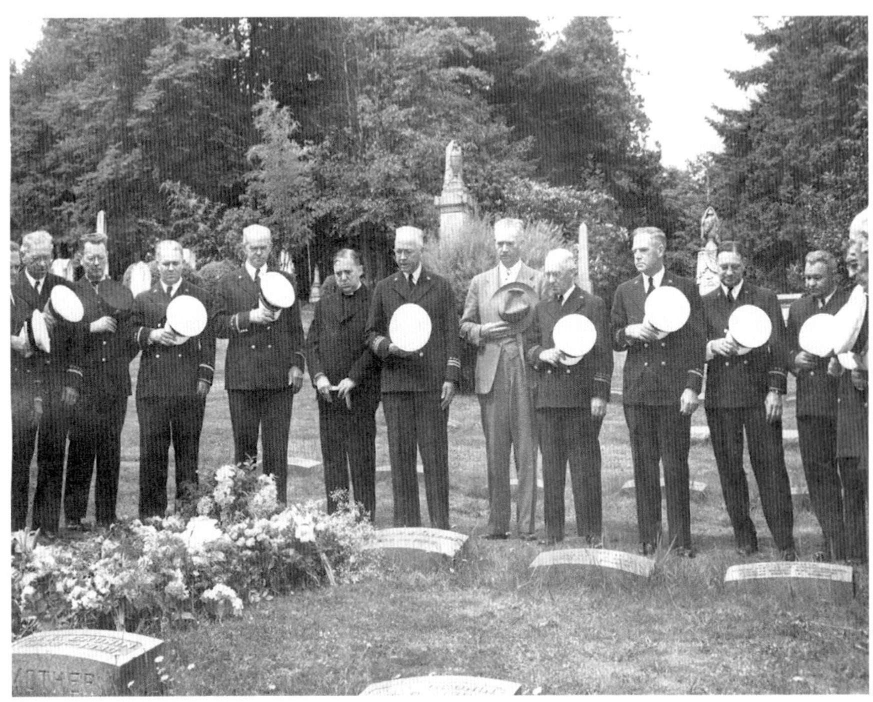

Campbell wasn't forgotten. Men pay their respects at a special service in 1947. *City of Portland (OR) Archives, A2001-083.*

financial panic of 1893 forced him to sell the house a year later, people dubbed the castle Piggott's Folly.[179] His book *Pearls at Random Strung; Or, Life's Tragedy from Wedding to Tomb: Including the Scientific Causes of All Diseases, Poverty, Premature Death and Longevity* is available from Amazon.

Carl William Mays (1891–1971) pitched in Major League Baseball from 1915 to 1929, playing for the Boston Red Sox, New York Yankees, Cincinnati Reds and New York Giants. Despite his high batting average of .268, he's most remembered for being the only pitcher ever to kill a player with a "beanball," a pitch intended to cause damage. After Mays's lethal pitch killed Cleveland Indians shortstop Ray Chapman in 1920, the sport began to think about requiring batting helmets.

David Campbell (1864–1911) joined the volunteer fire department shortly after moving from Pittsburgh, Pennsylvania, to Portland in 1878. He worked his way up through the ranks, becoming fire chief in 1895. He upgraded cisterns, hydrants and the alarm system and had Portland's first fireboat on the water by 1906. Campbell was one of the nation's top fire chiefs and was unanimously elected president of the Pacific Coast Fire Chiefs' Association. In 1909, Campbell bought Portland's first firetruck, the beginning of switching from horse-drawn apparatus. He was killed in the line of duty during a 1911 fire at Union Oil distributing plant at the age of forty-seven. More than 150,000 people crowded downtown for Campbell's funeral, almost three-quarters of Portland's population at that time.

Recreational Opportunities

River View is a huge and hilly green space, providing cardio challenges to bikers, runners and walkers. The cemetery offers several different self-guided walking tours. More solemn events include an annual Easter sunrise service, holiday memorial services dedicated to families who have lost loved ones and a National Children's Memorial Day candle lighting to commemorate children.

19

GREENWOOD HILLS CEMETERY

9002 Southwest Boones Ferry Road, Portland

This cemetery was especially popular with the many families who ran the dairies that once covered these hills of Southwest Portland. Volunteer-run Greenwood Hills is one of the few dog-friendly cemeteries in the Portland area.

History

Greenwood Hills was first platted as the Portland Masonic Cemetery, opening in 1884 with fifteen Masons transferred from Lone Fir. It joined several other cemeteries up on Palatine Hill, including the neighboring bigger and grander River View. At that time, Portlanders wanted bodies buried outside the city limits, and Palatine Hill was not yet part of Portland. The cemetery was built in the lawn-park cemetery style of the time with plenty of native trees, some of which are now close to 150 years old.

Immediately after opening, Greenwood Hills sold off two acres to the Grand Army of the Republic to bury Civil War veterans. Today the GAR cemetery is just across a path from Greenwood Hills. The Masons also sold a large plot to the Odd Fellows, who cared for this section until they handed it over to River View in 1943. Between 1950 and 1986, the cemetery sold off some of its property, reducing in size to its current twelve acres.

Greenwood Hills had a couple of different private owners over the years, the last of whom let the cemetery fall into ruin. In 1987, the *Oregonian* reported on knee-high weeds and confusion over who even owned the cemetery.[180] Eventually, the owner was tracked down and ceded the cemetery to about thirty family members of people buried at Greenwood Hills, who started the Greenwood Hills Cemetery Maintenance Association.

Over the next two decades, the number of participating association members dwindled due to age, death, moving away or waning interest. "They kept it going until about 2005," said Hattie Mead, currently president of the association. Then they posted a sign at the entrance saying they were relinquishing responsibility. "And if we did not want to see it abandoned again, then someone needed to step up and take hold of the reins."[181]

A surprising group came to the cemetery's rescue: neighborhood dog walkers. After years of allowing dogs, River View had banned canines. Neighbors had all started walking in Greenwood Hills instead. "So eleven of us said, how hard could this be? Let's step up. Little did we know. So we showed up at the meeting and volunteered. And some of the neighbors had brought their dogs to the meeting and the board members were not very pleased. But they were done, nevertheless. And the president kind of handed us the books and said, 'Here, bye.'"

While it may sound surprising that somebody would hand over the deed to land in a valuable neighborhood, a full cemetery isn't profitable. With twelve thousand people buried in Greenwood Hills—about one thousand per acre—the only new residents are those who bought plots many years ago. The cemetery has only a few new burials per year, and these don't bring in money. Instead, funds are outgoing for maintenance. The cemetery depends on volunteer work and donations to remain a safe and presentable part of the neighborhood.

Memorable Headstones

On first glance, the cemetery doesn't look full. That's because some large areas have only flat markers, and many of those have sunk under several inches of dirt and grass. These are the parts of the cemetery most popular with many dogs, as they can run unimpeded by headstones.

However, there are grander markers, too, including some beautiful examples of Woodmen of the World tree stones. Some families have large plots with tall markers, such as the Kelloggs, who have a row of markers

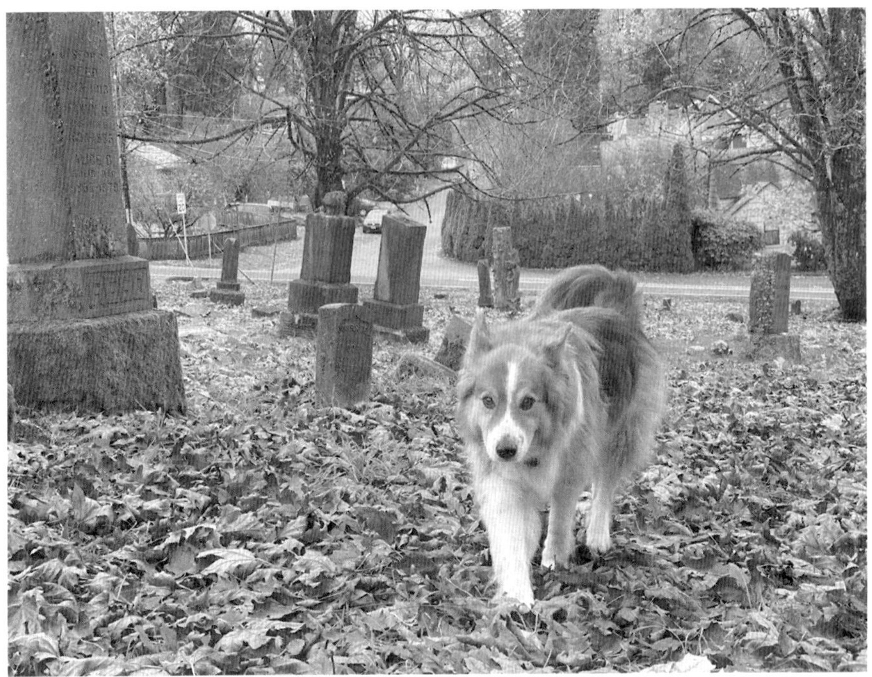

Canines welcome. Here, Friday romps between headstones.

shaped like cash registers. But some of the smaller markers are the beauties here. Rachel Ganty, who died in 1889 at the age of thirty, has an especially moving carved dead dove atop her stone. And the off-center stone of John Sixten Nelson, who died when only a year old in 1915, has a sweet lamb with the head still intact—a rarity, as pioneer cemeteries abound with headless lambs. But if you spot anything bordering on the ostentatious—say, a private mausoleum or a sarcophagus—you're probably looking across the property line into River View Cemetery. Greenwood Hills, River View and Grand Army of the Republic all butt up against one another so that it's hard to tell where one ends and the other begins. If you come to a sign prohibiting dogs, you've reached the end of Greenwood Hills.

Local Celebrities

Greenwood Hills has one U.S. congressman, Elton Watkins (1881–1956). He was born in Mississippi, the son of a Confederate soldier. Watkins worked for the FBI during World War I, enforcing violations of the Espionage Act, which made it illegal for anybody to convey information interfering with the war effort. He represented Oregon in Congress from 1923 to 1925.[182]

Many Portlanders will recognize the Raz name, perhaps from riding a Raz bus on a school field trip. Originally from a dairy family who owned the land now occupied by Wilson High School and Rieke Elementary School, Stefan Henry Raz (1908–1999) developed mechanic skills to keep the early milk trucks running. In 1937, he bought an old school bus from one of his customers, which began a family transportation business that lasted until 2004. Nearly twenty Raz family members are buried at Greenwood Hills.

Pioneers Simon Morgan and Catharine Abel Reeder and their son James traveled by covered wagon from Portersville, Indiana, to the banks of the Columbia. There they rafted down the river to Sauvie Island, landing in 1853. The family is still there running the Reeder Beach RV Park and Country Store. One of the main streets on the island is Reeder Road. Simon, Catharine and many of their descendants are buried at Greenwood Hills.

Greenwood Hills is the final resting place of George Jennings Ainsworth, commonly known as "Captain George." He was born in Oregon City in 1852. His father, John C. Ainsworth, was an Oregon pioneer and steamboat owner. Captain George was in one of the University of California's earliest graduating classes, where he studied civil engineering. His career in steamboats and railroads kept him moving between Oregon and California before he succumbed to anemia at the age of only forty-three.

Notable Resident

Mary Laurinda Jane Smith Beatty was an early Black suffragist who was born near Louisville, Kentucky, in 1834. Her parents were free persons of color. She was only fifteen when she married nineteen-year-old James William Beatty. They lived in Indiana and Victoria, British Columbia, before arriving in Portland around 1864.

Only 128 Black or mixed-race people show up in Oregon on the 1860 federal census. Oregon had discriminatory laws, such as the Black Exclusion Laws of 1857, but they were irregularly enforced. Mary Beatty worked in Portland as a dressmaker and let out rooms for rent. An early city directory shows that James Beatty worked as a kalsominer, which was somebody who painted structures with a mixture of water and plaster of Paris.

The Beattys did well for themselves, buying a substantial amount of real estate (despite laws prohibiting Black residents from owning property in

Oregon) and working for equal rights. In November 1872, Mary Beatty and three white suffragists attempted to cast their votes at Portland's Morrison Precinct. It was a bit anticlimactic. Unlike some places, where women were jailed for trying to vote, the Portland poll workers accepted the suffragists' ballots, placed them in a separate pile and didn't count them.

In 1873, Mary Beatty spoke at the first convention of the Oregon State Woman Suffrage Association. Minutes from the meeting record that Beatty "read an essay proving that the colored women are awake to their own interests."

Mary Beatty's involvement in suffrage waned when the couple moved out to a farm in Cornelius in 1874, but she kept up her friendships with fellow activists. They moved back to Portland in 1884 and spent fifteen years there before Mary died in 1899 of injuries after a fall.[183]

Recreational Activities

Mead stresses that Greenwood Hills is a cemetery, not a dog park. Friendly, well-behaved dogs are welcome. Misbehaving dogs and their people will be kicked off the private property by board members of the cemetery maintenance association.

Visitors are welcome to picnic at Greenwood Hills. Thanks to an Eagle Scout project, the cemetery has three nice picnic tables. The most scenic stands by a small pond.

Like most cemeteries, Memorial Day draws the most visitors to Greenwood Hills. If you want to meet other cemetery aficionados, join in the cemetery's annual cleanup on the weekend preceding Memorial Day.

Special Features and Highlights

The toy tree is a newer feature of the cemetery that started during the pandemic of 2020. With most parks temporarily shut down, the cemetery skyrocketed in popularity. Neighborhood children started bringing small toys and arranging them in and around a particularly large tree, drawing a whole new pint-sized clientele to Greenwood Hills.

20

GRAND ARMY OF THE REPUBLIC CEMETERY

9004 Southwest Boones Ferry Road, Portland

The GAR burial ground is on Palatine Hill, Portland's cemetery central, and butts right up against Greenwood Hills Cemetery, which in turn flows into River View. The many graves of Civil War veterans will appeal to military history buffs.

History

The Grand Army of the Republic, founded in 1866, was a fraternal organization for Union Civil War veterans. Its membership peaked at 490,000 in 1890, and it was an important force for veterans' interests. In 1882, fourteen Portland veterans formed the Grand Army Cemetery Association and purchased land. The Daughters of Union Veterans of the Civil War, a spinoff organization, managed the new cemetery for Civil War veterans and their families.

By the 1940s, passage of time and more recent wars started to overshadow interest in a Civil War cemetery. While the GAR cemetery still had big Decoration Day celebrations and some groups hosted activities like fundraising luncheons and card parties, GAR supporters had to fight harder in the legislature to get $1,000 or so in annual appropriations.

Still, the cemetery managed to acquire a special statue. In 1946, Theodore A. Penland (1849–1950), the last Civil War veteran in the area, unveiled a monument depicting a soldier, standing upon a seven-foot-tall granite marker.[184] Penland had enlisted along with his father and four brothers and was a well-known figure around town. By 1967, somebody had stolen the statue's rifle.[185] By 1970, somebody had managed to steal the entire soldier.

Pressed for funds, GAR descendants tried to find somebody to take over the cemetery. They offered it to River View in exchange for maintenance, but the larger cemetery wasn't interested. Federal officials declined care unless the bodies were moved to the newer Willamette National Cemetery on Portland's east side. The county turned the GAR cemetery down, too, but finally relented and took over in 1971 after the legislature cut off appropriations.[186]

In 1973, GAR's profuse flag display was vandalized over Memorial Day weekend. People tore flags from the ground, tied them in knots and threw them in bushes.[187] But the Civil War descendants carried on through the tumultuous '70s, planning Decoration Day programs featuring fife and drum music and rifle salutes.[188]

The county opened GAR for burials outside the Civil War lineage in 1996.[189] In 2009, forty years after the soldier monument disappeared, Sons of Union Veterans of the Civil War dedicated a replacement statue. The celebration included Civil War outfits, period music and musket salutes. Theodore Penland's great-grandson Richard W. Penland came all the way from Italy to speak.

Memorable Headstones

Just as the military emphasizes order over creativity, a typical headstone here is simple and neat, confining the info mostly to name, dates and affiliation and the design to upright with a military shield. It's interesting to walk through and look at all the states these men came from—Pennsylvania, New York, Ohio, Iowa, Illinois, among others—before winding up here with fellow veterans in Oregon soil.

If some of the military stones look too fresh to belong to longtime residents, it's because they were added later. For example, John Dunphy (1840–1908), an Irish-born Civil War veteran by way of New Hampshire, had an unmarked grave for one hundred years until the Sons of Union Veterans of the Civil War set things right. They weren't entirely sure where his body was located, so they put his headstone between the graves of two of his comrades. Dunphy was an ordinary seaman in the U.S. Navy on the steam sloop of war *Juniata*, which launched from the Philadelphia Navy

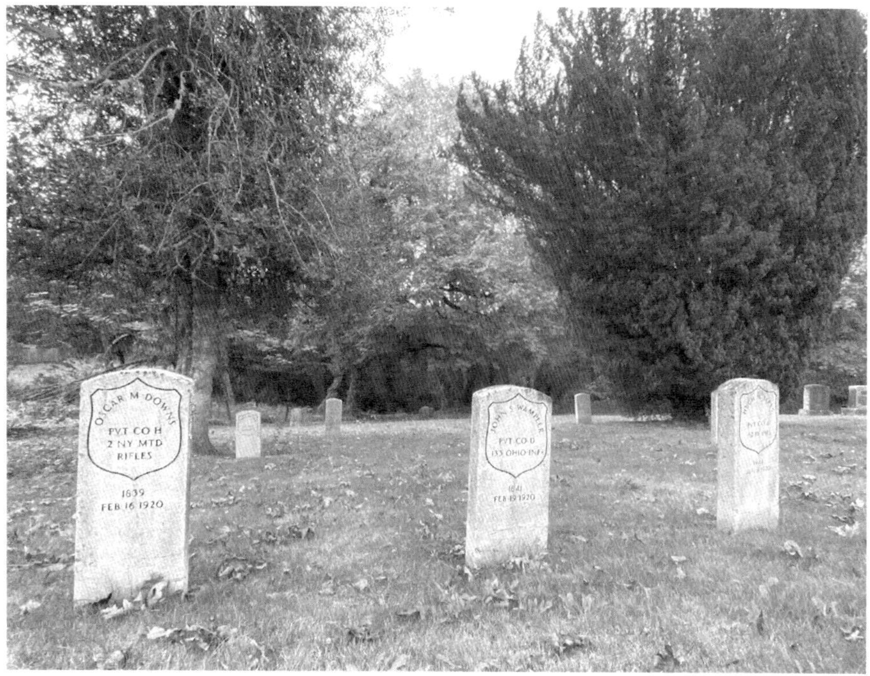

Typical military markers at GAR.

Yard in 1862 and was named after Pennsylvania's Juniata River.[190] But as seems especially common on military headstones issued long after the fact, there's a typo, and his ship will now be remembered as the *Juanita*, at least by visitors at the GAR Cemetery.

One of the more ornate stones is for George Washington Edward Frame (1886–1903), probably the relative of a veteran. Frame crossed the ocean from his birthplace of Oxfordshire, England, only to drown in the Willamette River at the age of sixteen. His stone has a nice framing of draperies and tassels over a crown and a cross. But GAR will be more interesting to military buffs than to people looking for artistic tombstones.

Notable Resident: Salmon Brown (1836–1919)

Salmon Brown was born in Ohio, the son of the famous abolitionist John Brown. In 1855, he went to Kansas with his father and brothers, where they brutally killed five proslavery men in what became known as the Pottawatomie Massacre. However, Salmon didn't participate in the even more famous raid on the arsenal at Harpers Ferry, a scheme to arm enslaved people for insurrection. Two of his brothers died in the raid, and his father was tried for murder, treason and slave insurrection, then convicted and hanged.

Salmon married Abbie Hinkley in 1857. During the Civil War, he served as an officer in the Ninety-Sixth New York Infantry, but he resigned because fellow officers worried that his infamous father would cause the enemy to target him. Brown and his wife moved out west, where they had ten children and raised sheep. They lived in California, Salem and eventually Portland. In the last years of Brown's life, a horse threw him, paralyzing him from the waist down. He shot himself in the head in 1919.[191]

EERIE TALES

At least one person has reported seeing a soldier standing guard over the cemetery in his blue Civil War uniform.[192] A more famous ghost is buried here yet haunts elsewhere. George Usherwood (1839–1909) killed himself by drinking wood alcohol and then inhaling gas in the courthouse where he worked as a janitor. He left a note that began: "No coroner wanted here—it is a little rest I am after—a little rest."[193] Instead of resting, his energetic spooking of the courthouse went on for years and repeatedly made the papers. In 1907, the *Oregonian* reported, "Since that time strange noises about the building and strange ghostly sights have been of almost nightly occurrence."[194] In 1909, Usherwood caused a ruckus while a bailiff and jurors tried to sleep in the courthouse. "Last night Bailiff Weinberger slept in the bed in which Usherwood killed himself, and this is presumed to have made the wraith uneasy," the *Oregon Journal* reported. Weinberger likened the noises to the rattling of pans or a chain, and vowed to not sleep in that bed again.[195]

21

BETH ISRAEL CEMETERY

426 Southwest Taylors Ferry Road, Portland

Like all the Jewish cemeteries in Portland, Beth Israel is tucked out of immediate sight. But once visitors enter the cemetery grounds, they'll be blown away by the workmanship and the high-quality maintenance that keeps markers looking practically new in the nation's oldest continuously operating Jewish cemetery.

HISTORY

In 1849, Jacob Goldsmith and Lewis May, two young Jewish immigrants from Germany, opened a general store in Portland. In the following years, more young Jewish men arrived in Oregon from California, setting up stores and supplying equipment to gold miners around Jacksonville.[196] Caroline Weinshank, the first Jewish woman in Portland, arrived in 1853 and opened a boardinghouse for Jewish bachelors.[197] Frontier life was hardly conducive to kosher kitchens and finding a quorum, but as the early pioneers started families and put down roots, they were able to establish their religion in the new city. And of course, they needed a place to bury their dead.

For German Jewish immigrants, establishing a cemetery often came before founding a synagogue. In 1855, Portlander Moses Abrams wrote to Jewish leader Isaac Leeser, "We are trying to get a Jewish burying ground. There are sum [*sic*] here who want to wait a while. We are all healthy persons, but I think it is better to prepare." In his master's thesis, Robert Scott Cline theorized that since Portland's early Jewish settlers were highly mobile, they were leery of investing in a burial ground that wouldn't be of use to them were they to move to a different city.[198]

In 1856, the Mount Sinai Cemetery Association formed and bought one acre of land from pioneer Finice Caruthers, whose land claim covered a broad area around the west end of where the Ross Island Bridge now stands. In 1858—the year before Oregon statehood—twenty-one members founded congregation Beth Israel, the first congregation west of the Rocky Mountains and north of California. Early services were held above a blacksmith shop, and San Francisco's Congregation Emanu-El loaned the Portlanders the torah (holy books) and shofar (ceremonial musical horn).[199]

In 1862, the congregation purchased and took over the Mount Sinai Cemetery Association and bought a large tract of Caruthers Addition. The *Daily Oregonian* wrote, "It looks as if the day is nigh at hand when the children of Judah and Benjamin will cease going to and fro, and become attached to the soil."

But as the city grew up around it, that cemetery would later be moved. Beth Israel bought new cemetery land in 1871 from John and Eliza Carson. When Corbett Street was widened, the city paid for residents of the old cemetery to be moved to the new land on Taylors Ferry Road. As the *Oregonian* explained, "Over a month was required in which to accomplish the work. Every grave was opened and the bodies or crumbling dust, as the case might be, were carefully removed to the new plot and there tenderly committed to the silent bosom of earth."[200]

As Portland's Jewish population expanded, so did its views on religious practices. In 1869, a splinter group of men from Prussia founded Ahavai Sholom, a more conservative congregation. Beth Israel developed into a reform congregation, with many members from the political and business elite. In the early 1900s, it had two rabbis of national prominence, Stephen S. Wise and Jonah Wise. Russian Jews established an Orthodox congregation, Shaarie Torah, in 1902, and Eastern European Jews founded Kesser Israel in 1916.[201] Other congregations formed as well, but these three also operate lovely cemeteries in Portland, not covered in this book due to space constraints but worth visiting. Portland's Beth Israel Cemetery has the distinction of being the oldest continually running Jewish cemetery in the United States.[202]

"As a reform synagogue in the modern era, you'll see that there is a certain flexibility with a lot of Jewish traditions," according to Bitsie Appleton, Beth Israel's office and cemetery coordinator. "For example, Orthodox Judaism does not allow cremation. We do." Beth Israel submitted its first request to the city to build a mausoleum in 1972. Now it has four, the last one built in 1999. The cemetery offers both niches for cremains and crypts for full body above-ground entombment. Appleton points out that Abraham and his wife were laid to rest in a cave—the first crypt.[203]

Memorable Headstones

The square-edged, urn-topped pillar of Leopold Hirsch (1825–1892) would be imposing, if not particularly unusual, in any Portland-area cemetery. But the marble would not be nearly as white. Beth Israel is the best local cemetery to visit if you want to see what old monuments looked like when they were new. While the cemetery has landscapers that do some headstone maintenance, the main cleaning happens on Mitzvah Day, Appleton said. On this day of service in the springtime, congregants use brushes and cleaning solution to keep markers looking sharp.

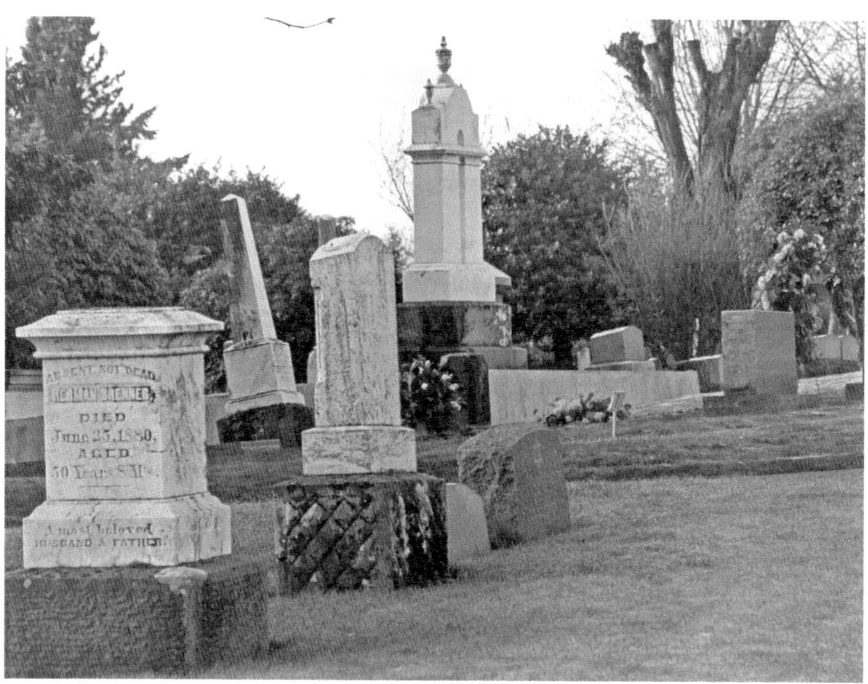

Well-kept monuments. *Oregon Jewish Museum and Center for Holocaust Education.*

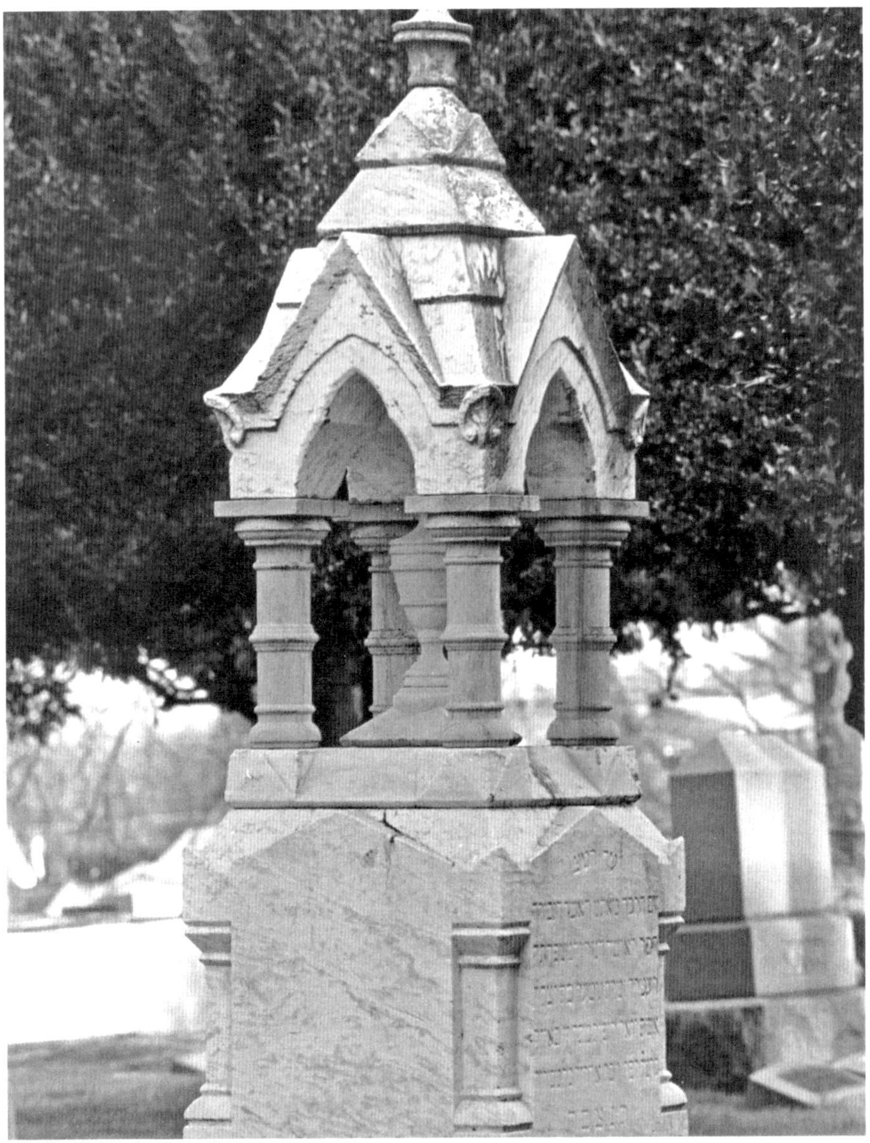

One of Beth Israel's more striking monuments. *Oregon Jewish Museum and Center for Holocaust Education.*

"Governing principles for Jewish funeral arrangements are simplicity and dignity," according to Appleton. "You'll see that there aren't many ornate headstones here. But there are many different types and personalizations." Especially in the last couple of decades, she said, personalization has become more common. Popular symbols include stars of David, usually on men's headstones, and menorahs, usually on women's.

The overall impression is order and a lot of obelisks, uprights and big monuments. Beth Israel seems more compact and organized than local pioneer cemeteries, with neat pathways, well-groomed plantings and lots of monuments packed in together. Despite a respect for simplicity, there are some fancier standouts, such as William Ellis's (1862–1914) big rectangular pillar with a row of rounded columns going up the sides, topped with leafy cornices. Levi (1833–1895) and Henrietta (1845–1889) White have particularly large monuments, his a sarcophagus shape, hers a chunky pillar. Leon (1861–1929) and Edith (1867–1950) Hirsch's tall Greek-style memorial looks like a doorway flanked by Doric pillars. Some stones are inscribed in English, some Hebrew, and others combine the two languages.

LOCAL CELEBRITIES

Beth Israel has many residents who played influential roles in Portland's civic life. Louis Fleischner (1827–1896) was president of the First Hebrew Benevolent Society of Portland. He donated money for Congregation Beth Israel to build a new sanctuary and secured a permanent water supply for the cemetery. He has an especially grand monument, with four tall classical pillars. Julius L. Meier (1874–1937) was the son of German immigrant Aaron Meier, co-founder of Portland's famous Meier and Frank department stores. Julius went into law and served as governor of Oregon from 1931 to 1935. Joseph Simon (1851–1935) immigrated to the United States from Germany as a young child in 1857. He grew up to serve as an Oregon state senator from 1898 to 1903 and was mayor of Portland from 1909 to 1911.

Millard Rosenblatt (1901–2000) made his mark both in medicine and golf. He taught at University of Oregon Medical School from 1930 to 1975 and served on St. Vincent Hospital's surgical staff for forty-five years. A lifelong golfer, he landed in the Guinness Book of Records for winning twelve cup championships from 1916 to 1968. In 1997, he was inducted into the Oregon Sports Hall of Fame.[204]

Comedy writer Daniel Simon (1918–2005) entertained millions with his work on classic TV shows, including *The Odd Couple*, *Facts of Life* and *Diff'rent Strokes*. He and his brother playwright Neil Simon began their careers together as writing partners for CBS radio just after World War II.[205]

Notable Resident: Rose Bauer

Rose Bloch Bauer was closely tied to Congregation Beth Israel. She was the director and soprano soloist and daughter of Jacob Bloch, Beth Israel rabbi from 1884 to 1900. At the time of her death in 1915, Bauer was one of Portland's leading singers.

Bauer went to study at the Vienna Conservatory of Music when she was only seventeen. After graduation, she was inundated with offers but chose to stay close to Portland. She sang in local operas, taught music and performed at charity shows. Her rendition of "The Star-Spangled Banner" was especially popular with audiences. Many people knew her as the director and soprano soloist in First Congregational Church, a role she held for eleven years while also serving in the same capacity at Temple Beth Israel. Bauer was a frequent guest soloist at Trinity Episcopal and also performed as a soloist with the Seattle Symphony Orchestra.

She helped scores of struggling young musicians find jobs to afford their musical education. "Her friends have said that she conducted a gratuitous employment agency for musicians," the *Oregonian* reported in her obituary. "The house was crowded to the doors by friends of the dead singer and their grief was manifest." Rabbi Jonah Wise conducted the service. Professor Edgar Coursen, who had accompanied her on piano for many years, played "Chanson Trieste" by Tchaikovsky. A wreath veiled in black hung in the place where she usually sang.[206]

Notable Resident: Maurine Brown Neuberger

At press time, Maurine Brown Neuberger is the only female Oregonian to have served in the U.S. Senate. She was born in Cloverdale, Oregon, in 1906. She earned her teaching certificate from the Oregon College of Education in 1924, then a bachelor's degree in English and physical education from the University of Oregon in 1929. She taught at Lincoln High School in Portland.

Maurine married journalist/politician Richard Neuberger in 1945. He'd served in the Oregon House of Representatives in 1941, before leaving for wartime army service. Maurine decided to go into politics, too. In 1948, Richard was elected to the Oregon Senate. Maurine won a seat in the Oregon House two years later, making them the first married couple to serve in a state legislature together. Both Democrats were reelected in 1952.

In 1954, Richard won his U.S. Senate race but died in 1960, near the end of his term. Maurine ran for his seat in November 1960 and won with 54 percent of the vote. During her six-year term, she advocated for consumers, notably in the tobacco and meatpacking industries, and worked on legislation to improve women's rights. She served under Eleanor Roosevelt on Kennedy's Presidential Commission on the Status of Women, which identified economic, social and political inequities.

Maurine married Philip Solomon of Boston in 1964. After finishing her term, she moved to Cambridge, Massachusetts, and taught American government courses at Radcliffe College and Boston University. The couple divorced in 1967. Maurine moved back to Portland and taught at Reed College.[207]

Special Feature: Torah Scrolls

Beth Israel Cemetery has one especially unusual marker, which reads: "Here lie Torah Scrolls from Simferopol, in the Crimea. Survived the Nazi Occupation hidden from 1945–1990. Buried by the Children of Beth Israel, May 14, 1995." Simferopol was a center of Jewish life that was contested between Ukraine and Russia for many years. When Nazis captured the city in 1941, they murdered fourteen thousand residents, mostly Jews. By the time the Russians liberated Simferopol in 1944, the death toll had risen to twenty-two thousand.

Meanwhile, Simferopol's Torah scrolls were hidden away from the Nazis—and remained hidden. In 1990, Dr. Joe and Cathy Thaler visited Simferopol as part of a medical delegation. The man who had hidden the scrolls for decades gave them to the Thalers, who carried them back to Portland in two large paper sacks.[208] Unfortunately, the scrolls had deteriorated beyond repair by that point. Back in Portland, photographer Elizabeth Collings carefully photographed the scroll fragments for the Oregon Jewish Museum. In 1995, a group of religious schoolchildren reverently buried the scrolls in Beth Israel Cemetery, in accordance with the Talmudic prohibition against destroying or desecrating sacred texts.[209]

22

MOUNT CALVARY CEMETERY

333 Southwest Skyline Boulevard, Portland

Monument aficionados who've been wondering where to find angels in Portland cemeteries need to drive directly to Mount Calvary. This enormous Catholic cemetery on Portland's west side has grassy, rolling hills, views of Mount Hood and plenty of angels, crosses and ornate—at least by Portland standards—monuments.

History

The Roman Catholic Portland Archdiocese established Saint Mary's, its first cemetery, in 1858 across from Lone Fir. But Saint Mary's was getting full by the late nineteenth century, so in 1888 the archdiocese bought one hundred acres in Portland's West Hills, including twenty and a half acres from the Nathan B. Jones Donation Land Claim and ten acres of the William and Levina Naylor Donation Land Claim. More than one thousand people turned out for the consecration on September 30, 1888—despite the proceedings lasting for hours on a rainy day.[210]

Meanwhile, across the river, the four-block Saint Mary's was becoming an eyesore. No financial provisions had been made for perpetual care, and the neighbors were complaining. When Archbishop Edward D. Howard began leading the Portland archdiocese in 1926, he appealed to the city to

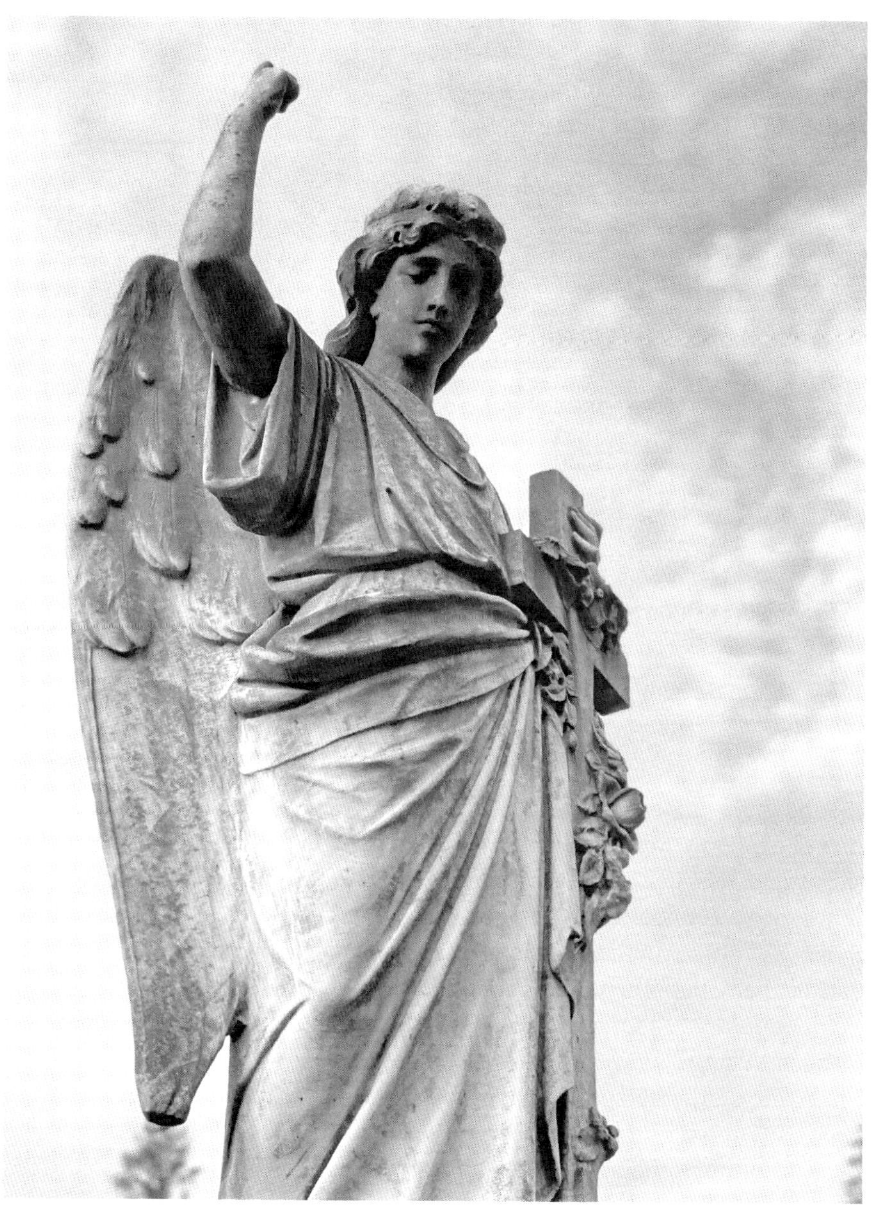

One of Mount Calvary's many angels.

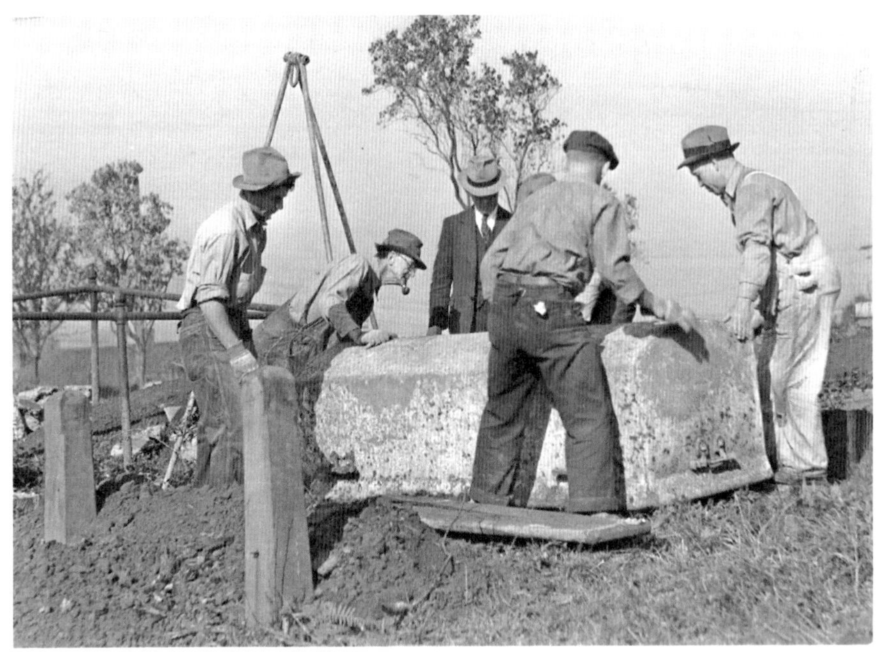

Workers exhume a Mount Calvary–bound casket from Saint Mary's, 1937. *From the* Oregonian.

take over care. The city refused. Then the church tried to raise money from descendants of those buried in Saint Mary's, but few were left. Eventually, the church decided to move the bodies to Mount Calvary, which had the foresight to be built with a perpetuating fund. It took about four years to get all the bodies moved. Many of the coffins had rotted away, so workmen constructed cedar boxes to transfer the remaining bones.[211] Central Catholic High School was built on the old Saint Mary's site.

In the early 1900s, Portlanders were intrigued by *Oregonian* reports that something in the Mount Calvary soil was turning bodies to stone. Fourteen-year-old Mary Owens was buried in 1895 and exhumed in about 1903 to be moved to another spot in the cemetery. Workers found the casket much heavier than it should have been. They looked inside and found "a crust about an inch thick had become petrified over the entire body, forming a stony shell, and the corpse was in as perfect condition otherwise as it was the day it was buried." The girls' relatives were easily able to recognize her features. Theories about why bodies were petrifying included a leaking standpipe and the soil itself.[212] What's striking about the accounts—aside from the petrification—is the intimate relationship with death and decay.

It's hard to imagine Portlanders of today wanting to look at their exhumed relatives or newspapers printing details of a corpse's appearance.

Starting in 1946, the cemetery began building mausoleums. It didn't have a columbarium until 1989, twenty-six years after the Catholic Church lifted its ban on cremation. There's now a small green burial ground as well. Mount Calvary currently covers 120 acres.

Memorable Headstones

Mount Calvary sprawls across both sides of Northwest Skyline Drive/West Burnside—the two streets join here for a short time—with distinct sections on each side. An enormous white Greek-looking altar dominates a hill on the north side of the street. This is where the area's top-ranking male clergy are buried in semicircles down the hill, archbishops on top. The north side also has two mausoleums, a columbarium, a separate children and babies' cemetery and the folks relocated from Saint Mary's in the 1930s.

The south side has the more interesting markers, with a wider variety of headstones, ledger stones and monuments than most Portland cemeteries and some outstanding pieces of funerary art. There's a good assortment of angels, including baby angels, a child angel, full grown, one-winged, one-armed and even a headless angel.

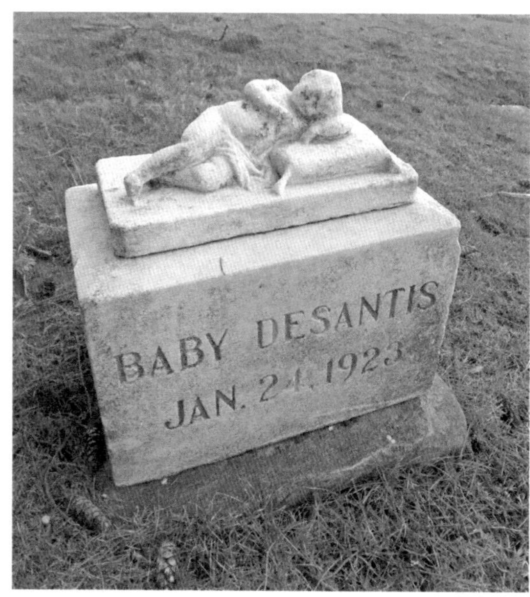

A baby's marker.

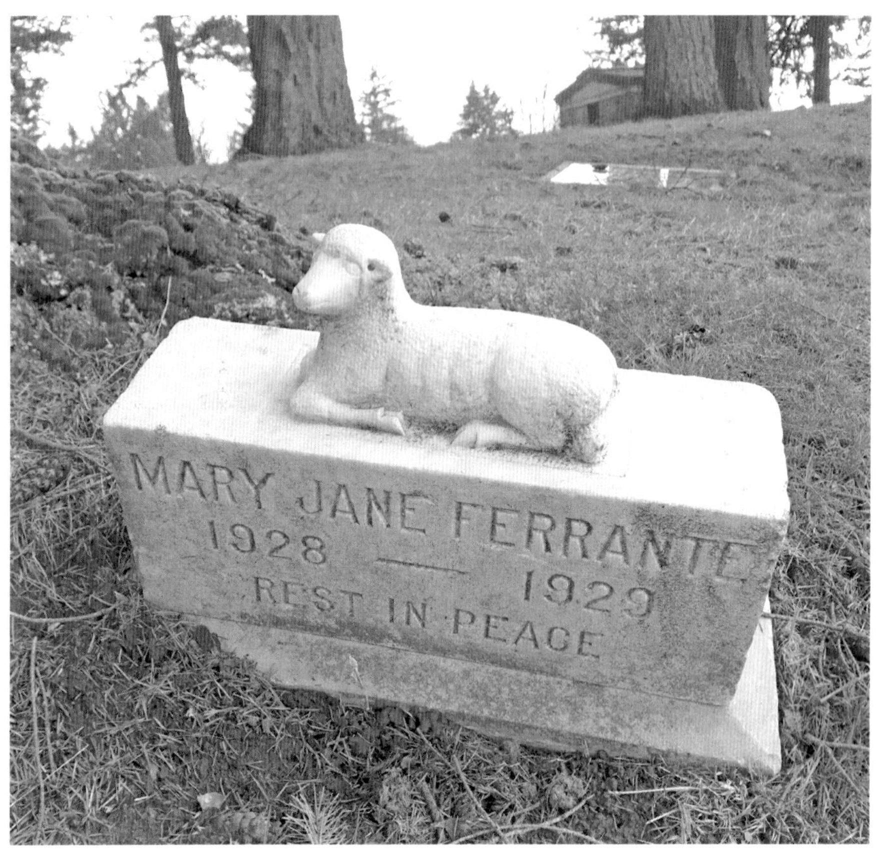

Glass-covered, cameo-shaped photo inserts are popular here, with many well preserved from early in the twentieth century. Some monuments bear carved portraits, such as the huge granite slab for the Munly family, which depicts small oval pictures of all the male Munlys. Nixon E. Munly (1929–2017) warranted two portraits: a bust in his Coast Guard uniform and a full-length of him in weightlifting trunks hoisting a barbell over his head. Munly, an incredible athlete, won amateur titles around the globe in sports, including Olympic weightlifting, boxing, tennis and arm wrestling.[213]

Mount Calvary has few Woodmen of the World monuments but one remarkable specimen. John H. Glennon (1858–1897), born in Queens County, Ireland, has a tree stone with a cross growing out of the top. The cross is in the same log style as the stump.

Minnie E. Burns Miller (1849–1866) has a particularly lovely stone, carved and signed by leading Portland stonemason John Gruber. The seventeen-year-old had just been married that year. Her monument is a large tablet

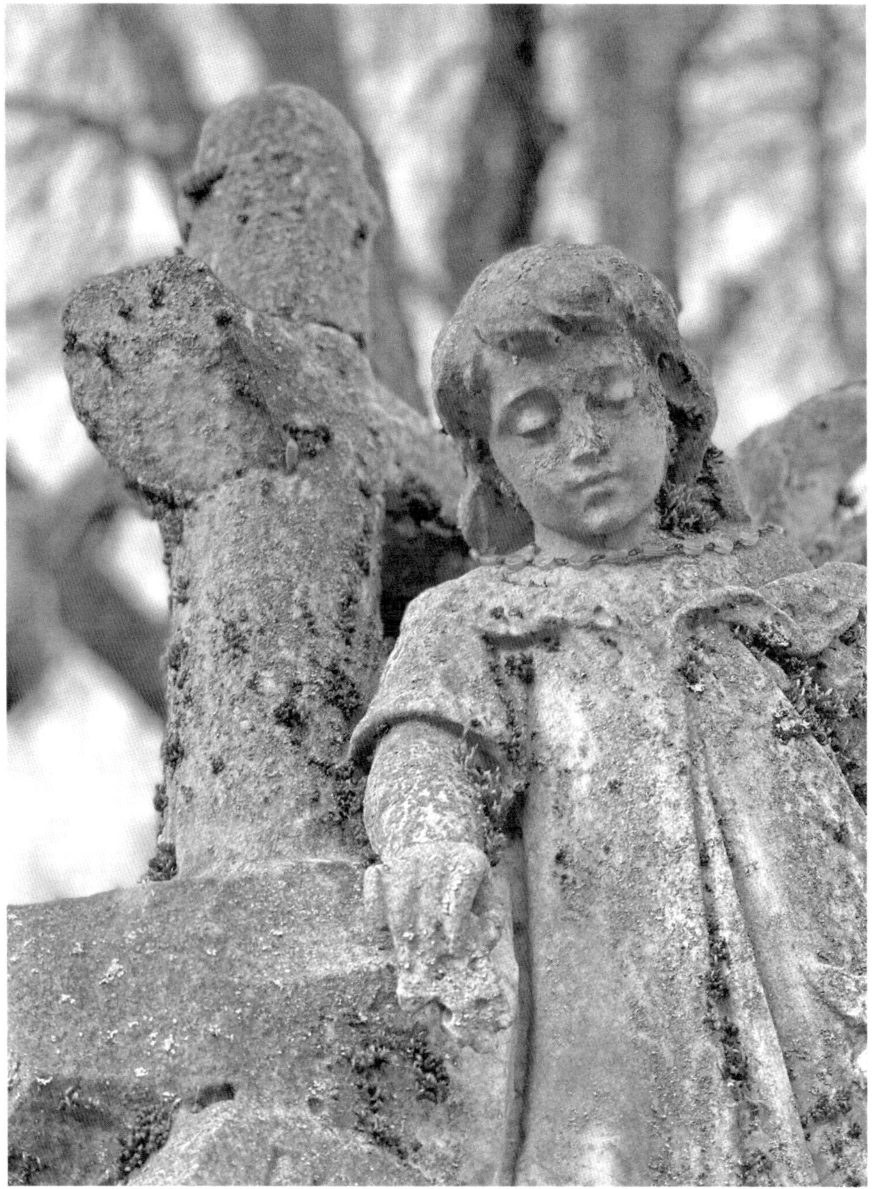

Opposite: A lamb is the most common symbol for babies and small children.

Above: Little girl angel.

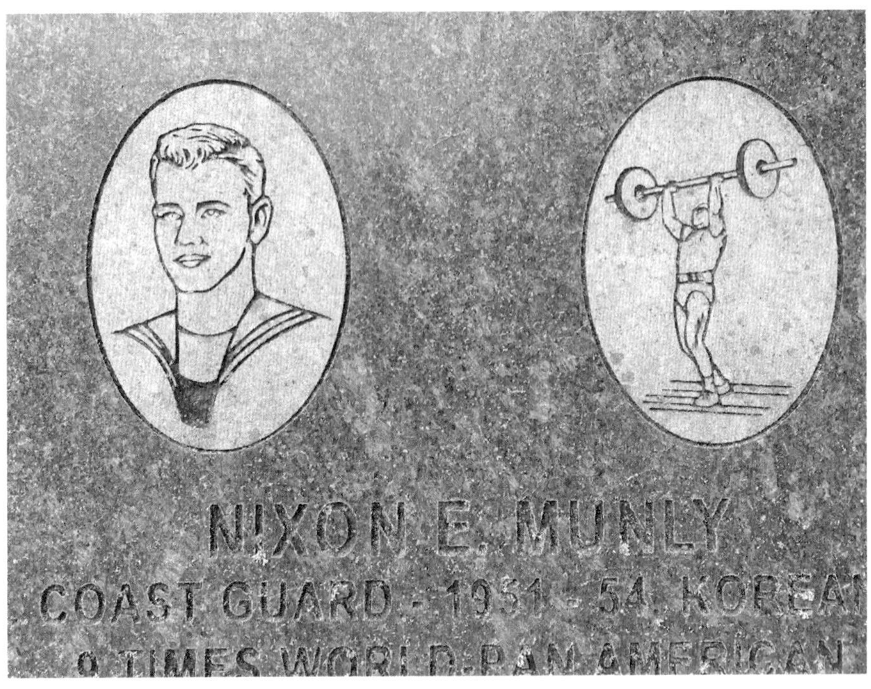

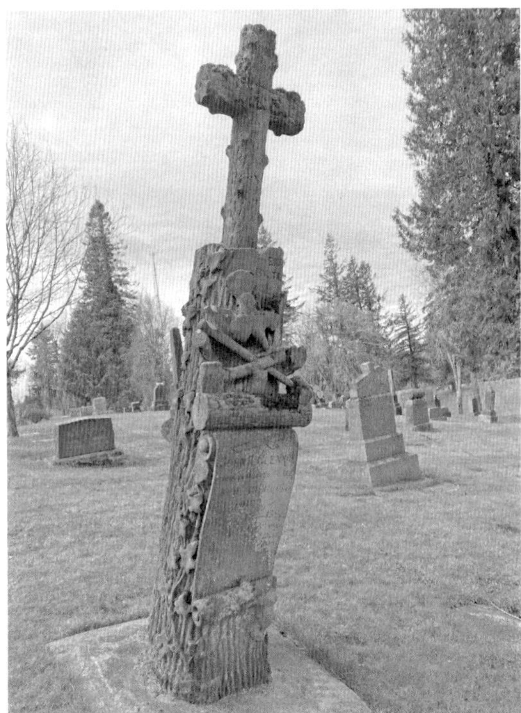

Above: Nixon Munly's carved portraits.

Left: This unusual Woodmen of the World tree stone includes a cross.

Opposite: A marker by the early master stonemason John Gruber.

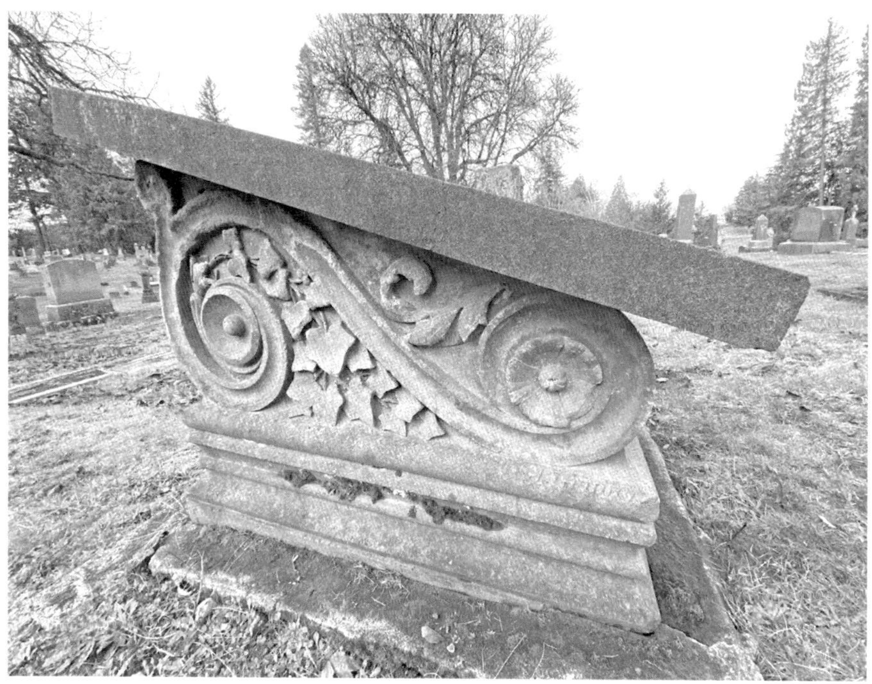

held up by a slanted base of scrolls and ivy. Since Mount Calvary wasn't founded until 1888, hers must be one of the many bodies and stones that was reinterred here.

Quite a few private family mausoleums are scattered around the grounds. Other large monuments include statues of religious figures and scenes. Our Lady of Consolation towers over a huge base inscribed with *Consolatrix Afflictorum*, the Latin name for this form of Mary. The flat area around her includes burials of many nuns and offers views of hills to the west.

Even the section markers at Mount Calvary are worth a look. Instead of adhering strictly to ordinary numbering or lettering systems, here you'll find sections named for religious figures, such as Queen of Peace, Saint Nicholas and Saint Benedict, each marker carved with a likeness.

Local Celebrities

In addition to practically everyone who's anyone in Portland's Catholic Church hierarchy, politicians like U.S. Representative John M. Gearin (1851–1930), federal judge James M. Burns (1924–2001) and Chief Justice of the Oregon Supreme Court and U.S. Senator Hall S. Lusk are buried here. Ben Holladay (1819–1887), aka the "Stagecoach King," created a stage route to California during the 1849 gold rush.

Mount Calvary's sports and entertainment greats include Irish-born Jack "Nonpareil" Dempsey (1862–1895), world middleweight boxing champion from 1884 to 1891 who died of tuberculosis at age thirty-two, and Francis William Leahy (1908–1973), who coached the University of Notre Dame football team from 1941 to 1943. Actor Lawrence Keating (1899–1963) played a neighbor on talking horse sitcom *Mr. Ed.*

Notable Resident: Eileen Darby

Eileen Darby (1916–2004) is remembered as the greatest photographer of the Golden Age of Broadway. She was born in Portland and was a champion swimmer as a teen. Her father, an engineer who photographed government projects, taught her camera and dark room skills. In 1937, she moved to New York to make it as a photographer. She worked for Pix Agency, which sent her on the theatrical assignments that became her specialty. *Life* magazine regularly assigned her work. In 1941, Darby formed Graphic House, where she both took photos and used her excellent darkroom skills to process film for other photographers. Darby became famous for her photos of the late 1940s productions of *Death of a Salesman* and *A Streetcar Named Desire* and was much in demand. She stopped taking photos after her husband, Roy Lester—she used her maiden name for her work—died in 1976. Eventually, she moved back to Portland, where she died at age eighty-seven after a fall.[214]

Special Feature: Famine Monument

During and after the Irish Famine of 1845–51, Portland's Irish population swelled from 1 to nearly 10 percent. Many of these famine Irish, as they were sometimes called, are buried at Mount Calvary. To honor them, the cemetery and archdiocese partnered with the Oregon Chapter of the Ancient Order of Hibernians to commission a monument. Irish artist Brendan McGloin replicated the ninth-century Cross of the Scriptures at Clonmacnoise. This fourteen-foot-high sandstone cross weighs seven tons and depicts biblical scenes. Mary McAleese, the president of Ireland, came to Mount Calvary to dedicate the Oregon Famine Memorial Cross in 2008.[215]

23

JONES AND HAVURAH SHALOM CEMETERIES

5763 Southwest Hewett Boulevard, Portland

While many of Portland's once remote cemeteries are now in the middle of busy, less-than-peaceful commercial neighborhoods, Jones is tucked away in an affluent residential area in Portland's West Hills with views of the Chehalem Mountains. Except for the sound of close-by Highway 26, this is a quiet place to contrast the original Jones Cemetery with the Jewish cemetery it now shares space with.

HISTORY

Nathan B. Jones was this land's first American owner, thanks to the Donation Land Claim Act of 1850. Jones buried his father, William Jones, on his homesteaded land in 1854. He planned to lay out the cemetery in sixteen-foot squares. Walkways would lead between the squares, starting at his father's grave.[216] However, he didn't get around to it. In 1872, shortly before his death, he donated the land to Multnomah County as a cemetery, in order to protect his father's grave.

Jones had a steady influx of new residents in the late 1800s. But things got pretty quiet in the old pioneer cemetery in the middle of the twentieth century. By the 1960s and '70s, burials had slowed down to a trickle, and most new interments joined family members who already resided there. But then in 1986, Congregation Havurah Shalom bought 750 grave sites at Jones Cemetery and made them available to Jews, their spouses and children. The presence of Havurah Shalom is what makes this cemetery so spotless and well tended. And even fans of older headstones will probably enjoy the Havurah markers, which are moving and show a lot of personality and creativity. The Havurah renaissance also spurred more burials in the Jones Cemetery.

MEMORABLE HEADSTONES

Instead of a neatly laid out cemetery, the older stones seem to be placed almost randomly. Many stones are missing, lost to neglect or vandalism or perhaps never set on the graves in the first place.

Jones lacks any especially grand headstones. Most of the older pioneer stones are toward the back. The largest is the Jones headstone, which marks the resting place of William, the father, who died in 1854 at the age of seventy-six, and Nathan, who died in 1894, aged seventy-four.

Sophia Adline Morriss's (1848–1904) heart-shaped marker is one of the prettiest stones. She's identified as "Our beloved wife and mother" on the front and "a native of Missouri" on the back. Anna Fuhrer (1863–1894) has a nice carving of a hand holding an open book, perhaps to indicate that she died young, in mid-story. Her inscription states, "As a wife, devoted. As a mother, affectionate. As a friend, e'er kind and true."

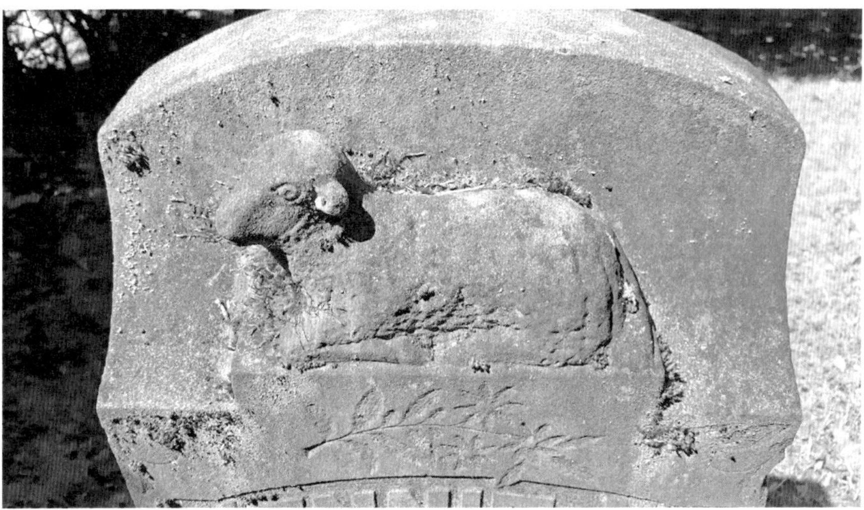

A carved lamb.

The Havurah headstones display a diverse range of symbols and epitaphs, ranging from traditional Jewish themes like menorahs and stars of David to individualistic tributes, such as lines from Mary Oliver's poem "The Summer Day" and a marker depicting what appears to be a drawing of a 1950s-era TV set. Several markers are rough-hewn stone, about the size of small tree stumps, concave at the top so that the rain turns them into water features. Some markers are inscribed in both Hebrew and English. Most of the Havurah headstones are piled with the remembrance rocks that people leave when visiting Jewish graves.

NOTABLE RESIDENT: NATHAN JONES

Born in 1820, Nathan Jones came to Oregon as a pioneer of 1847. In 1850, he settled at Tanner Creek and planned a community named Zion Town, named for a nearby summit called Mount Zion. But Oregon already had two towns called Zion, so Jones couldn't get a post office in that name. Instead, he took a neighbor's suggestion to call the post office Sylvan, named for Silvanus, a Roman god of animals and the countryside. But Jones still became known as the "sage of Zion Town."

"Jones, a hermit who would today be called an eccentric old hippie, splash-painted the outside of his house with psychedelic colors and confided to those who would listen that his great aim in life was to make Zion Town the political and cultural capital of Oregon," according to *In Search of Western Oregon*.[217] He named his house The Hermitage and adorned it with a huge painting of the City of Zion descending from heaven.[218]

His dreams of Zion's glory never came true. Jones was assaulted during a robbery in his cabin in 1894. It took a week for him to die.[219] Fortunately, he'd thought ahead and already had his headstone erected, though he couldn't have foreseen the full inscription: "Mr. Jones was the founder of Zion, and came to his death by the hand of an assassin." Charles Davey was charged with Jones's murder, but Portland lawyer Edward Mendenhall got him acquitted. Zion Town died with Jones, and this area is now known as Sylvan.[220]

NOTABLE RESIDENT: ORPHA GERULF

Orpha Gerulf's tale is an example of the tragic consequences of putting too much trust in fortunetelling, although it did make the *Los Angeles Herald*. The

Jewish Stones

If you visit a Jewish cemetery, you'll probably notice stones on top of grave markers. "The stones are a Jewish custom that replace flowers, as flowers die but stones will last forever," said Bitsie Appleton, cemetery coordinator for Congregation Beth Israel. A group called Libe Shteyn, or Love Stones, hand-paints rocks with colorful designs, weather seals them and delivers boxes of them to Jewish cemeteries around the Portland and Vancouver area. People who didn't bring their own rock can leave a love stone. According to Appleton, it's fine for non-Jewish people to leave a stone on a Jewish grave when they visit.

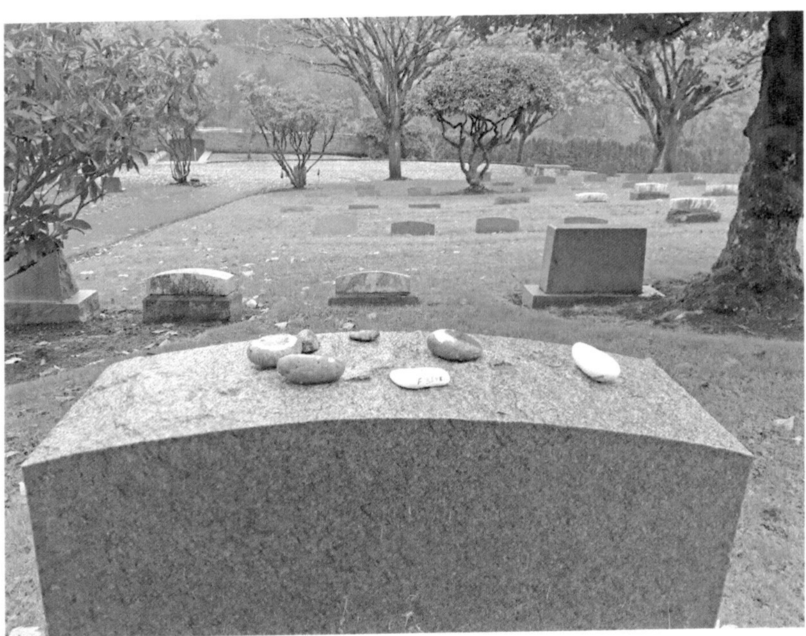

Stones for a Jewish loved one.

October 27, 1909 edition reported, "Orpha Gerulf, 25 years old, a waitress, despondent over a quarrel with a man who had been attentive to her, told her fortune last night with a deck of playing cards to see how her love affair would turn out. After the cards had been laid out, she told her friends she was 'all surrounded by death.' A few hours later, she shot herself through the heart."[221]

Notable Resident: Benjamin Martin Deutsch

In the Havurah cemetery lies Benjamin Martin Deutsch. Born in New York City in 1912 to a family with roots in Germany, Austria and Hungary, he spent much of his career in Connecticut. Deutsch was a butcher. He worked at Daw Packing Plant in Hamden, Connecticut, which was known locally as "The Baloney Shop" before a two-alarm fire totaled it in 1978. The packing plant, which disgruntled firefighters described as "a coffin," was known for making corned beef and pastrami, among other meat products.[222] This may have been where Deutsch honed the skills that eventually earned him this epitaph: "Pioneered the introduction of pastrami into the United States & Jewish culture." He outlived his wife of many years and wound up dying in Multnomah County in 1994 at the age of eighty-two.

Recreational Activities

Geocachers can search for a cache at Jones,[223] although some debate the propriety of hiding containers in cemeteries. An enthusiast in one online forum instructs fellow geocachers to avoid hiding anything on a grave, under a marker or in a place that would force a searcher to climb on a monument.[224] Good advice.

24

OSWEGO PIONEER CEMETERY

17401 Stafford Road, Lake Oswego

This cemetery in the Palisades neighborhood of Lake Oswego is closely tied to the town's history of steel producing. While it's full of historic characters, Oswego is more active than many pioneer cemeteries, as it's still selling plots.

History

The sloping, triangular-shaped Oswego Pioneer Cemetery occupies a tiny fraction of what was once the Bullock family's 319-acre donation land claim, registered in 1850. Pioneers Jesse and Nancy Bullock were from North Carolina and Tennessee, respectively. The first burial on this land was their son Solomon in 1856. Other burials followed, and in 1881 Jesse Bullock and George Prosser, his son-in-law, allowed other families to start burying their dead there. Early maps show the cemetery as a rectangle, but by 1927 the blueprints reflect the current triangular shape.[225]

Many of the town's early settlers came to Oswego specifically to work for Oregon Iron & Steel Company (OI&SC). Skilled workers came from the Hanging Rock Iron Region of Ohio, which had produced charcoal iron during the Civil War. At the time, Oswego was a company town. Iron production dominated, and the company also owned the post office, general store and workers' housing.[226] More than ninety steel workers wound up buried in here or in next door Sacred Heart, making Oswego Pioneer a

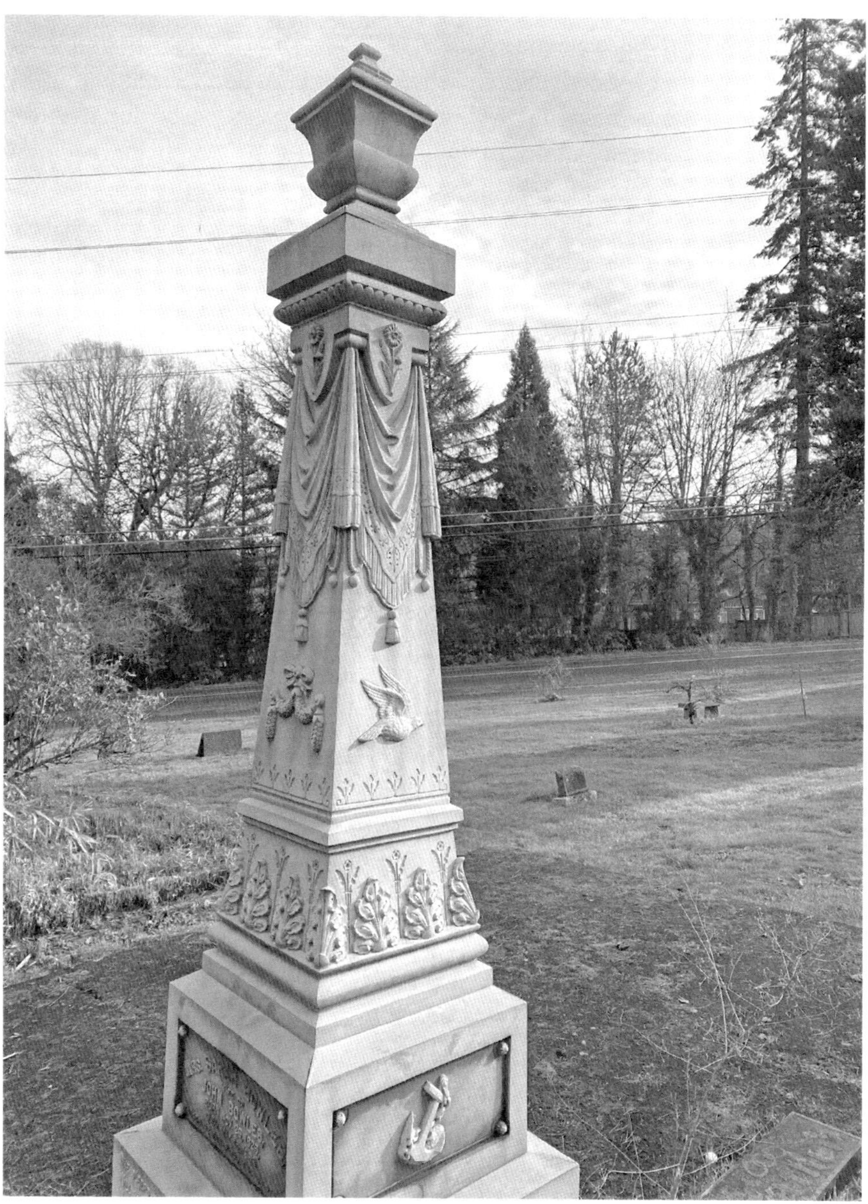

A white bronze monument.

company cemetery as well. The blast furnace closed in 1892, the same year that OI&SC took over cemetery operations. By that time, the company had amassed a huge amount of increasingly valuable real estate, and the owners started focusing on developing the land into an upscale residential location and recreation destination. They also had the good sense to change the name of Sucker Lake to Oswego Lake.

By 1934, OI&SC had had enough of the cemetery biz, so they turned management over to the Methodist Episcopal Church. Four years later, the church handed the cemetery over to the International Order of Odd Fellows. But as Odd Fellows membership declined throughout the twentieth century, so did the care of the Oswego Pioneer Cemetery.

In 1976, Ethel Schaubel visited her mother's grave after spending several years living in Hawaii. This granddaughter of Oswego pioneers was shocked to see weeds, brambles and general disrepair. The practice of tending family graves had apparently gone the way of the dodo bird since her childhood. She decided to do something about it. Schaubel and Bill Blizzard, editor of the *Lake Oswego Review*, formed a board and recruited a group of volunteers to clean up the cemetery.[227] Their efforts have continued for more than forty years now, making this one of the strongest volunteer cemetery efforts in the area. Boy Scouts built pathways, a driveway and flower boxes. Volunteers organized old records, wrote grant applications netting $25,000 and mowed the cemetery grounds.[228]

Perhaps the most significant twenty-first-century upgrade so far was moving a donated house to the cemetery grounds to serve as a caretaker's cottage. Joe Collins has occupied the house since 2010. "In the ten plus years I have been here, I cannot recall any acts of vandalism, i.e. monuments tipped over or graffiti. My presence here is known and I can see a good portion of the grounds from the house."[229] No tipped monument surely makes Oswego the envy of many a pioneer cemetery. Right beside Oswego Pioneer, Sacred Heart Cemetery provides a contrast. As Collins points out, Sacred Heart's bigger crew and herbicides make the Catholic cemetery resemble a golf course. "That's not who we are here," he says, proudly embracing the less manicured look of history.[230]

Memorable Headstones

While curbing—raised concrete perimeters around family plots—is present in areas of many pioneer cemeteries, it's especially noticeable in Oswego

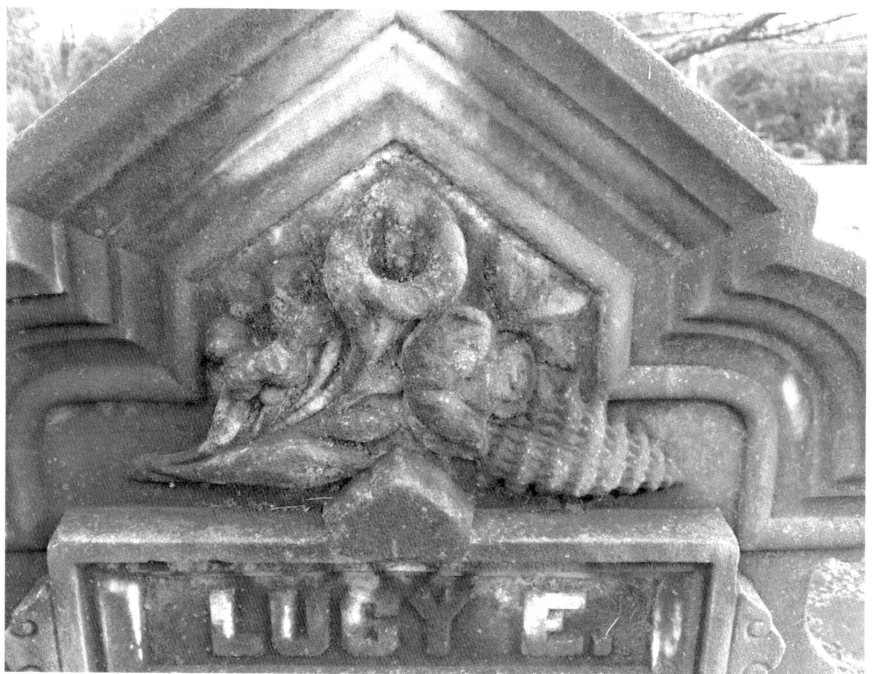

Detail on a stone.

Pioneer. The older part of the cemetery is divided into clearly delineated ten-by-twenty-foot plots, resembling raised beds in a vegetable garden. Inside each plot is a mixture of flat and upright headstones, trees and shrubbery. Some pioneer graves sport one-hundred-plus-year-old roses, which a local garden club periodically tidies up.[231]

In the newer part of the cemetery, Lake Oswego lives up to its present-day upscale reputation with a preponderance of leisure-themed tombstones. Markers commemorate the deceased's love of sailing, golf, skiing, snowboarding, basketball and flyfishing. One stone, apparently the final destination of travelers, depicts the Eiffel Tower, Egyptian pyramids and a cruise ship. The cemetery has an unusually high number of markers for people who are still alive. Collins said that they encourage preneed customers to add their stone within a year of buying a plot. It does seem a good way to get the most control over and enjoyment out of your memorial.

Local Celebrities

Oswego Pioneer is a true local cemetery. Visitors will see many prominent families buried here—including Clinefelter, Childs, Wanker, Ek, Prosser, Pollard, Pauling, Bullock, Worthington and Shipley—all the early movers and shakers, many with streets named after them. You'll find six former mayors, including Jerome Thomas, Oswego's first. Arthur "Red" McVey, who was born in England and became Oswego's first fire chief, is buried here, as is Lucia Bliss, the city's first librarian. James Campbell, a chief justice of Oregon's supreme court, has the inspiring epitaph, "A life devoted to the task of making the world a little better place to live in."

William and Alice Worthington came to Oswego in the 1880s from the Hanging Rock Iron Region of Ohio. William was one of many Ohio men recruited by his brother Theodore to come out west to take a job in the iron works. The arduous two-week journey entailed taking migrant trains from Ohio to San Francisco via El Paso, then a steamship from San Francisco to Portland. Once settled in Oswego, William Worthington's job was making charcoal for the furnace. He was the grandfather of Ethel Schaubel, who later resurrected the cemetery.[232]

Notable Residents: Linus and Ava Pauling

Oswego Pioneer's most famous resident is Linus Pauling, scientist, humanitarian and twice Nobel Prize recipient. Linus's grandfather Charles Pauling came to Oswego to work for the iron and steel company. Linus was born in Portland in 1901 but spent summers with his German-speaking grandparents in Oswego. After his pharmacist father died when Linus was nine, his mother ran a boardinghouse on Hawthorne Street in Southeast Portland. Even as a child, Linus was fascinated with chemistry and spent many hours in his makeshift lab in the boardinghouse basement. He got his bachelor's degree in chemical engineering from Oregon Agricultural College (now Oregon State University) in Corvallis. Ava Helen Miller was a student in chemistry for home economics majors, a class Pauling helped teach. They married in 1923. He went on to get his doctorate at the California Institute of Technology.

Pauling was an extremely influential chemist in the 1930s and 1940s. Among other accomplishments, he discovered basic protein structures, determined the cause of sickle-cell anemia and advanced the fields of x-ray crystallography, quantum mechanics, nuclear physics and electron diffraction. During World War II, he also worked on topics related to war. But after the bombing of Hiroshima, he and Ava turned their attention to peace. They became leading antinuclear activists from the 1950s on, suffering such indignations as FBI surveillance, revoked passports, losing scientific funding and being falsely branded as communists. Pauling won the Nobel Peace Prize in 1962.

Later, Pauling became fascinated with the possible healing powers of vitamin C. He published the bestselling *Vitamin C and the Common Cold*, founded a research institute to study vitamins and nutrients and greatly boosted vitamin C sales.[233]

Pauling died in Big Sur in 1994. His sister Pauline Pauling Emmett had a cenotaph, or monument honoring a person whose remains are elsewhere, placed in the family plot in Oswego Pioneer. In 2005, the ashes of Linus and Ava Pauling were moved from Big Sur to the Oswego plot.[234] Collins said people who come to pay their respects are often surprised that these outsized personalities have such a humble and ordinary marker.

Eerie Tales

Russell DeLashMutt was captain of an 1852 wagon train to Oregon. When he had a stroke in 1901 at the age of eighty-two, the *Medford Mail* recounted this story as his doctor and Mrs. Hellen, his caretaker, awaited his imminent death: "In 1854, Mr. DeLashMutt bought a clock in Oregon City which he placed upon his mantel. The clock kept good time for years until one day in the year 1876 it stopped short. Some time afterwards news was received that Mr. DeLashMutt's youngest son had died on the day the clock stopped. The ancient timepiece withstood all efforts to make it go and Mrs. Hellen gave Mr. DeLashMutt a smaller clock. On the day that Mr. DeLashMutt received the paralytic stroke, this clock also stopped and the old clock, which had not run since 1876, gathered itself together, emitted a ghastly sound, and gave six solemn strokes, and then stopped again. The number of strokes is understood to have meant that Mr. DeLashMutt had but six days to live, and Dr. Strickland says this will probably prove to be the case."[235]

RECREATIONAL OPPORTUNITIES

The pioneer cemetery is a stop on the Oswego Iron Heritage Trail, a self-guided walking tour that links historic sites from the town's early iron industry. The other stops are Prosser Mine, the charcoal pit site, pipe foundry site, 1888 iron furnace site, a worker's cottage and the 1866 iron furnace. Interpretive signs help visitors understand the importance of each site. Oswego Pioneer also welcomes leashed dogs.

SPECIAL FEATURES

Locals who want to get involved with the cemetery can inquire about the adopt-a-plot program. About a dozen plots have already been adopted by volunteers who tidy them up a couple of times a year.

A large display board lists the sixty or so veterans buried here from World War II, Korea, Vietnam and Iraq. A peace pole stands nearby, inscribed "May Peace Prevail on Earth" in eight languages. Sponsored by the Rotary Club, it was installed in 2016 as part of the international Peace Pole Project, which has placed more than 200,000 such memorials around the world.[236]

25

MOUNTAIN VIEW CEMETERY, OREGON CITY

500 Hilda Street, Oregon City

This don't-miss cemetery is located in Oregon City, about fifteen miles southeast of Portland. Oregon City was founded in 1829 and incorporated in 1844, seven years earlier than Portland, and was the first capital of the Oregon Territory. So the cemetery is filled with important people of the time and the most fabulously carved stones available.

History

The original cemetery land was part of William Livingston Holmes's donation land claim, which he gave to the city when asked for a burial place. The first burial was the infant John Barclay, son of Dr. and Mrs. Forbes Barclay, in 1848.

An 1848 letter to the *Oregon Spectator* highlights the spontaneous spirit of Old West city planning. "Called upon this morning to bury a young man brought in from the country for interment, I was surprised to find, that a change had been made in the location of the Cemetery," wrote William Roberts, grave digger, in a letter to the editor. Roberts was distressed about having to walk twice as far to this newly designated bit of land and about what would become of the former cemetery. "What is to be done with the eight or more dead bodies already buried in it and when, probably, will the location be changed again?"[237]

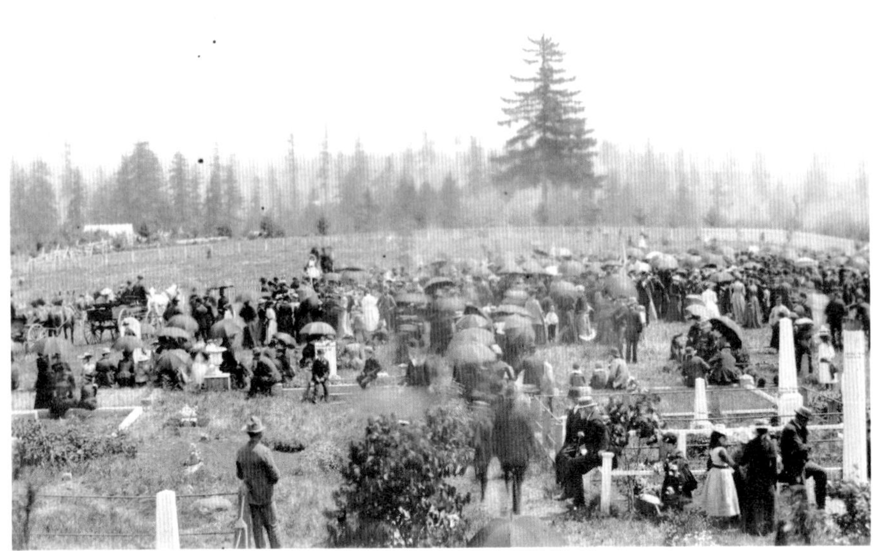

Decoration Day, 1895. *Friends of Mountain View Cemetery.*

Despite Roberts's worries, the new location caught on. It was considered the city cemetery from 1848 onward, making it the oldest municipal cemetery in the Oregon Territory. However, current records set the founding at 1856, though at least twenty people were already buried there by then. The Holmes family officially deeded five acres to the city council of Oregon City in 1863 for use as a public cemetery, plus an adjacent acre for a Masonic cemetery. Oregon City had the first Masonic lodge west of the Mississippi.

Oregon City is now overshadowed by Portland in size, but in its early days it was the end of the Oregon Trail and the seat of government. It supplied flour, wheat and timber to the miners during California's 1848 gold rush. In the 1860s, the town added a woolen mill and the first modern paper mill.

In 1882, the name officially changed to Mountain View Cemetery.[238] As the city thrived, it had to buy more and more land to bury its dead. In 1897, the city purchased what's called the First Addition. Several plots in the First Addition were reserved for potter's field burials of unknown and indigent people. Newspapers published notices about these mysterious deaths, but they often stayed unidentified. "The unfortunate wanderer appeared to be about 30 years old, clean shaven, without any marks or scars which might give some clue to his identity," the *Oregon City Courier* reported in 1910 about

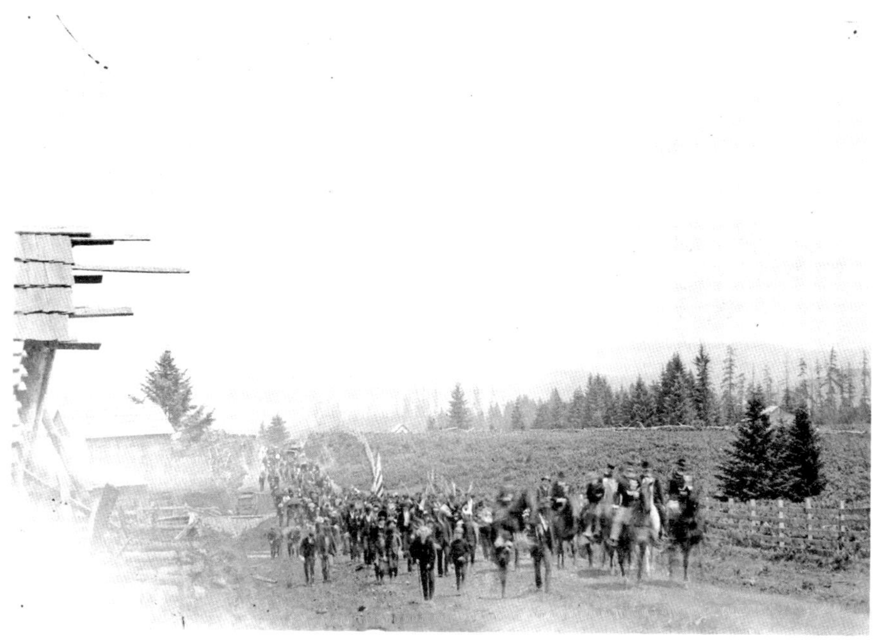

A 1900 GAR Decoration Day procession. *Friends of Mountain View Cemetery.*

a body found mangled on the Southern Pacific tracks.[239] Such a body might still go unidentified today, but one hundred years ago cemeteries were even likelier to have quite a few such burials.

Like most old cemeteries, upkeep has waxed and waned. In 1899, the *Oregon City Enterprise* described an effort to straighten out poorly kept early records and map the cemetery. "The job was a most complicated one and necessitated an immense amount of labor and research into the musty archives of the dim past," the newspaper said. "The work of investigating reveals the fact that many of the graves are in a most deplorable condition of neglect, for which there is almost no excuse at all."[240]

The city council declared an emergency need to appoint a sexton in 1918. The council set payments to the sexton ranging from six to twelve dollars for interments and six to ten for disinterments. If digging a grave required blasting through a rock formation, the sexton would make an additional dollar per shot.[241] Around that time, the council rearranged lot boundaries to correct the problem of some bodies having accidently been buried in two different lots.

In 1926, the old section of the cemetery was full and a bit rundown. So many people wanted to remove bodies and rebury them in the new

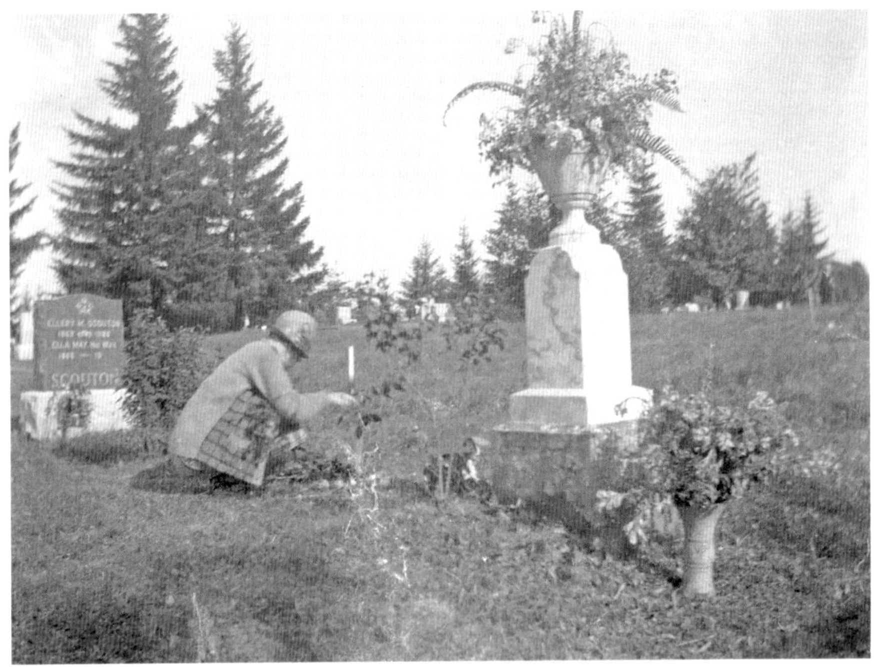

Woman tending a grave. *Friends of Mountain View Cemetery.*

part—where there was room for plots for additional family members—that the city council instituted a credit of thirty-five dollars for each grave turned back to the city. However, if the body was moved to a different cemetery, they forfeited the credit.[242]

The county bought the Second Addition in 1909, allocating several more lots for indigent burials. The cemetery continued to expand over the twentieth century until it reached today's total of fifty-four acres. After years of deliberation, the city commission finally decided to proceed with architectural drawings of a proposed mausoleum in 1965.[243] Aboveground burial proved a popular choice in Oregon City, and the mausoleum expanded several times over the next decades.

In 1971, the Masonic and Odd Fellow lodges both wanted to release their interest in the cemetery and give the land to the City of Oregon City. It took a few years for this to happen officially, but now these formerly separate cemeteries are among the oldest parts of Mountain View.[244]

The city was questioning the cost of running the cemetery by 1978. Despite the mausoleum additions, Mountain View was having a hard time covering operation costs. The city commission discussed options like raising prices of cemetery services, instituting stacked burials and even selling or closing down the cemetery.[245] Fortunately, Mountain View raised fees and pulled through.

The Friends of Mountain View Cemetery formed sometime around 1980 to keep up the long tradition of Memorial Day observances. The group has also spearheaded many cleanups, helped staff document graves, identified veterans from all wars and conflicts and planned for a newly restored Veterans Memorial Area.

Nowadays, Mountain View is perhaps the best-maintained pioneer cemetery in the area. In 2018, the Oregon Commission on Historic Cemeteries gave the Friends of Mountain View an $8,109 grant to repair and restore twenty-three markers. Most had been badly repaired in the past and broken again. Headstone expert Bruce Howard restored the stones, assisted by staff and volunteers.[246] Later, Howard and experts from Historic Preservation Northwest restored the larger and more complicated 1868 Masonic column-style monument of Frederick Wellington Charman.[247] Grants also bought security cameras to help protect the cemetery from further vandalism.

Memorable Headstones

Some family plots are set off with curbing or, in a few cases, short fences or wrought iron gates. Many of the stones are astonishing works of art, and several have still legible signatures of stonemasons. Jane Ainsworth's (c. 1833–1859) graceful obelisk with a cut-out nook containing a broken pillar—symbolic of a life cut short—is signed by W. Masters of Portland. Martha G. Kester's (1832–1880) stone, adorned with a weeping willow, is signed by Merces & Vospers Marble Works in Portland. In 1880, N.C. Merces and Alfred Vospers had their marble works at 47 Stark Street in downtown Portland. Another weeping willow stone, this one for James E. Rhoades, who died in 1868 when he was only a year old, is signed, "J.A. Kelly, OR City."

Rebecca Rinearson's (1829–1862) beautiful stone features carved theater curtains with tassels and an upside-down rose hanging above her name. There's a rare double obelisk for two brothers, Michael (1847–1879) and William (1837–1856) Mann. A couple of tree stones show that Woodmen of the World had members in Oregon City, as well as several stones for members of the related female organization, Women of Woodcraft. A

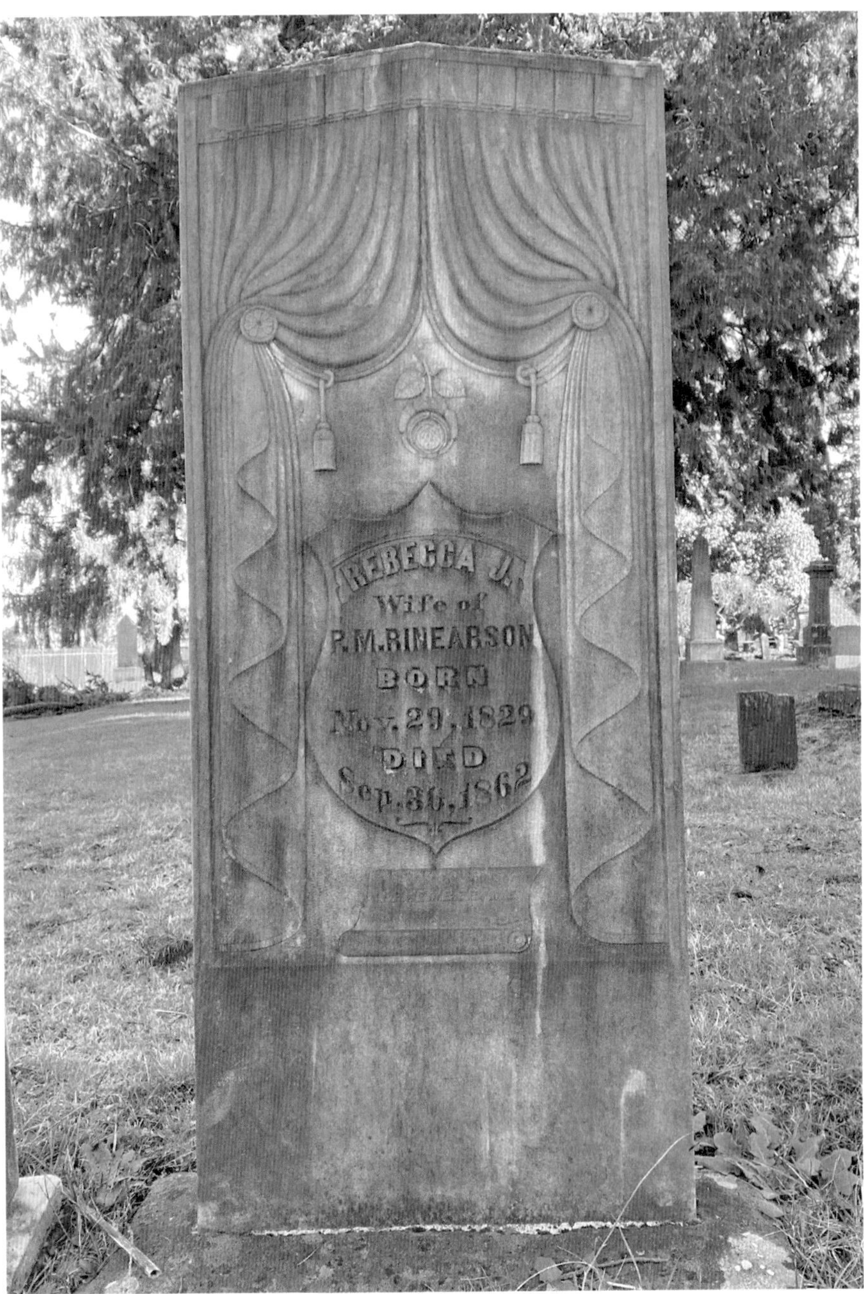

Carved draperies.

marker for Owen Pugh Owens (1869–1891), born at Llanegryn, Wales, has the words *er cof* written on top, which is Welsh for "in memory of."

Herman Werner's (1857–1915) podium marker is topped by an open book, the right side of the book draped with a cloth. On the front of the podium is a picture of the heavenly gates ajar, an anchor and the words "Peace Perfect Peace." The gates ajar became an extremely popular motif after Elizabeth Stuart Phelps published her book *The Gates Ajar* in 1868, which especially comforted women who'd lost husbands and male relatives in the Civil War. The book describes a heaven of blissful domesticity where their loved ones who have gone before are waiting for them behind the open gate of heaven.[248] By 1900, 80,000 copies of Phelps's book had sold in the United States and 100,000 in England.

Mountain View has many evocatively inscribed markers. Henrietta Winckler's (1810–1892) stone reads, "We are going to her. But she will not return to us." Lewis Hadaway's (1856–1886) marker bears lines that also showed up in other cemeteries around the United States in the 1870s and 1880s: "Rest Husband in the silent tomb, Rest for the shadow and the gloom of death is passed." Mary Ann Cuttridge (1871–1898) got this inscription: "Insensate form once animated with life, now lies lifeless in her lonely silent cell. No matter how the storms of life may rage above, she hears them not. She is resting well."

Siblings Horton (1839–1853) and Josephine (1840–1853) Hunsaker share a double headstone. Children of pioneers Jacob T. Hunsaker and Emily M. Collins, the whole family was exposed to typhoid fever. The siblings died within a month of each other. While Josephine was sick, famous Oregonian Dr. John McLoughlin brought her a rosebush to cheer her up. The family planted it outside her window. After she died, her mother transplanted the rose to her grave site. The rosebush has survived more than 150 years, despite run-ins with the sexton's power mower. A fence now protects the grave site. If visitors examine the back of the stone, they'll catch a typo, where the stonemason misspelled the surname as "Hunsuker." Materials being costly, they seem to have remedied the mistake by turning the stone around and starting over.

A sloped part of the cemetery leading into a wooded canyon serves as Mountain View's potter's field. Some of Mountain View's unknown residents are buried in this mostly forgotten area, where thick moss completely covers many of the markers. By 1930, the cemetery had buried nearly twenty unidentified adults, babies and children. Some were suicides who were never identified.

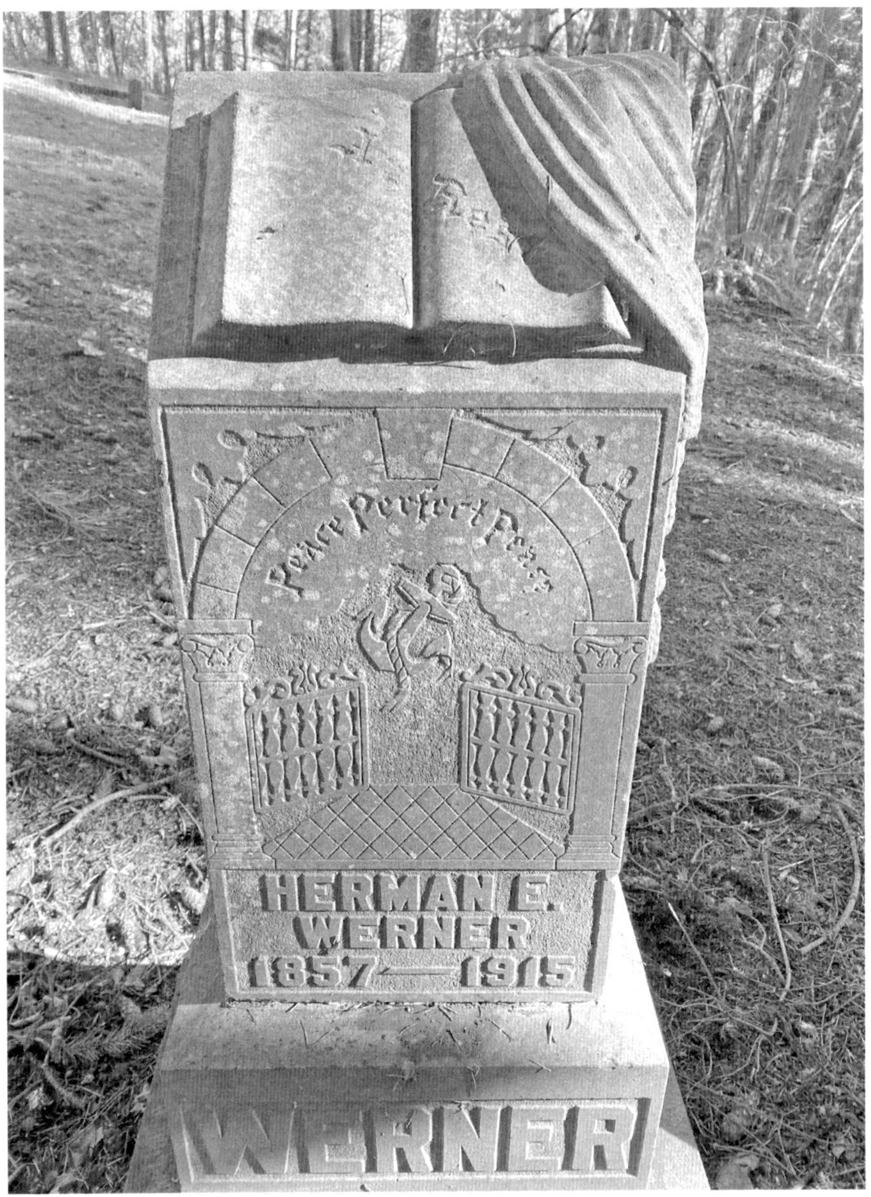

The popular gates ajar motif suggesting a permeable boundary between heaven and earth.

Local Celebrities

Many important local and state officials are buried in Mountain View. William Livingston Holmes (1807–1879), an 1843 pioneer, was the first sheriff of Clackamas County, serving in the 1840s and 1850s. John T. Apperson (1834–1917) served in the Oregon State Legislature, was a state senator and a Clackamas County sheriff in the 1870s and 1880s, and later became president of the Oregon State Agricultural Society and the Oregon Pioneers Association. Peter Paquet (1839–1896) served three terms in the Oregon State Legislature and was an Oregon City mayor and city councilman. He also built boats and bridges and worked for the Hudson's Bay Company.

Early pioneers had to be versatile to survive, and many were entrepreneurs. Peter Skene Ogden (1794–1854) is thought to be the first white man to explore central Oregon. He worked as chief factor for the Hudson's Bay Company and was responsible for ransoming survivors of the 1847 Whitman Massacre near Walla Walla, Washington. Stonecutter Sidney Moss (1810–1901) established both the first hotel and the first store (excluding the Hudson's Bay Company) west of the Rocky Mountains. Forbes Barclay (1812–1873), born in the Shetland Islands, was the Hudson's Bay Company's physician and surgeon in the 1830s and 1840s. He also served as city coroner, mayor, Oregon City school superintendent and city councilman. Absalom Hedges (1817–1890) established the community of Canemah just south of Oregon City in 1849 and helped build *The Canemah,* one of the earliest steamships on the Willamette River.

While pioneer women were often relegated to the role of mother and helpmate, some helped in their husbands' businesses, such as Jane Caufield (1805–1891), who ran a store on Main Street. Jennie Barlow Harding (1853–1926) was one of Oregon's leading flower culturists. She promoted Oregon City's first rose show and helped establish the Rose Society, which she served as president.

Notable Residents: Frank "Ta-Tanka-Ska" Whitebuffaloman (1903–1977) and Ruby Lang (1916–1982)

Frank Whitebuffaloman was born on the Standing Rock Reservation in South Dakota in 1903. His Sioux name was Ta-Tanka-Ska, and he's believed to be the last grandson of Sioux Chief Sitting Bull. In addition to stints working on railroads and ranches, Whitebuffaloman had a life of both cultural performance and show biz. He and his whole family traveled with the Buffalo Bill Wild West Show in the 1920s. This famous vaudeville show introduced cowboys and Indians to an international audience. Whitebuffaloman later appeared in movies, including *A Man Called Horse* and *Crazy Horse*.[249] He portrayed his grandfather Sitting Bull at festivals and consulted with college professors on Indian history and traditions. His name made him keeper of the ceremonial buffalo-cap peace pipe.

Whitebuffaloman's wife, Ruby Lang, descended from Chief Joseph of the Nez Perce. She and Whitebuffaloman formed the Sitting Bull White Buffalo dancers and performed around the Northwest. The couple were prolific foster parents in addition to raising four biological children.

When Whitebuffaloman died in 1977, more than three hundred Native Americans attended his memorial service in Milwaukie's Crystal Lake Church. Some came from as far away as North Dakota. Chiefs from the Umatilla and Siletz tribes attended the service, which was followed by a traditional funeral feast featuring deer meat and Indian fry bread.[250] Ruby Lang died in 1982 and is buried beside Whitebuffaloman.

Notable Resident: Clarence Chesterfield Howerton (1913–1975)

Clarence Chesterfield Howerton, born in 1913, was the third of five sons in his family but the only one to stop growing at twenty-eight inches. Life as a little person wasn't easy in the rough lumber camp of McCleary, Washington, where a specialist diagnosed him with a "deranged ductless gland." Howerton's mother—herself only four feet tall—kept him out of school. But his short stature led to a performance career. In 1923, when only ten years old, he started traveling with Ringling Bros. and Barnum & Bailey. Billed as Major Mite, he performed off and on with Ringling Bros.

until 1946. In 1938, Howerton played one of the trumpeters who heralds the mayor of Munchkinland in *The Wizard of Oz*.

Off duty, Howerton liked to dress up in spats and top hats and smoke cigars. He was known for a demanding nature and incredibly foul language. According to one account, "When Prohibition ended, the Major would march into a tavern in full top hat regalia, kick the shins of the nearest person, and order, 'Set me up on the bar, you bastard!' If he felt really mean, he would run the length of the bar, drop-kicking anything in his path."[251]

After his performance career, Howerton lived with a niece in Dayton, Oregon. He died of pneumonia in 1975.

Special Features

Mountain View is home to the Parents of Murdered Children Memorial, a garden plaza and wall commemorating homicide victims and those killed by drunk drivers. It's the first of its kind in Oregon and the eighth in the country. This is a moving tribute to the surprisingly many people in the area who've lost their lives to murder.

A Veterans Memorial Plaza, founded in 1951, honors locals who served in foreign wars. The City Commission of Oregon City donated property for the plaza in 1951. Plaques honor soldiers and sailors and include recipients of the Silver Star, Bronze Star and the French Croix de Guerre.

NOTES

1. Lone Fir Cemetery

1. Sarah Mirk, "The Ghosts of Lone Fir Cemetery," *Portland Mercury*, October 29, 2009.
2. *History of the Pacific Northwest—Oregon and Washington*, vol. 2 (North Pacific History Company, 1889), 466.
3. *Oregonian*, September 28, 1904, 10.
4. *Oregonian*, October 7, 1905, 11.
5. Haunted Lone Fir Pioneer Cemetery, http://americashauntedroadtrip.com/lone-fir-pioneer-cemetery.

2. Multnomah Park Cemetery

6. *Oregonian*, November 17, 1888, 8.
7. Author interview with Eric Cordingley, 2020.
8. *Oregonian*, February 16, 1906, 10.
9. *Oregonian*, January 9, 1908, 9.
10. *Oregonian*, December 15, 1908, 11.
11. *Oregonian*, April 1, 1923.
12. *Oregonian*, August 27, 1899, 24.
13. "Woman Shot Three Times, Paramour Wounded with Revolver and Slain with Hatchet While Helpless on Floor," *Oregonian*, January 1, 1922.

14. "Purdin Retrial Begun," *Oregonian*, February 22, 1922, 2.
15. *Oregonian*, January 15, 1925
16. Author interview with David Anderson, 2020.
17. *Oregonian*, March 21, 1911, 9.
18. Cameron Addis, "Whitman Massacre," Oregon Encyclopedia, https://www.oregonencyclopedia.org/articles/whitman_massacre/#.X-f65RaIY2w.
19. Author interview with David Anderson, 2020

3. Brainard Cemetery

20. *Morning Oregonian*, December 5, 1913.
21. *Morning Oregonian*, January 9, 1914.
22. *Morning Oregonian*, January 13, 1914.
23. Lao Iu Mien Culture Association, "Community Brief," https://limcacenter.org/lc/wp-content/uploads/2017/06/Iu-Mien-brief-2013.pdf.
24. *Oregonian*, August 23, 1892, 8.

4. Rose City Cemetery

25. Fred Lockley, *History of the Columbia River Valley From The Dalles to the Sea*, vol. 3 (Chicago: S.J. Clarke Publishing Company, 1928), 114–15.
26. Author interview with Jay Ollerenshaw, February 2021.
27. *Oregonian*, June 28, 1995
28. Carol Silverman, "Oregon Roma: Gypsies: A Hidden History," *Oregon Historical Quarterly* 118, no. 4 (2017).
29. Eric Lundgren, Bike Portland, February 16, 2009.
30. National Governors Association, "Gov. Albin Walter Norblad," https://www.nga.org/governor/albin-walter-norblad.
31. Hall of Valor Project, "Alaric B. Chapin," https://valor.militarytimes.com/hero/51.
32. Hall of Valor Project, "John Alphonsus Murphy," https://valor.militarytimes.com/hero/1839.
33. *Statesman Journal*, April 10, 1955.
34. *Oregonian*, March 2, 1975.
35. *Oregonian*, September 19, 1975.
36. *Oregonian*, October 29, 1975

37. *Morning Oregonian*, March 2, 1908.
38. *Morning Oregonian*, March 3, 1908.
39. *Morning Oregonian*, March 15, 1908.
40. *Morning Oregonian*, March 6, 1908.
41. *Morning Oregonian*, May 24, 1908.

5. Japanese Cemetery

42. Court records, Japanese Ancestral Society of Portland vs. Portland Japanese Benevolent Cemetery Association.
43. *Oregonian*, May 8, 1910.
44. *Oregonian*, May 31, 1927.
45. *Oregonian*, August 15, 1943.
46. Ollerenshaw, interview.
47. *Oregonian*, August 14, 1943.
48. *Oregonian*, August 17, 1946.
49. *Oregonian*, November 3, 1946.

6. Columbia Pioneer Cemetery

50. East Portland Historical Overview & Historic Preservation Study, 2009, City of Portland Bureau of Planning and Sustainability, https://www.portlandonline.com/portlandplan/index.cfm?a=346260&c=51427.
51. *Sunday Oregonian*, August 27, 1899, 24.
52. *Morning Oregonian*, October 28, 1898, 3.

7. Powell Grove Cemetery

53. Rachel Blumberg, ed., *The Wheel Keeps Turning: An Oral History of Parkrose (Portland)* (FamilyWorks, 2002), 17.
54. *Oregonian*, September 30, 1959, 9.
55. John Branch, "The Town of Colma, Where San Francisco's Dead Live," *New York Times*, February 5, 2016.
56. *Oregonian*, August 18, 1960, 1.
57. Chronological List of Oregon's Legislatures, https://www.oregonlegislature.gov/citizen_engagement/Reports/Chronological.pdf.

58. *Morning Oregonian*, April 12, 1887, 5.
59. *Morning Oregonian*, February 6, 1893, 5.
60. *Morning Oregonian*, July 18, 1907, 10.
61. *Morning Oregonian*, January 22, 1866, 3.

8. Historic Columbian Cemetery

62. Oregon Historical Society Digital Collections, "Love, Capt. Lewis," https://digitalcollections.ohs.org/love-capt-lewis.
63. *Oregon Daily Journal*, July 7, 1903, 12.
64. Author interview with Ed Bixby, February 3, 2021.
65. W.J. Ghent, ed., *The New Appeal Socialist Classics*, vol. 7, *Socialism and Organized Labor* (Girard, KS: New Appeal, 1916).
66. *Oregonian*, July 19, 1965, 16.
67. *Oregonian*, November 17, 1902, 12.
68. *Oregonian*, December 10, 1903, 11.
69. *Oregonian*, September 5, 1949.
70. Jeff Dwyer, *Ghost Hunter's Guide to Portland and the Oregon Coast* (Gretna, LA: Pelican Publishing Company, 2015).
71. KOIN CBS6, May 14, 2013.

9. Humane Society Animal Cemetery

72. Edith Knight Hill, "Faithful Friends of Many Varieties Find Resting Place in Humane Society's Burial Place," *Sunday Oregonian*, March 22, 1931.
73. "Pet Cemetery Offers Outlet for Animal Lovers' Grief," *Oregonian*, October 11, 1982, 31.
74. Conversation with Kaylee Guerrero, December 21, 2020
75. Mary Henry and Elizabeth Mehren, *Pioneering Compassion: 150 Years at the Oregon Humane Society* (Oregon Humane Society, 2018), 158–61.
76. Bob Walters, "Final Resting Place for Hundreds of Pets," *Oregonian*, February 7, 1961.
77. "Loyal Dog Sees Master," *Oregonian*, July 17, 1923, 2.
78. Susan Stelljes, "Bobbie the Wonder Dog," Oregon Encyclopedia, https://www.oregonencyclopedia.org/articles/bobbie_the_wonder_dog/#.X-WJfhaIY2w.

79. "Portland Woman Educating Four-Year-Old Orangutang Young Native of the Wilds of Borneo to Be Trained for Career in Movies," *Oregonian*, October 22, 1925.
80. *Oregonian*, October 21, 1923.

10. Douglass Cemetery

81. *Sunday Oregonian*, June 22, 1958.
82. City of Troutdale, "Richard Knarr, Troutdale Sand and Gravel," https://www.troutdaleoregon.gov/community/page/richard-knarr-troutdale-sand-and-gravel accessed December 5, 2020.
83. *Bygone Times*, the Newsletter of the Troutdale Historical Society, October–December 2019, 3.
84. David Goran, "Fish Wheels: They Were So Effective and Therefore Banned in the United States Because They Threatened the Salmon Population," Vintage News, September 17, 2016, https://www.thevintagenews.com/2016/09/17/fish-wheels-effective-therefore-banned-united-states-threatened-salmon-population.
85. Metro, "Douglass Notable Burials," https://www.oregonmetro.gov/sites/default/files/2020/03/20/Douglas-cemetery-tour.pdf.
86. BBC News, "UK Politics: Screaming Lord Sutch Found Dead," http://news.bbc.co.uk/2/hi/uk_news/politics/371216.stm.
87. "Kent Henry: Guitarist with Steppenwolf and Blues Image," Independent, https://www.independent.co.uk/news/obituaries/kent-henry-guitarist-with-steppenwolf-and-blues-image-1657169.html.

11. Mountain View Stark Cemetery

88. Stark Street Mile Markers, http://starkstreetmarkers.blogspot.com/2008/05/blog-post.html.
89. *Gresham Outlook*, September 29, 2009.
90. *Morning Oregonian*, May 28, 1910.
91. *Morning Oregonian*, June 30, 1910.
92. *Morning Oregonian*, July 1, 1910.

12. Pleasant Home Cemetery

93. "Old Church Makes Way for Huge Supermarket," *Oregonian*, January 19, 1960, 3.
94. Pleasant Home UMC, "History," http://www.pleasanthomeumchurch.org/History.
95. *Oregonian*, April 16, 1908.
96. *Oregonian*, January 27, 1907.
97. *Morning Oregonian*, August 7, 1904.
98. *Morning Oregonian*, July 7, 1911, 1.

13. Mountain View Corbett Cemetery

99. "Joel Bates," https://sites.rootsweb.com/~ormultno/Stories/EMPA/bates-j.htm.
100. *Portrait and Biographical Record of Portland and Vicinity, Oregon* (Chicago: Chapman Publishing Co., 1903), 256–57.
101. George Katagiri, "Japanese Americans in Oregon," Oregon Encyclopedia, https://www.oregonencyclopedia.org/articles/japanese_americans_in_oregon_immigrants_from_the_west/#.YNYLRhNKiXw.
102. Sharon Nesbit, "Corbett Farmer Lived Quiet, Gentle Life," *Gresham Outlook*, March 17, 2009.

14. Gresham Pioneer, Escobar and White Birch Cemeteries

103. *Webfooter Extra*, December 2018, newsletter of Webfooters Post Card Club.
104. Interview with Mike Andrews, Gresham cemeteries tour guide, February 24, 2021.
105. Ibid.
106. Ibid.
107. W.R. Chilton, ed., *Gresham: Stories of Our Past, Campground to City* (Portland, OR: Gresham Historical Society, 1993).
108. Master Plan for the Gresham Section of the Springwater Trail Corridor, 1991, https://scholarsbank.uoregon.edu/xmlui/bitstream/handle/1794/4099/Gresham_Springwater_Trail_Master_Plan.pdf?sequence=3&isAllowed=y.

109. *Gresham Outlook*, June 25, 1964
110. Metro, "White Birch Cemetery," https://www.oregonmetro.gov/historic-cemeteries/white-birch-cemetery.
111. Gresham Historical Society.
112. Discover Nikkei, "Oregon Nikkei History: A Brief Summary—Part 1," http://www.discovernikkei.org/en/journal/2010/5/21/oregon-nikkei-history.
113. Amy K. Buck, "Alien Land Laws: The Curtailing of Japanese Agricultural Pursuits in Oregon" (master's thesis, Portland State University, 1999), https://doi.org/10.15760/etd.5872.
114. Matt DeBow and Christopher Keizur, "A Show of Respect," *The Outlook*, May 14, 2019.
115. Daryl C. McClary, "Forty-Three Passengers Die in a Trolley Car Accident in Tacoma on July 4, 1900," *History Link*, 2005.,
116. "Evidence of a Murder: Box of Bones Found in Gresham Graveyard," *Oregonian*, December 11, 1900, 8.
117. "Mystery Solved," *Oregonian*, December 17, 1900, 8.

15. Lincoln Memorial Park

118. *Oregonian*, October 12, 1909.
119. *Oregonian*, August 29, 1999.
120. *Oregonian*, January 23, 1910.
121. Author interview with Eric Cordingley, December 13, 2020.
122. *Oregonian*, May 31, 1912.
123. *Oregonian*, May 31, 1913.
124. *Oregonian*, December 6, 1914.
125. *Oregonian*, March 10, 1915.
126. *Oregonian*, February 29, 1928.
127. *Oregonian*, June 28, 1995.
128. *Oregonian*, July 20, 1915.
129. *Oregonian*, August 14, 1914.
130. *Oregonian*, May2, 1928.
131. *Oregonian*, July 8, 1929.
132. *Oregonian*, October 21, 1930.
133. *Oregonian*, June 12, 1923.
134. *Portland Telegram*, June 12, 1923.
135. *Oregonian*, June 2, 1925.

136. *Oregonian*, July 6, 1924.
137. *Oregonian*, September 14, 1926.
138. Author interview with Randal Houle.
139. Child Bereavement UK, "Grief and Bereavement in Gypsy and Traveller Families," https://www.childbereavementuk.org/information-grief-in-gypsy-traveller-families.
140. *Oregonian*, October 9, 2018.

16. Wilhelm's Portland Memorial Funeral Home, Mausoleum and Crematory

141. *Sunday Oregonian*, February 18, 1900, 6.
142. *Morning Oregonian*, February 19, 1900, 3.
143. *Morning Oregonian*, February 21, 1900, 12.
144. Oregon Burial Site Guide.
145. Preservation Artisans Guild, "Nine Interesting Facts about Portland's Historic Mausoleum," https://www.preservationartisans.org/2019/08/04/nine-interesting-facts-about-portlands-historic-mausoleum.
146. Eileen G. Fitzsimons, "Wilhelms Buys Portland Memorial," *Bee News*, March 4, 2008.
147. Ciara Dolan, "Dissolving the Dead: A Look Inside Portland's First Aqua Cremation Machine," *Portland Mercury*, May 9, 2019.
148. Tom Hallman Jr., "Secrets, Scandal Entombed in Portland Funeral Home," *Oregonian*, May 23, 2009.
149. *Oregonian*, February 19, 1917, 9.
150. Preservation Artisans Guild, "Povey Brothers Studio: The Art of Stained Glass," https://www.preservationartisans.org/2016/10/12/povey-brothers-studio-the-art-of-stained-glass.
151. Heather Arndt Anderson, "The Original Portland Eccentric," https://narratively.com/the-original-portland-eccentric.
152. Mike Houck, "Anatomy of a Mural: A 70-Foot Heron Transforms a Lifeless Wall," https://www.theintertwine.org/outside-voice/anatomy-mural.
153. Portland Wild, "Portland Memorial Mausoleum Mural," https://portlandwild.com/art/103.

17. Milwaukie Pioneer Cemetery

154. Val Ballestrem, "Milwaukie," Oregon Encyclopedia, https://www.oregonencyclopedia.org/articles/milwaukie/#.X96_BBaIY2w.
155. *Western Star*, December 26, 1850.
156. "East Side Affairs," *Morning Oregonian*, January 7, 1899, 8
157. Milwaukie Pioneer Cemetery Association Inc. Newsletter, third quarter, 2004.
158. Milwaukie Pioneer Cemetery Association Inc. Newsletter, third quarter, 2007.
159. Sons of Union Veterans of the Civil War, http://suvcw.org/LGAR/History.html.
160. *Sunday Oregonian*, April 20, 1913.
161. Find a Grave, "Cornelius D. Young," https://www.findagrave.com/memorial/141463169/cornelius-d.-young.
162. Matthew Westfall, *Devil's Causeway: The True Story of America's First Prisoners of War in the Philippines, and the Heroic Expedition Sent to Their Rescue* (Lanham, MD: Rowman & Littlefield Publishers, 2012).
163. "Gravedigger, as Ghost, Scares Man," *Morning Oregonian*, January 5, 1910, 1.

18. River View Cemetery

164. "Death's Silent Home," *Morning Oregonian*, April 25, 1879, 3.
165. Stephen Leflar, *The Pursuit of Happiness: A History of South Portland* (Portland, OR: self-publishing, 2008), 2008.
166. Sellwood Bridge, http://www.sellwoodbridge.org/?p=river-view-cemetery.
167. United States Department of the Interior, National Park Service, National Register of Historic Places Continuation Sheet for Lone Fir Cemetery, 2007.
168. Harvey Scott, *History of Portland* (Portland, OR: Mason & Co., 1890).
169. United States Department of the Interior, National Park Service, National Register of Historic Places Continuation Sheet for Lone Fir Cemetery, 2007.
170. *Morning Oregonian*, November 14, 1904, 4.
171. *Morning Oregonian*, May 28, 1906, 1.
172. *Morning Oregonian*, June 5, 1906, 7.

173. Anna Griffin, "Burials Are Out, So Cemetery Hopes It Can Cash In," *Newhouse News*, August 7, 2007.
174. Jonathan Maus, "In off-Road Plan Letter, Parks Board Supports Trails in Forest Park and River View Natural Area," BikePortland, https://bikeportland.org/tag/river-view-natural-area.
175. Steve Law, "Portlanders Shall Rest in Green Peace," *Portland Tribune*, July 8, 2010.
176. Mike Francis, "Memorial Day 2012: Remembering Oregon's First Foreign War," *Oregonian*, May 28, 2012.
177. Michael Schepps, "Seid Back (1851–1916)," Oregon Encyclopedia, https://www.oregonencyclopedia.org/articles/back-seid/#.YNYLoRNKiXw.
178. "Chinese Admitted to Bar," *Morning Oregonian*, June 18, 1907, 10.
179. *Portland Tribune*, May 10, 2007.

19. Greenwood Hills Cemetery

180. *Oregonian*, June 4, 1987.
181. Author interview with Hattie Mead, November 5, 2020.
182. Charles Carney, *History of Oregon Illustrated*, vol. 3. (Chicago: Pioneer Historical Publishing Company, 1922).
183. Jean M. Ward, "Mary Laurinda Jane Smith Beatty," Oregon Encyclopedia, https://www.oregonencyclopedia.org/articles/beatty-mary-lj-smith/#.X7YBZ1CIY2w.

20. Grand Army of the Republic Cemetery

184. *Oregonian*, April 1, 1970.
185. *Oregonian*, May 31, 1967.
186. *Oregonian*, June 18, 1970.
187. *Oregonian*, May 31, 1973.
188. *Oregonian*, May 31, 1977.
189. Oregon Burial Site Guide.
190. Naval History and Heritage Command, "Juniata I (Sloop-of-War)," https://www.history.navy.mil/research/histories/ship-histories/danfs/j/juniata-i.html.
191. Kansas Historical Society, Kansapedia.

192. Hattie Mead, interview.
193. *Oregonian*, August 5, 1905.
194. *Oregonian*, December 9, 1907.
195. *Oregon Journal*, November 20, 1909.

21. Beth Israel Cemetery

196. Virtual Jewish World: Oregon, United States, https://www.jewishvirtuallibrary.org/oregon-jewish-history.
197. "Where We Were," *Oregon Jewish Life*, September 1, 2013.
198. Robert Scott Cline, *Community Structure of the Urban Frontier: The Jews of Portland, Oregon 1849–1887* (master's thesis, Portland State University, 1982).
199. Oregon Jewish Museum and Center for Holocaust Education.
200. "Early Cemeteries," *Morning Oregonian*, April 26, 1887.
201. Ellen Eisenberg, "Jews in Oregon," Oregon Encyclopedia, https://www.oregonencyclopedia.org/articles/jews-in-oregon/#.YNTnthNKiXw.
202. Oregon Burial Site Guide, http://orgenweb.org/OR-Burial-Site-Guide/Multnomah,OR.pdf.
203. Author correspondence with Bitsie Appleton, March 2, 2021.
204. *Stanford Magazine*, July/August 2000.
205. *New York Sun*, July 28, 2005.
206. *Morning Oregonian*, June 16, 1915, 9, 11.
207. Kimberly Jensen, "Maurine Brown Neuberger," Oregon Encyclopedia, https://www.oregonencyclopedia.org/articles/neuberger_maurine_1907_2000_/#.YNToYRNKiXw.
208. Bob Hicks, "Yads, Torahs, History's Pointing Hand," *Oregon Arts Watch*, January 12, 2016.
209. Text panels from exhibit at Oregon Jewish Museum and Center for Holocaust Education.

22. Mount Calvary Cemetery

210. Daniel Curran, "Mount Calvary Catholic Cemetery," Oregon Encyclopedia, https://www.oregonencyclopedia.org/articles/mt-calvary-catholic-cemetery/#.YNToiBNKiXw.
211. *Sunday Oregonian*, October 24, 1937.
212. *Oregonian*, November 4, 1906.

213. *Oregonian*, November 10–12, 2017.
214. Broadway Photographs, "Eileen Darby," https://broadway.cas.sc.edu/content/eileen-darby.
215. Curran, "Mount Calvary Catholic Cemetery."

23. Jones and Havurah Shalom Cemeteries

216. *Cemeteries of Multnomah County: Brainard, Douglass, Havurah, Jones* (Portland: Genealogical Forum of Oregon, 2006).
217. Ralph Friedman, *In Search of Western Oregon* (Caldwell, ID: Caxton Printers, 1990), 170.
218. "County's Cemeteries Abound with Touchstones of History," *Oregonian*, March 24, 1981, 73.
219. "Jones Pioneer Cemetery: Portland, Multnomah County, Oregon," http://www.interment.net/data/us/or/multnomah/jones/pioneer.htm.
220. Joseph Gaston, *Portland, Oregon, Its History and Builders*, vol. 2 (Chicago: S.J. Clarke Publishing Company, 1911).
221. *Los Angeles Herald*, October 27, 1909.
222. *New Haven* (CT) *Register*, February 3, 1978.
223. Geocaching, "Zion's Founder RIP II," https://www.geocaching.com/geocache/GC7E3ZF_zions-founder-rip-ii?guid=d2f741e7-7a97-4442-9ef7-60a1c8d30a7e.
224. Geocaching, "Is It Disrespectful to Hide Geocache in Cemeteries?" https://forums.geocaching.com/GC/index.php?/topic/306404-is-it-disrespectful-to-hide-geocache-in-cemeteries.

24. Oswego Pioneer Cemetery

225. Oregon Inventory of Historic Properties Historic Resource Survey Form, 2016, https://www.ci.oswego.or.us/sites/default/files/fileattachments/boc_hrab/webpage/18307/pioneer_cemetery_lakeo_survey_form.pdf.
226. Grant McOmie, "Discover Oregon's Historic Pioneer Cemeteries," Travel Oregon, October 28, 2011, https://traveloregon.com/things-to-do/culture-history/historic-sites-oregon-trail/discover-oregons-historic-pioneer-cemeteries/.
227. Janet Goetze, "Memorial to Honor Ethel Schaubel, Guardian Angel of Oswego Pioneer Cemetery" *Oregonian*, May 20, 2014.

228. Cliff Newell, "Pioneer Cemetery Celebrates New Era Monday," *Lake Oswego Review*, May 26, 2011.
229. Email from Joe Collins to Teresa Bergen, December 14, 2020.
230. Conversation between Joe Collins, Teresa Bergen and Heide Davis, December 7, 2020.
231. Ibid.
232. "Where the Workers Rest," https://www.ci.oswego.or.us/sites/default/files/fileattachments/parksrec/webpage/12126/7_oswegopioneercemetery_whereworkersrest.pdf.
233. Tom Hager, "Linus Pauling (1901–1994)," Oregon Encyclopedia, https://www.oregonencyclopedia.org/articles/pauling_linus_1901_1994_/#.X96TThaIY2w.
234. "Who's Buried in Linus Pauling's Grave?" The Centennial, Lake Oswego's Centennial Celebration 1910-2010, July 1, 2010, https://www.ci.oswego.or.us/sites/default/files/fileattachments/publicaffairs/webpage/13678/centennial_july2010.pdf.
235. *Medford Mail*, November 15, 1901, 4.
236. "Peace Pole for the Oswego Pioneer Cemetery in Lake Oswego Oregon-USA," https://www.worldpeace.org/2016/12/peace-pole-for-the-oswego-pioneer-cemetery-in-lake-oswego-oregon-usa/.

25. Mountain View Cemetery, Oregon City

237. *Oregon Spectator*, April 20, 1848.
238. City Council of Oregon City meeting notes, July 5, 1882.
239. *Oregon City Courier*, December 2, 1920.
240. *Oregon City Enterprise*, October 6, 1899.
241. *Morning Enterprise*, October 4, 1918.
242. City Council of Oregon City meeting notes, March 3, 1926.
243. City Commission meeting notes, August 12, 1965.
244. City Commission meeting notes, March 11, 1971.
245. City Commission meeting notes, March 5, 1978.
246. Karin Morey, correspondence with authors, February 18, 2021.
247. Oregon City, "Volunteers Repair 150-Year-Old Monument in Mountain View Cemetery," https://www.orcity.org/community/volunteers-repair-150-year-old-monument-mountain-view-cemetery.
248. Elizabeth Stuart Phelps, *The Gates Ajar*, https://americanliterature.com/author/elizabeth-stuart-phelps/book/the-gates-ajar/summary.

249. *Aberdeen* (SD) *Daily News*, March 18, 1977, 10.
250. *Oregonian*, March 17, 1977.
251. Howerton Heritage Newsletter, Winter 2000.

SUGGESTED READING LIST

Baugher, Sherene, and Richard F. Veit. *The Archeology of American Cemeteries and Gravemarkers*. Gainesville: University Press of Florida, 2014.

Byrd, Dean, Stanley Clarke and Janice Healy. *Oregon Burial Site Guide*. Portland, OR: Binford & Mort Pub., 2001

Cemeteries of East Multnomah County. Portland: Genealogical Forum of Oregon, 2001.

Cemeteries of Multnomah County: Brainard, Douglass, Havurah, Jones. Portland: Genealogical Forum of Oregon, 2006.

Kidd, Julie, ed. *G.A.R. Cemetery*. Compiled by Friday Morning Research Group, Genealogical Forum of Oregon, Portland, 2003.

Loeffel-Atkins, Bernadette. *Widow's Weeds and Weeping Veils: Mourning Rituals in 19th Century America*. Gettysburg, PA: Gettysburg Publishing, 2012.

Mathiesen, Johan. *Lone Fir: The Cemetery: A Guide*. Portland, OR: DeadManTalking, 2012.

———. *Mad as the Mist and Snow: Exploring Oregon Through Its Cemeteries*. Ashland, OR: Ashland Creek Press, 2011.

Neighbors, Joy. *The Family Tree Cemetery Field Guide: How to Find, Record and Preserve Your Ancestors' Graves*. Cincinnati, OH: Family Tree Books, 2017

Sloane, David Charles. *Is the Cemetery Dead?* Chicago: University of Chicago Press, 2018

———. *The Last Great Necessity: Cemeteries in American History (Creating the North American Landscape)*. Baltimore, MD: Johns Hopkins University Press, 1991.

Snyder, Tui. *Understanding Cemetery Symbols: A Field Guide for Historic Graveyards*. N.p.: Castle Azle Press, 2017.

Stout, Annette. *Pioneer Cemeteries: Sculpture Gardens of the Old West*. Lincoln: University of Nebraska Press, 2008.

Widing, Roy. *Whispers from the Tomb: A True Love Story Discovered in a Century Old Mausoleum*. N.p.: Quality House, 2012.

ABOUT THE AUTHORS

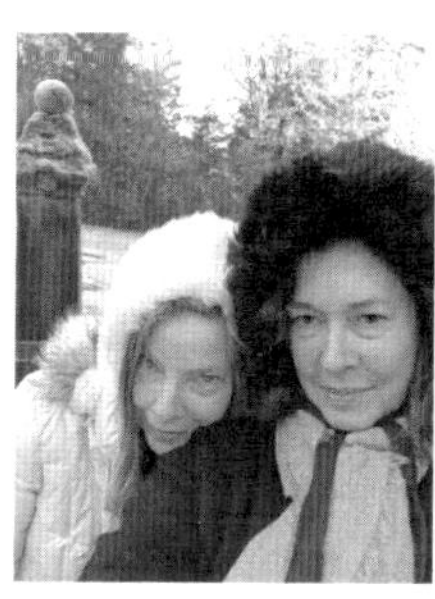

Heide Davis and Teresa Bergen are good friends and cemetery sleuths who live in Portland, Oregon. Heide is a painter who loves vintage stuff. Teresa is the author of *Easy Portland Outdoors* and *Transcribing Oral History*. They like to explore old cemeteries and antique malls, go on ghost tours and otherwise poke around in the past.